OCEANS

M000303149

The Patterns & Techniques of

EmoTrance™

Vol. 1

Silvia Hartmann, PhD

First Edition 2003

ISBN 1 873483 73 2

Published By

DragonRising

Oceans of Energy

The Patterns & Techniques Of EmoTrance Volume 1
© Silvia Hartmann, PhD 2003

ISBN 1 873483 73 2

First Edition 2003

Published by
DragonRising
18 Marlow Avenue
Eastbourne
East Sussex BN22 8SJ
United Kingdom
http://DragonRising.com

All Rights Reserved in all media, including future media.

Printed and bound by Antony Rowe Ltd, Eastbourne

Other titles by this author:

Adventures In EFT
The Advanced Patterns Of EFT
Project Sanctuary
The Story Teller
Energy Healing For Animals
In Serein

TABLE OF CONTENTS

OCEANS OF ENERGY 9

Welcome To Oceans of Energy 10

PART 1 - EMOTRANCE & THE ENERGY BODY.................................. 15
Re-Drawing The Maps Of The Energy System.................................... 16
The Basics Of EmoTrance.. 22
The Basics Of EmoTrance.. 23
Affecting Energy With Intention 24
Quantum Time Resolutions.. 25
The Energy – Intention Principle 28
The Basics Of Energy Exchanges... 29
The Hardest Energy Exchange Of All 29
Better Than "Tranquil" 34
The Core of The Physiological Responses.................................... 41
"It's Only An Energy!" 42
Client Centred, Led By Physiology 45
Energy States & Energy Manifestations 46
Energy & Water... 47
EmoTrance As A Physical Skill 49
EmoTrance Self Help.. 50
Riding The Lightning 53

PART 2 - THE CONCEPT OF ENERGY NUTRITION 57
Saying YES To Energy Flow 59
Having The World – And Eating It 64
Becoming An Energy Vampire 65
Jealousy & Envy 66
Making Room For New Energy 69
Making Room For New Energy 70
Play EmoTrance With A Friend! 74

PART 3 - INTRODUCING SHIELDS... 77
Reluctance To Dropping A Shield.. 82
Shielding From "Frightening Energies" 83
Dissolving Shields 84

PART 4 - ENERGY HEALING WITH EMOTRANCE..................................... **89**
Skills & Abilities – I AM A Healer.. 89
Laying On Of Hands... 91
The Jaw Healing Posture 92
"Hands Of Ghost"... 94
Working With Healing Energy - Adding Energy 96
Removing Energy 97
Greeting The Day, Greeting The Night 98
Clearing Channels 100
Repairing Broken Channels 101
Tracing A Channel 102
Overall Healing With Innocent Energy 102
Healing The Fault Lines 106
Healing Fault Lines..107
Notes On Fault Line Healing...108
Concluding A Fault Line Session 109
Healing & Resting 110
Natural Healing - While You Sleep 110
Healing Shame 113
True Forgiveness – Finally Healing The Oldest Wounds 115
Proxy Work 117

PART 5 - EMOTRANCE AS A HEALING TUTOR................................... **119**
EmoTrance Contra-Indications 119
Intuition VS. Feedback 122
Self Healing For The Healer 125
Healing Beyond "Conscious Contortions"...126
Ecology & Aspects 128
"Infallible Healing" 128

PART 6 - ENLIGHTENING COGNITION **129**
Learning "With The Heart"..133
Opening To True Learning 135
The Clear Blue Field And The Problem Of Erosion 136
All The World Your Teacher 137
The Doors Of Perception ... .139

PART 7 – PATTERNS FOR HEALING & TRANSFORMATION.............. **141**
Eating With Love 142
Now, Where Do You Feel THAT In Your Body? 144
Raising Sexual Energy 145
The 360' Field Clearer 146

The Fairy Wish 148
Giving & Receiving Gifts 149
The Energy Of Money 151
Prejudice Removal 153
Energy Dancing 155

PART 8 - RAISING ENERGY FOR MAGIC, HEALING & FOR LIFE...... 157

Performing Powerful Blessings 159
Curses 161
Thoughtfields & Reality Creation 163
A Different Dream – Goal Setting To State 166
A Developmental Model Of The Energy Body........168
Managing Major Life Shifts......................................170

ADDENDUM 1 – THE ROAD TO EMOTRANCE..................................... 177

EmoTrance – The Developmental History...............177
Energy Not Emotions 184
All You Need Is Love ...? 187
The Storm Drains...192
The Benefits Of "Bad" Energies! 193
"In The Field"...197
More Repercussions, More Surprises......................199
"Where in your body is the sadness ...?"...............201
EmoTrance As A Healing Teacher...........................207
EmoTrance Self Help...212

ADDENDUM 2 – QUESTIONS & ANSWERS 215

Feelings, Blocks & Shields..215
Channelling Energies...217
A Natural Ability? 221
Energy Pathways 223
EmoTrance & Hypnosis 228
EmoTrance & The Auric Field 230
Metaphors & Energy 234
Physical Pain & Disease 241
Distance Healing, Proxy Healing 242
Explaining EmoTrance 243

ADDENDUM 3 – EMOTRANCE ARTICLES.. 247

Introduction To EmoTrance.. 247

Back To Physicality 248
Re-Establishing The Even Flow................................248

Repercussions & Energy Nutrition..249
Playing In "The Oceans of Energy" 250
Endless Possibilities, Endless Applications...........................251

Starving For Love Amidst The Oceans of Energy 253
No Even Flow ... .253
"Could Do Better ..." 255
Kundalini 256

Energy Nutrition – Essential Health For The Energy Body 259
What Is Energy Nutrition? 259
Intention & Energy 259
Energy Reversals or "Saying NO To Healing" 260
All You Need Is Love 261
Shields To Joy & Ecstasy 263
Human & Other Energies..264
The Essential Flow Of Energies 265
Re-Learning To Process Energy Correctly 267
In Conclusion 268

Heal Your Energy Body 269
Energetic Bodies, Energetic Health 270
A Healthy Mind in a Healthy Body 271
Emotional "Freedom"?..272
What Are Emotions? 273
The Progression Of Disease 274
Healing The Energy Body 276
Healing In The Quantum Realms..277

ADDENDUM 4 - EMOTRANCE SESSION STORIES 281
Fibromyalgia And Old Emotions...282
Low Self Esteem 283
Birth Issues...284
PTSD From A Car Accident..286
Johnny...287
A Poor Relationship With Father..289
Anxious About Being Too Far From Home 290
Severe Depression 291
A Wonderful Person ...?...291
Changing A Life Pattern...292
Guilt 294
Weight, Insecurity, Age Issues...294
Experiences From A Training Weekend 295
Panic Attacks & Pain In The Heart.......................................296

Fear Of Criticism 296
Understanding Shame In A New Way 297
Aspergers Boy's Fear Of Others...299
Low Self Esteem & Depression 301
Completing The Diamond Transformation 301

ADDENDUM 5 – EMOTRANCE IN THE FIELD................ 305
No More Tears On The Pillow..305
Old Car Crash Pain In The Heart Area.................................306
There In The Present 307
Aging..307
Calmly Facing A Turning Point..309
Lost Lover Found 310
Weight Issues 311
Getting More Luck Into My Life 311
Falling In Love With Your Demons.......................................312
Frightening The Relatives With Emotional Control 313
Calming a Severely Distressed System 314
Physical Awakening Of An Abused Energy Body....................314
Speaking "His" Name 315
The Sandwich, The Enemy ... .317
Love For My Father 318
4am Chakra Expansion 319
The Energy Of Best Sellers 320
ET Makes Housework Easier! 321
Friendship Is ... .322
Even Sceptics Can Heal ... .323
The Realms Of The Psychics 324
The Onion Induction 325
EmoTrance - The Ultimate Challenge 327
Learning From Our Children..328
Throwing Away Books 329
First Successful Complaint 330
The Nurse Who Dared To Care 331

Conclusion To Vol. I... 333

GLOSSARY OF TERMS... 335

FURTHER INFORMATION... 339

About The Author.. 339

OCEANS OF ENERGY

If you could shift
your point of view
for just a moment, as you
now grow still
and silent within,
without a thought or care,
without a thought of worry or desire,
then you might just begin to feel:

A power tingling in your fingertips
a breath that draws to you
a part of all there is, of which
you are a part,
and that surrounds you
buoys you, nourishes, protects

and reaches far and wide, and further still
into the deepest blues of oceans,
the deepest greens of mountain lakes
and all the creatures that reside
in forest groves, eternal deserts
as above,
the stars are dancing.

Oceans of Energy
and they lie at your fingertips,
for you to navigate and learn
to know the ancient arts
of balance, deep release
and once again restore
the Even Flow,
the Perfect State of Being.

Silvia Hartmann, 2001

9

Welcome To Oceans of Energy

It is my pleasure to welcome you personally to EmoTrance – a system that goes quite beyond simply healing and restoration and one, that if you understand it even just a little bit, will bring a great deal more pleasure, joy and excitement to your life.

That is really what EmoTrance is about – not just dour fire fighting, making things a bit more bearable, but to experience and find whole new realms of joy, of peace, of tranquillity and of admiration for yourself and all of creation – the Oceans of Energy of which we are but a part.

It has always been my deep belief that this universe is fantastically beautiful and entirely awesome. It is beautiful in destruction as well as in genesis – always. It could be no other. For many years it seemed that people just forget this somehow, enmeshed in their own worries, fears and pains as we all still are most of the time, and I have always wanted to do something about that.

I know how marvellous I can feel, how totally connected to everything and everyone about me and yet so incredibly free at the same time.

I am sure you have experienced such a thing too and if you have not, then – wow, just know that there are wonderful things awaiting you.

It is never to late to fall in love with the universe itself all over again, and you don't have to have young eyes to see this beauty. You don't have to have sharp ears to hear the music of the stars. You don't have to have slender, strong limbs to soar to the heavens and become one with life itself. You don't have to be accomplished, clever, intelligent or beautiful to come home to life and know in every atom of your being that you belong here, that you are welcome here, and that all the grace and love of the universe is indeed yours by all rights.

You don't have to live amidst beautiful nature in a rich castle full of gems and jewels to be joyful and absolutely eternal – all these things are nothing but states of being, and every human has both the ability and the right to move into these states of being at will and with volition, like a swimmer would dive into a sparkling, refreshing ocean that will buoy them up and give them of its own life, to the fullest and in every way.

When I suggested that such things could be obtained through the system I have chosen to call EmoTrance, many bitter accusations were thrown in my direction of over-exaggeration or promising more than could possibly be fulfilled – and yet, it is so simple, so clear and so very obvious that people can and do experience these other states of being, often by accident, entirely unexpectedly. And it is also true that people will spend an entire lifetime trying to recreate these states of being, with objects, with people, with settings, with landscapes and with behaviours, never even suspecting that none of these things had anything at all to do any of these things but instead, was only about **their own ability to experience the world in a whole new way**.

So, here we are and this is what EmoTrance is for – a device designed to help us re-learn the ways of the Oceans of Energy, for us to repair ourselves with volition and prepare ourselves for a true opening to what there really is, all around us, all the time. EmoTrance is a device to make it easy for us to let go of old hurts and injuries which are precluding true enjoyment and pro-activity in this life. It is a device to help us come to a point where we can drop our shields to incoming energies from our environment and from other people and once again, use these energies to fuel our own growth and re-emergence into these states of being that seemed as lost to us as paradise itself.

In the very act of using the device called EmoTrance, we are learning things about our energy bodies and our relationships with the energies of the universe that are often surprising, always healing in the most profound sense of the word and these learnings re-build the connections that were damaged or had shattered – including the connections within our own totalities to our minds, hearts and physical bodies.

EmoTrance is not something you read about in a book and keep as an interesting theory on a metaphorical shelf in the laboratory of your conscious mind.

It is something you need to do. Something you need to try out, experience for yourself because the real learnings are NOT in this book but are to come in YOUR EXPERIENCE with the Oceans of Energy. EmoTrance is the bridge, an invitation if you will, to get to know yourself and the universe in a deeply personal fashion, a truly unique interaction that will be different for every single person who tries it.

I can only encourage you to use the techniques and principles for real. I have done the very best I can to make it easy and exciting for you to be wanting to do this, to allow yourself to really forget all you thought you knew about what works and what doesn't, or how long or difficult certain healings might need to be.

Allow yourself to be surprised.

If you cannot yet allow yourself to be far more than pleasantly surprised, at least allow yourself the possibility of such a thing, and the possibility that you personally can experience the states of being once thought to have been reserved for mystics only, quite naturally and simply – and without years of study.

One of my teachers once told me that we have more neurons in our brains than there are stars in the visible sky, and that the connections between them are to all intents and purposes, infinite.

I've always known that there was so much more we can be, do, have and experience than what we see modelled around us. I don't know how I know, I just know that it is so.

There was a time not too long ago when it was deemed to be impossible for a human being to be accelerated faster than 25 miles an hour lest they would explode. Now, we laugh at that. But in truth, are we any better? How many things which are thought to be impossible can we achieve and better still, how many things can we achieve that have never even been thought about at all because there were no models to show us the way, because no human has achieved it so far? How many things do you think – you, very personally YOU, dear reader! – can be achieved by others but not by you? What is it that you think you could never have? The mental clarity to instantly compute vast system dynamics in an instant, or the experience of true love that was returned in kind?

EmoTrance teaches us that these things are not skills, they are not talents and they are not genetic – but simply states of being we can learn to slide in and out of at will, and simply because we were designed **by nature** to do exactly that in the first place. Before we go into these realms, however, a little basic repair work and preparation needs to be done. After all, when you plug yourself into a super-high voltage power line, you will have to have the internal systems on line to cope with that kind of power or else, you will simply fry. In our passage through human society, our energy bodies were not taken care of as they should have been and many systems an adult human needs to give and receive love, for example, are non-existent, broken or stuck in an infantile stage – they simply cannot handle that kind of power yet. As we set about repairing and restoring the first and most urgent systems for the most basic kinds of energy – attention and negativity from humans, fear and pain from the physicality, loss and bereavement, to mention but a few – incrementally, our ability to handle more powerful and wider ranges of energy without hurting ourselves in the process increases. Many of us are very right to fear love, for example, because it would indeed, cause enormous pain and suffering if an energy form of that power and brilliance was to be allowed to rush through our systems if they are still damaged and broken and unable to cope.

So this is the first task and the first natural usage of EmoTrance – namely to repair things, unblock channels and pathways, restore some basic survival functions for the energy body and to give it the nutrition and care it always needed to grow and evolve into the star a human energy system, fully adult and fully online, was always meant to be.

But it is centrally important to me that you remember all the way that EmoTrance is not just about healing but about **evolution** – about going beyond mere cessation of symptoms and into new realms of experience, entirely re-writing who we thought we were and what we can be, do, learn to know and experience in the process.

Now, you might have heard such words spoken before and you might have listened with an amount of sadness and regret, perhaps a thought that it's nice in theory but that "the hard reality of real life" (aka suffering, pain, death and misery) is all there will ever be for you, personally because you (don't have what it takes, don't deserve it, aren't smart enough, aren't enlightened enough, don't work hard enough at enlightenment, blah blah blah ...).

If that is response, come back to this introduction once you have learned the EmoTrance process and allow yourself to let go of all of that, to find the place in your body where it hurts, to know that this is "just an energy" and that you can release it, once and for all, if you choose to do so now.

It really is that easy. It was always meant to be THAT easy. We were designed absolutely by nature, by God or by accident if that's what you want to believe to be able to do just that – with volition in the quantum spaces, take charge of our energy bodies and have them flow towards health, power and beauty that will have **immediate** repercussions in The Hard and thus, prove its validity in the most incontrovertible way – by YOUR own personal experience.

Now, and having said all of that, let us begin at the beginning and if you would, I would share with you the stages and pathways by which I came to EmoTrance and the presuppositions behind the system. As you will find, I did not arrive at EmoTrance by accident or by channelling a superior being, but simply by following evidence and trying out things for myself, so that I would learn for myself what worked, and what did not.

I hope that you will do exactly that with this manual, namely not taking anyone's word for it but your own; to try out EmoTrance and the "Patterns and Techniques, Volume 1" for yourself and make your own personal experience the final adjudication on whether this is useful and correct.

In this spirit, I thank you sincerely for the time and your open mind and I wish that you will find a similar sense of excitement and wonder as I did when I discovered EmoTrance.

Silvia Hartmann, PhD

January 15th, 2003

PART 1 - EMOTRANCE & THE ENERGY BODY

For at least 12,000 years human beings have been making maps of the energy system.

These were passed down through the many, many generations of healers working with the human energy system in many different ways but then modern science came along and at least for the First World, for two hundred years, it all came to halt right there.

The problem is that we cannot measure the energy system.

Science has not yet come up with the underlying mathematics to create the machinery to measure what we call energy flow, the meridians, the chakras, subtle energy, Auric layers and all of that.

We do not have machinery to make the energy system visible or to measure it; unlike X-rays, whereby we take a picture of a persons arm and then hold it up to the light and say, "There, you can see the bones quite clearly," for the energy body and all its systems, we do not have anything at all to show it to us.

Now, there are some people who can see auras, and others who can see parts of the energy body, but that is a special skill; I wanted something different.

I wanted to develop a way to work with the energy system which anyone can do; where you need no special skills or talents; where you do not have to study for years.

We all have an energy system; we are all born with one.

There simply MUST be a way – a natural way, at that – for us to be able to naturally work with this system and for me, EmoTrance is that way.

Re-Drawing The Maps Of The Energy System

This is a book on energy magic – not just healing, but a great deal more than that.

It is a book about the human energy body and its systems, yet you will not find a single map as you might have been used to seeing in books on this topic.

Maps of meridians, acupoints, chakras, Auric layers – you will not find anything like this here.

Rather than working with standardised maps, we are going to be working with your own specific energy body **directly** instead; and believe it or not, the map of your own energy system has never been drawn.

Even in our physical bodies, the veins shift beneath the skin in response to muscle tension and the temperature in the room to which our skin reacts by contracting or relaxing; they are not always in the same place.

Our energy body is far, far more fluent than that and very difficult to pin down in the first place as it is so very interactive to all the other energetic occurrences around it and within it.

But that is the very least of it.

The maps of the energy system we do have are either thousands of years old, or they were channelled by some person, some where, at some time – you could say they simply made them up, if you were of that mind.

Also, the ancient and revered maps we have handed down from civilisations way back when have severe structural limitations.

The first of those is that the map makers did not know how to represent a three dimensional object back then; this is why chakras, for example, always look like flat dinner plates with lotuses painted on them.

As we are talking here not even three dimensional – and just imagine trying to get some sense of what a human being really looks like through their developmental stages by studying an Egyptian tomb painting! – but indeed, the energy system is n-dimensional and thereby impossible to represent at all on flat paper, or even on a screen with the most advanced of computer technologies.

16

Chakras are not flat dinner plates; and of course, my meridian points are not in the same place as yours, or his, or hers – acupuncture, for example, relies on the practitioner intuiting the correct placement within a vague area.

That is just for starters. There is more.

For example, the ideas of what a fully functioning energy system should look like were originated in extremely conservative, extremely strict patriarchal societies which were feudal in nature; and of course, they were modelled absolutely and **only** by and on men.

A Chinese peasant of 5000 BC would truly have an energy system that is so unlike any of ours, a map drawn using him as a model would have to be next to useless to a 21st century 1st world inhabitant.

In these ancient traditions, it is held for example that the centre of the body is midway between the navel and the genitals.

This may have been so way back when with our Chinese peasant but if you were to ask one of **us** to point to the center of their body, it would be much higher in most cases – stomach and up. Please don't take my word for this. Try it out for yourself. Take any group of people, or individual 1st worlders and ask them to close their eyes. Then say, "I want you to show me the real center of your body, the place where you put your hand when you say, yes that is me – put your hand there or point." I can promise you, people will NOT point at their genitals, unless they have been conditioned to think of their center as that low down by, for example, doing a great deal of martial arts drills.

Conditioning is the key here. If you were to run a feudal society which is as strictly conservative as those societies which gave us the old maps of the energy systems, of course a key point in shaping your inhabitants energy systems would have to be **conformity** to a standard ideal – and this is indeed still a major value in the Eastern civilisations to this very day.

When you shape people's energy systems using **standardised** techniques, manoeuvres, drills, then of course their whole being will be shaped by and through this – they will think the same things, believe the same things and generally, turn out to be very well behaved citizens.

Make the whole thing heavily ancestor-worship based and we have something so stable and so non-evolutionary, it can indeed survive for tens of thousands of years basically unchanged.

However, and much as I am in awe of the idea of creating standardised well conforming citizens via prescribed energy drills to turn out cloned minds and bodies as a concept, and as much as I admire how well this has worked over the past ten thousand years, I really do think now its time to stop and to do something else instead.

First of all, let us now forget about those old maps, no matter how many grains of truth may be hidden amidst the distortions and disturbances, for we don't actually know yet which bits are the truth and which bits are completely wrong.

In order to find out what is what, I suggest we go back to the drawing board.

Only this time, it isn't one single drawing board for all of us, but a single drawing board each on which we get to draw **our own energy bodies** as they are in reality.

Not many of us look like Barbie or Action Man. None of us can sustain this for more than a few years at the most – and most especially not if we lose our legs in an accident or have our face burned off in an explosion.

Where is Barbie then? What good is the model then? What good does it do to treat someone with maps based on the old ideal?

It is of course as pointless and as painful as it would be to cover a real human being with a table cloth upon which the organs are marked out and then to procede with the operation according to the table cloth and NOT according to the real person who lies, screaming, below.

We have highly personalised energy bodies.

They were always highly personalised, from the moment of conception when a totally unique being came into physical existence with a genetic structure unlike any other. It starts right there.

Within seconds, this personalisation unfolds into n-complexity – so many variables that they can no longer be computed by the greatest computer in the world, so complicated that there doesn't even exist a form a mathematics yet to even try to describe it.

The developing being is subjected to the environment his mother provides; it shifts and changes endlessly as do her moods, what she eats, the environment she herself lives in, and which interacts with her own genetic uniqueness and all of that interacts with the individual's unique uniqueness too.

By the time a human baby is born, even if they started out as an identical twin, they are so personalised, it is extraordinary.

But then, life happens.

We sustain injuries and traumas, experiences, sensations. We live and we eat and grow and with every little thing we become more and more individual. This is a natural and extraordinary process and societies across all the ages of men have tried to counteract this trend by social conditioning and learning to do and be the same as those who went before.

Not to be too different because that is a threat to the tribe and the continuity of that which went before.

Schoolchildren and soldiers get to be dressed the same and taught the same drills and to sing the same songs so they learn to think the same; nowadays, this has escalated into one desirable body shape only (one each for men and women), everyone having to have the same "perfect" teeth and other limiters to individuality of that nature.

I have worked in psychology and related fields for a very long time.

Therefore I have met with very many people who cannot fit into these societally prescribed "conceptual corsets" and they are wearing the scars of trying to squeeze themselves into those.

What I particularly wanted for all those people, and myself included, was to get out of those corsets so that we can firstly, really see what's actually there, and secondly, do something about it so these people can live a good life too.

It is true that I was astonished to find these very same kinds of corsets in energy healing of all places too. If you don't have chakras that are stacked up like dinner plates up the front of your body, there's something wrong with you and you need to be fixed through "healing and meditation".

If your meridians don't run this way or that, then you need to do twenty years of yoga or chi gung in order to fix that and become the same as everyone else – you wouldn't want to feel left out now, would you?

This is not my idea of healing.

Over the last 25 years, I have made some new ideas of healing that suit me personally much better than to turn me into yet another sandal wearing, mineral water slurping health & fitness freak automaton.

No thanks. That isn't my desire and it isn't my path. I would like to heal my injuries and enjoy my life – in whichever way this may come my way. I would like to learn what **my own** energy body actually looks like, what it does, what it can do for me, how it works.

My life has been such that I have been through the "personalisation process" to the extent that I simply cannot now go to work 9-5, come home, lie on the couch and drink a beer, have sex, go to bed, and do the same again until I retire.

I have an energy body that I don't know about, and when I look at the diagrams of "the perfect energy system" they have as little to do with me as Barbie has to do with the way I look.

Some people might wish to deny this fact, but almost everyone who is in the field of personal development, psychology, or healing similarly has a highly personalised energy system also – else they'd quite happily work in a factory and wouldn't even be here.

I am going to say this quite clearly now – a great many of us are in pain.

In constant pain. This may not always be physiological pain but if you wait long enough, you'll get that too.

Our lives are not **working** as they should, as we want them to, as we had always hoped they could.

We are deeply unhappy with who we are and what we are doing, yet quite powerless to change any of it, for all our efforts with all these different healing modalities.

Sparks of enlightenment states of true joy, grace, connectedness with the universe are far and in between, unpredictable and unreliable; for the rest of the time we fill our lives with worries of one kind or the other, addictions to this and that, idle chatter and all sorts of things to keep the underlying pain at bay.

If you are now very appalled at these statements, I would apologise to you and simply say that I have been around healers for long enough to know that it is themselves they seek to heal and that their journey with their teachers, their clients and healees is a healing process for themselves, first and foremost.

It is the healers who are in the most pain, so much so that they try to become their own cure.

And, as we shall see, this pain is caused by the conditions in the energy system.

Which is exactly why I wish to repair the energy system, restore it to its proper glory and help it come back on line as nature intended.

And that is why I have rejected the standardised maps of the energy system, especially for use in **human psychology** because these have failed to make a material difference to the pain of wrongness, chaos and confusion I and the other healers I know have experienced for so long.

So instead, I would invite you to come along and find out how **your own** energy body works; what has happened with it to make it be in such pain; and to use a simple system of healing based entirely on **your own feedback and experiences** to make it work better for you so you can feel less pain, and still less, until we turn the corner and our underlying states are no longer states of misery and despair that need to be kept at bay with friends and red wine, with work and sex, with spending countless hours on a typewriter or drowning oneself in meditation but **instead** our underlying states of being are of joy, of happiness and delight so that when allow ourselves a moments silence, we can hear the universe sing in harmony with our own selves at last.

So, to sum up, we make a new map of each individuals energy system in EmoTrance and then work with this new map to give us directions as to what needs healing and what does not.

Here are the main points once more in brief.

The Totally Individualised Energy System

It is more effective to work with what really exists in your energy system than trying to first re-shape your energy system to a standard and then manipulate it from there.

It is more effective because:

- It saves years of painful work attempting to re-shape the energy system to an idealised standard ...

- ... which might prove a futile endeavour anyway if it is too individualised to start with ...

- Working on your own energy system rather than with an imaginary template gives immediate and direct results.

- You are guided to your own true ecology immediately and cannot violate it.

In order to work with your own individual energy system, we:

- pay attention to the existing conditions

- learn about what is there and what is not

- are guided with direct physiological and emotional feedback in all our interventions.

The Basics Of EmoTrance

Energy is about flow, and flow is about constant movement – no excuses, no obstacles; there is no situation in nature that doesn't have this aspect of constant flow.

Even a black hole is flow. Suns are flow and every little thing, from atomic decay to the rain that falls in nature is constantly shifting, flowing and evolving.

We as people are also constantly flowing and evolving. We eat, we digest, we expend energy, we eliminate; there are cycles within cycles, short and long but in the end, everything flows.

That **is** the number one rule of energy.

Intellectually, we know this and we understand this. Practically, we do a great many things with our bodies and our minds that are in direct opposition to this – a direct violation of the basic law of the universe that decrees nothing is finite and everything is in constant flow.

Instead, we try to keep energies out. We will hold on to them tightly, we will block them away, try to slow them down, reverse them, stop them from moving.

This of course causes widespread repercussions on the physical and mental states of well being, as these are a part of the interlinked systems that comprise the **totality** of a human being.

EmoTrance rests on a number of presuppositions and the most important one of those is that we have three levels of events taking place in an interlinked fashion for a human being in their totality.

- **The first level is that of physicality – the physical.**
- **The second level is that of emotions and sensations which are not directly rooted in physiology.**
- **The third level that of the energy system**.

The energy system and what happens at that level causes changes and manifestations in the second level, that of emotions and feelings; this in turn impacts the physiological level.

This three step chain is one of the main precepts of Energy Psychology.

When one works with any one of these levels, through this interlinkage all the other systems are also affected. If you have a massage, for example, and someone says nothing but simply sensuously slides their warm hands over your body and loosens strictly physical muscle tensions, this will impact your sensations, feelings and emotions and also, your energy system.

Likewise, if someone was to come up you and do nothing but just say, "You are a wonderful person," your emotions and sensations would respond, causing an effect on your body and your energy system.

If we were to work on the energy system alone and not do or say anything, this too would have an affect both on the emotions as well as on the physical body.

Now the problem for most people in this system lies in the mid step, the emotions and non-physical sensations.

Energy bodies are fine things with superb structures to maintain themselves and their integrity; physical bodies are simply amazing in their resilience and ability to keep on going in spite of the most adverse environmental conditions imaginable.

Why am I saying that there is a problem with the mid step? Well, if you cut your body, it heals a few days later. But someone is told when they are three years old, "You don't deserve to have been born at all." and a person can spend the rest of their lives in an institution!

Clearly, something has gone very wrong indeed somewhere in this system.

If indeed, all energies must flow and if humans exchange energies in their interactions with each other, then something must have gone wrong for someone after fifty years in therapy **still** to be holding on to something their father said to them when they were five years old.

EmoTrance is designed to change exactly that.

Affecting Energy With Intention

The old adage goes, "Where attention goes, energy flows."

This is actually structurally incorrect; it should say, where intention goes, energy flow changes.

We can and do use intention and attention, conscious instructions transmitted via all media of thought (such as "saying things to yourself", "seeing pictures", pure black space thought etc) to **influence and change** existing energetic realities.

Although we cannot move a rock by staring at it, switch off a panic attack in mid-occurrence by simply saying, "Ok, I've had enough now, stop," nor will a wound to close or a splintered bone to re-fuse in an instant, we can indeed influence energetic realities with intention.

This is because intention and thought and energy are **of the same realm** and structurally designed to work with one another.

This process is natural and in action all the time; humans sometimes turn deliberately to trying to shape energetic realities with their intention, for example in the act of prayer, spell casting, making a wish, or the more modern versions of affirmations, goal setting, visualisation and so forth.

What has been forgotten and this is proving to be perhaps one of the most major causes for ill health and unhappiness amidst a well fed, well sheltered and well supported population in the First World today, is that **our intention is interfering with energy exchanges ALL THE TIME.**

This is entirely unconscious; "energy awareness" is restricted to the few in our societies who make an effort to find out more about energy healing, come into contact with the powers of the energy system because of ill health or because they are studying martial arts perhaps.

In EmoTrance, we are going to start reversing this trend and instead of using intention to hurt ourselves, use it to heal our energy bodies, which is where it works beautifully and perfectly, and in quantum time.

Quantum Time Resolutions

As we are working strictly with energy and intention in this system, it is extremely important to always remember that these occurrences are not governed by the laws of nature which we are used to.

This entrainment into mechanical, Newtonian/Aristotelian cause-and-effect thinking **limits totally** what you can do and expect to do in these realms.

For example, we think of the problems of someone who was brutally traumatised by torture as being "huge".

Huge, like a mountain. With that comes a sense, emotion and belief that it must "logically" take a correspondingly huge effort to remove these problems – we are used to thinking that if you want to move a mountain, you will have employ a hundred thousand elephants to pull it down. This sense of hard work is completely based on mechanical thinking and the problems you would face if you were to consider such an endeavour – where will you get that many elephants from? How will you feed them?

Another example would be someone who has spent their entire youth in dreadful circumstances – 15 years of misery, every day, every hour, every second. That is a long time and once again, there is this sense that we by needs have to spend a corresponding time in therapy – at least 15 years if we were to do it every day, every hour, every second.

I know you know that in the quantum realms time and space do not work like that.

There, you can move not just a mountain but a million of them with a single thought.

There, the past and present are interchangeable and ten thousand years are structurally no different from a single second.

I know you know but it is important to remind ourselves about this every so often, especially when our own problems are concerned that seem so "huge" and have gone on for so "long".

In order to really work with intention in the quantum spaces, we have to let go of these notions and prepare ourselves to accept that healing is actually **easy**, and **fast** – just as fast as it can be accepted.

Our conscious awareness **is** where our attention and intention comes from and the intention for healing for example will be as effective as the conscious awareness allows this to be.

Please note that I am **not** speaking about physical healing. I am only speaking about the energy body which is entirely quantum based and entirely unbound by mechanical, "hard universe" laws of nature whereas the physical is not, at least not whilst our energy bodies are not working as they should.

All problems therefore **which derive directly from the energy body** can be truly healed easily and quickly – and the main repercussions of this, the fastest indicators how true and right this actually is, do not come from the physicality (a step removed) but **from the system of emotions, sensations and feelings** that are based on responses to non-physical realities.

These systems are **directly in touch** with the energy body; it is these systems that are responsible for the "mental health epidemic" in the First World; it is these systems that cause aggression, submission, sadness, self destruction, hatred and wars; and it is these systems which respond like a dream to these instant, quantum interventions via the energy body.

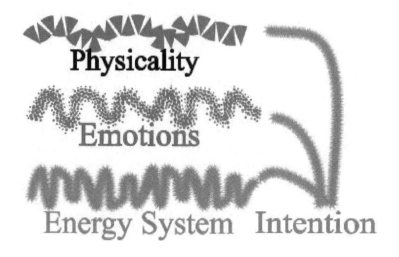

Intention does NOT move the Physicality.
Intention does NOT move Emotions.
Intention ONLY moves Energy.

Intention moves Energy:

Instantly
Rapidly
In Quantum Time
In Quantum Space
Easily

Intention is <u>designed</u> to move energy.

The Basics Of Energy Exchanges

We have already noted that energy needs to flow in, through and out in a natural and systemic function of any energy body at all – and this is indeed the case.

People are, it seems, the only life form on this planet who is using their reflexive consciousness to deliberately interfere in these natural, systemic flows.

As we are all "beings amidst the Oceans of Energy", people's energy bodies are of course designed to partake in many, many energy exchanges with everything around us.

I would say that people have managed to create absolute chaos in all of their energy exchanges with absolutely everything there is, from leylines to beetles and the rest of the universe; but if we start somewhere, we can begin to restore the Even Flow at least there and then hopefully, the lessons will be learned and become resourceful patterns that we can apply to everything else.

So, and seeing that the most pain anywhere is as usual caused not by landslides, natural disasters or lions, I thought we might as well start with the source of this pain, and that would be the energy exchanges that take place between people.

The Hardest Energy Exchange Of All

People have the most extraordinary contortions in their energy systems and more specifically, on the topics of handling incoming energies – giving and receiving energy, if you will.

This is the most basic necessity of energy exchanges within the same species; and I would like to now share with you the transcript of a real session with a person which demonstrates what EmoTrance does and how it works far better than another 20 pages of theoretical discussion.

Here is a Client (C) with an EmoTrance practitioner (ETP) and they have agreed to work on a problem – negative emotions, bad feelings and limiting beliefs with their resulting behavioural disturbances all rolled into one – which can be triggered when someone says to them: "Oh dear, but you have so much potential."

In EmoTrance, we consider that (or any other) sentence, spoken by a real human being with force and meaning, very much as an "incoming energy" and then we note the response of the intended recipient.

Here is what happened in real life.

> ETP, with feeling: "Oh dear, but you have **so much potential!**"

> C (face screws up in disgust, moves backward on the chair as though she was trying to get away from this "incoming message"): "Yuck. That feels awful."

> ETP: "Where exactly do you feel that in your body?"

> C (places both hands on the top of the chest, around the thymus area): "Here. It feels hard, hot – really horrible."

Now, let us consider this for a moment. We have just observed that energy needs to flow. Clearly, the energy form of this statement, "You have so much potential" is not flowing into this person's energy system, is not being processed there nor is it allowed to flow out to complete that pathway.

Indeed, and bearing in mind that the client moved backwards in the chair as though **she was being pushed** by this energy form, as well as the sensations she is describing, we can see clearly this energy is being blocked in her mid chest and it doesn't go any further.

Now, it is my supposition that in this lady's energy body, there exist channels naturally which are absolutely designed to handle this kind of energy (or any other kind of human-generated energy possible, for that matter). It is further my supposition that if and when these channels can be found and activated, the energy will be able to enter her energy system. That it will not only then pass through her energy body without causing damage but quite on the contrary, will be nutritious to her and allow her to feel **better** than if this energy had never come her way at all.

This lady's inability to "digest" this form of incoming energy can be reversed, and it can be reversed easily.

We have already clear and positive proof as to where **exactly** it seeks to enter her energy body and where exactly it is stuck; the lady showed us this with her hands and with her words because **that is where she felt it**

in her physical body which is the natural feedback device for the underlying conditions in the energy body.

Now please note that we are talking now not of games, of suppositions, of "intuitions" or of ideas. This lady **felt** the energy disturbance clearly and perfectly and told us where it was.

Now we know this, we can begin to impact that system.

And this is remarkably easy, because energy is impacted by intention – indeed, this is what intention is for, namely to shape, shift and control **energetically based manifestations** and including very much our own energy body.

Let us now return to the lady and her ETP and find out what happened next.

> ETP: "Now, I am going to say that sentence again to you and when I do, I want you to place your intention on this blockage in your chest and to simply pay close attention. We want to find the natural channels through which this energy would move if it was allowed to do so. Are you ready?"
>
> C: "Yes."
>
> ETP: "Oh but you have so much potential."
>
> C: "It seems to want to move sideways, towards my collarbones."
>
> ETP: "Help it with your intention. Help it to soften and to flow as it should, encourage the process."
>
> C: "I can feel it beginning to flow down my arms."
>
> ETP: "Very good."

Now, most people who see a demonstration like this for the first time are quite amazed and say, "But isn't it really difficult to move energy like that? How did the lady know which way it wanted to go? How do you learn that?"

The truly wonderful and surprising thing about doing this is that it is completely natural and easy – apart from a very few highly disassociated individuals who also cannot make any of the other energy therapies work (such as EFT, TFT, TAT and so forth), the vast majority of the population can just do this, without any training, any meditation, anything at all really. Even and especially small children simply respond to the suggestion or idea that this stuck thing could be softened and allowed to go where it needed to will simply nod and say, "Ok, yes, it's beginning to move ..."

I would now invite you to try the following exercise for yourself.

Get a piece of paper, and on that paper write down something you really don't like to hear about yourself or that people have said to you in the past and which has caused you pain, if not agony. Good candidates are comments such as, "You are useless." – "You are ugly." – "You are worthless." – "You are stupid." – "I don't love you anymore." or any suchlike energy messages that you would experience as being very painful to you and best prevented from ever happening again.

This piece of paper will broadcast the energetic message to you in the absence of a helpful other who can shout the words at you with meaning. Write out the statement in the "you" form as suggested above, turn the paper face down and take a deep breath.

Now, turn it right side up, allow the energy of the statement to come to you and take note as to **where you feel this in your body**.

If you feel nothing at all as you are reading such a statement, you will need to back up and find something really hurtful to you personally. Perhaps you have body image issues that could be used with this such as believing you have a big nose, your hips are too wide or your arms too puny. Perhaps your parents, caretakers or teachers had a particularly nasty phrase with which to hurt you on a regular basis; use that for this exercise.

The important first step is to **feel the response to the incoming energy in your body**.

With EmoTrance beginners, we use these negatives because many people are used to not paying attention to body signals of this nature or have trained themselves to block them out or ignore them completely; a heavy shot across the bows provides a clear cut experience for a first trial and that is always very useful in order to give you both the confidence and the experience to start working with more subtle forms of energies later on.

Now that we have located the place where you feel these sensations in your body we turn our attention to this erea. You might like to place your hands on that place to help you keep your focus and now, consider that these sensations are simply caused by a **disturbance or blockage in your energy body** and that the channels absolutely exist to move this energy in, through and out very successfully.

Pay attention and ask yourself, "Where would this energy like to go?"

Most people get an immediate idea – it might want to go up or down, left or right, it matters not. If you do not get such an indication, read your statement again to bring the sensations right back to full strength and this time, be ready to soften the energy which is causing these physical sensations (when there is actually nothing physically visible at all touching you in physicality) around the edges, just a little bit, like a little steam would come off a block of ice and as it rises, it will show you the channels that were supposed to take this energy if it was in flow (but cannot take or transport this energy in the form of a big blocked up ice cube, if you will).

Then, you let it soften more and flow out entirely.

Repeat this process until you can look at the statement on the paper, and the energy flows freely and readily into you, through the requisite channels and out, leaving you feeling energised and entirely undisturbed by this particular form of energy.

Existing Energetic Realities

If you remember, I said at the start that we are not working with pre-existing ideas of what anyone's energy system should look like, feel like, work like or be like in any way.

We therefore do not talk about meridian points, meridian channels, acupoints, heart centres, governing vessels or chakras on the grounds that we really don't know yet what we are dealing with in a person's energy system and to ask ourselves if this "pain in the chest" is being caused by a this, that or the other is only a mental contortion or blockage to using the basic EmoTrance technique fast, effectively and to its fullest potential.

I therefore refer to all forms of energy manifestations (invisible stuff that nevertheless has a directly observable impact on physical reality) as "ereas" which is short for "Existing Energetic Realities".

Ereas are literally anything of an energetic origin that we have not found another name for yet, don't know the name of, can't describe and/or don't really know what exactly they may be in and of themselves.

I use this term for all manner of energetic manifestations and including disturbances/vortices in the energy body, ghosts, dense thoughtfields, "spirit attachments", "demons" for the simple reason that by refusing to be any more specific about what these ereas may be, we leave our conscious minds wide open to learn something new about them, about their nature, and to really be able to keep scientific in our processes of discovery.

Better Than "Tranquil"

Now you might be forgiven to think that once the original blocked energy has been freed and left the building, the client feels better, all is well with the world and we are done. That is a very interesting and very common limitation in our belief systems, namely that the best we can hope for is a cessation of pain, a relief from the torment and all goes blissfully still and quiet. This view of health is only to be expected from us who don't know any better because all we know is living in constant pain and we'd give anything for that blissful moment of pain cessation.

A child born and raised in a refugee camp will have as his highest dream that one day, if he is very lucky and behaves himself, he might be able to live the day when he will have a whole bowl of gruel, all to himself.

You can understand how this sad state of affairs comes into being; yet we must always, always remember that there is more to expect from life than a bowl of gruel, and there is more to be expected from EmoTrance than simply a cessation of pain – even if we have no experience of such exalted states and therefore, are in no position to even be asking for them! Indeed and in this spirit, for us here learning EmoTrance there is some more work left to be done after the energy flows freely – we can do much, much better than tranquil.

Now, look back to your piece of paper but this time, move the energy faster – draw it into yourself instead of being simply accepting of it and let it **swish** through the channels and out fast. What does that feel like?

It should tingle and make you feel energised, happier and altogether **stronger** than you felt before. Do it again until you can really, really feel yourself buzzing with this energy, laughing, delighted or simply astonished.

This effect is known as the **"energised end state"** of any EmoTrance process and what I would say to you is, "Please don't stop before you have reached this state."

Indeed you could say that doing EmoTrance but not reaching the energised end state is like doing sex but not having an orgasm – interesting but essentially pointless.

And just as in that particular metaphor, I cannot tell you about what that feels like when a previously scary or depressing, frightening or deeply hurtful energy form simply rushes through you, leaving you feeling light and delighted, strong and energised, proactive and **alive**.

You will have to experience it for yourself.

Now, please **stop** and try this most basic EmoTrance move by yourself or call a friend and try it out with them on the telephone.

Basic EmoTrance – Step By Step

Here are the simple steps of the Classic EmoTrance technique for the first time at a glance:

1. Decide on something that has been said to you or about you in the past and that has caused pain.

2. Allow yourself to interact with this "incoming energy" by either: a) Writing it down on a piece of paper, turning the paper face down, taking a deep breath and then flipping it over so the statement's energy "jumps out at you" or b) by calling a friend and having them say the statement to you with meaning and with energy.

3. When the energy has impacted you, pay close attention to where you feel this in your body.*

4. If you can, place your hands there and now pay attention to where this energy would want to go if it was allowed to move. If you don't get an immediate indication, begin to soften the energy blockage by gently massaging the erea with your hands, warming and loosening the energy blockage as you do so.

5. Now, begin to move the energy through the channels that are becoming apparent, all the way through and out, wherever they want to go. Don't argue with the pathways, simply allow the process to unfold until a natural exit point has been found.

6. Repeat the "incoming energy" and do the softening and moving through the channels again. This time, it will already be much easier and faster and you will find that the channels are clearing and flowing much better than they did before.

7. Repeat the "incoming energy" until it simply rushes in, through and out and you are tingling, light, bright and joyful.

8. Take a moment to consider how this one change will affect your actual behaviour and your thoughts because you no longer have to be afraid of this energy or seek to avoid it.

* If there is more than one impact site, concentrate on the most painful one for now; we will talk of having multiple injuries or blockages later and the order and sequence of correcting these.

Now, let us return to our lady client who was having problems with the notion of unfulfilled potential and find out how she is doing.

ETP: "What is happening in your body?"

C: "It is not just going out of my arms, it is also going down my legs. They tingle. Can I stand up? I feel like I need to move."

ETP: "Of course! Energy makes its needs known to us and we must immediately respond."

C (gets up and moves her legs, shakes out her feet): "Ooh, that feels really strange. It is going out through the soles of my feet. I feel much lighter, tingly!"

ETP: "That is probably because we have relieved that pressure on your chest. Come on, let's try it again - "Oh but you have so much potential!"

C (looks surprised): "That feels very different. Much better."

ETP: "But it hasn't entirely gone yet, has it. What do you feel?"

C (indicates a place on her upper chest, to the left of the original site): "There is something left here, something stuck."

ETP: "That's alright. Just soften it up and let it find its pathway. Where does it want to go?"

C: "Hm, it seems to want to go upward. Up my neck. It's sludgy, uncomfortable."

Energy & Movement

EmoTrance is all about movement – freeing up that which was stuck and allowing it to sparkle and flow, dance like a bright sunlit brook dances over smooth worn river rocks.

EmoTrance – whether you do this by yourself or with a client – is not something you do lying down in a state of catatonia (only if you want it to be).

It is expressive – use your hands to show your were disturbances are; let your face show how you really feel about this, give your body free reign for once to respond and back away to show you the reality of your energy exchanges.

When your legs tingle, get up and move about; shake your hands out to help the energy flow, writhe and move your head and neck as the energies flow through you.

You can do EmoTrance to music – indeed, I recommend that you do so, to your favourite sad and happy songs alike, it is a truly wonderful experience.

When you are treating clients, let them move, do it standing up so you can really get 360' access to their energy bodies.

EmoTrance can help those amongst us who are very disassociated to really get back into our own bodies; to have our energy bodies really re-mesh with our feelings and with our physicality.

Allow yourself to feel that movement.

Now here we come to a classic energy occurrence which is very common in EmoTrance, namely that the energy is trying to move through a channel but has not softened up sufficiently to be able to flow properly. It is still too "thick" and viscous and not running freely yet and that creates an unpleasant and sometimes even painful sensation.

When this happens, it means that you need to slow down and **soften the energy further** before it can flow as it should.

Here is what happened next:

ETP: "This energy is still too thick, we need to soften it more. Just put your intention on it and tell it to soften up. Keep your hand there too, that helps."

C: "Yes, it is better now. I was pushing it too hard, trying to get rid of it I think."

ETP: "Just soften it and let it flow. Where is it going?"

C: "This is strange. I thought it was going to go up my neck and out of the top of my head at first, but then it came back around, down the side of my face ..." (starts to yawn heavily)

ETP (smiles and waits)

C (in between much yawning): "It is going through my jaw where I grind my teeth and out of my mouth ... oh that feels so much better ..." (yawns again)

ETP (waits until the yawning has ceased)

C (starts to giggle): "I feel really light headed – this is funny, I don't know how it could be but it just is."

ETP: "Ok, shall we try it again? Here we go: Oh but you have SO much potential!"

C (raises eyebrows, then starts to giggle, then laughs convulsively, tries to speak but can't stop laughing)

ETP (laughing also): "So this doesn't bother you anymore?"

C (struggles for composure): "No, it's just funny. This is so strange! Where did it go???"

The answer to this clearly is – it went in, through and out and that's it.

It was just an energy, nothing more and certainly nothing less which had become stuck, confused the energy body and now, it was flowing cleanly and **there was no longer a problem**.

This is a very unusual and truly amazing aspect of EmoTrance and in and of itself, the proof of the theory, namely that if you restore the Even Flow in an energy body, the emotions follow suit immediately and predictably and there is no need for talking therapy or conscious investigation of the problem **at all**.

Can you begin to imagine what a saving in time, effort and money in therapy hours alone this simple fact represents?

Just for fun, consider the statement of "Oh but you have so much potential" and this "Client". We don't know any details about her but with normal investigative talk therapy, where would we have gone? What would we have done, could have done, to affect such a drastic change in just under five minutes? A change that has stayed absolutely, didn't erode and the problem never came back; further, it had some interesting and wide ranging repercussions on a whole range of related and seemingly unrelated areas.

Another important aspect of treating the energy system, purely and simply, and NOT trying to work out with the conscious mind what is happening is that the treatment is **by definition** ecological – there is no need to worry about whether it is "good for you" or not to change your mind, let go of obsessions and anxieties, release limiting beliefs and negative feelings about the self or others because clearly, we are "just" repairing and putting to rights a natural system and help it to work better.

There can be no objection to this, as there can be no objection to healing a physical injury rather than having it remain an open sore for eternity with all the suffering it entails – and not just to the owner of said sore.

Someone in pain is NOT a good or a healthy person to have around for a partner, for growing children, for friends, for houseplants and pets even – their unhappiness makes proper, satisfying relationships very difficult if not impossible.

Short term, of course we want to help someone get better and we are patient and make allowances. But having someone around who is in constant agony for 20, 30, 50 years or more is intensely damaging to their surroundings and for that reason alone, namely to save your friends, your family and your pets from such suffering it really is clearly a good idea to allow yourself to heal.

The Core of The Physiological Responses

I would now like to pick up on something that really is centrally important about EmoTrance – namely the focus on the body, on the **physiological sensations** relating to your problems and disturbances.

Human beings have amazing minds, and they can make up all sorts of things, misjudge all sorts of things, make wrongful attributions and mistakes about cause and effect.

No-one is safe from that, not even the most strict of scientists who have been making mistakes in their calculations and getting things wrong for longer than most of us.

Physical input breaks through all illusions, all imaginings, all false learnings.

Pain and extreme pain, pleasure and extreme pleasure are undeniable realities in our neurology.

If you have a toothache, no amount of meditation can keep this at bay as the infection spreads and the pain becomes more and more unbearable, as the physicality is drawing attention to itself and calling to you, then screaming at you, louder and louder still, to do something because survival is at stake.

Physicality and the preservation of physicality is the first commandment of a physical being, and if we focus not on auras, or chakras, or meridians, or this and that and simply **stay with the physical reality of what we feel** in our bodies then we **simply can't go wrong** and will never get lost in madness or illusion.

For energy healing, you can imagine how centrally important it is to distinguish between reality and make belief, between actual learnings about the nature of energy body and guess work or hallucinations which might sound great and sell a million books, but do not help you a bit when you are writhing on the floor in agony of mental and emotional pain yet again.

When we do EmoTrance, we do not slide off into metaphors – my pain is like a big black sword stabbing at my solar plexus.

You cannot move "a big black sword" through a meridian. That what has been **interpreted** as "a big black sword" is **only an energy** that needs to soften and flow through its requisite channels – AND it will do so, but for the asking of it, if it is **NOT** encased in a hard metaphor which makes it basically incompatible with the energy system directly.

Please note that **all talking therapy** is a form of metaphor therapy, as words are just labels for experiences, thoughts, feelings and sensations just as much as swords, fiery balls or Katherine wheel chakras or nothing but labels, albeit of a slightly different kind.

As soon as we label our feelings and experiences, we are in the same position as the user of a personal computer would be – namely dealing with the programmes through **an interface device**. There are **NO** little dustbins or little yellow file folders in a computer. Those are representations and behind them is the reality of the computer and its workings – a million lines or more of code.

When we let go of the metaphors and labels and deal with the energy body directly rather than through an interface (which distorts, deletes and impoverishes what the reality is and what you can actually do with it!) we become **far more effective** immediately. Whatever we are attempting to do is faster, has less errors in it, and the effects are much, much more profound for the same effort expended – exponentially so, in fact.

So, we only have two realities – one is the physical sensation the person who is working with EmoTrance is really feeling and the energetic reality beneath which is actually causing the physical sensation.

"It's Only An Energy!"

In theory, this is clearly a very good way to go about "repairing injuries in the energy body" – focussed, fast, easy and absolutely in accordance with the laws of nature as they pertain to the quantum energy systems.

In practise, you would be surprised how very difficult it is for most people to stop thinking of their problems as unfathomable, mysterious, complicated madnesses that need at least fifty years in therapy to make the slightest bit of headway (but probably can never be resolved at all).

Here is an example:

> C (crying, on the telephone):"My husband has left me! I am all alone! My heart is broken and all is lost!"

ETP: "Where do you feel that in your body?"

C: "In my stomach. It is so horrible!" (sobs out loud)

ETP: "It is only an energy. Soften it and allow it to move."

C: "But it only wants to protect me!"

ETP: "It is only an energy. It can't want anything. Let it move."

C (surprised): "Oh alright then. Yes, it is moving into my back, into my spine and down my legs."

ETP: "How do you feel now?"

C (amazed): "Much better! My goodness, that was so easy ... Thank you!"

Because we think a lot and we are used to thinking a lot with our conscious minds, we literally anthropomorphize energetic occurrences, giving them a will where none exists: "It only wants to protect me" – "It's only an energy – it can't want **anything**!" is an example of this.

Here is another example.

This client had "forgiveness and anger" issues. Now if you have ever been involved even at the very periphery of counselling or psychology at all, you would be forgiven for heaving a deep sigh and see a therapeutic landscape of years stretching out in front of you – causative issues, repressed memories, trauma by the bucket, interrelations, parts conflicts, habitual belief formations, secondary gain, ecology and, and, and and ...

Here we go with EmoTrance:

C: "I am so furiously angry. There's no way I am going to forgive this person for what they did, not ever!"

ETP: "Where do you feel that in your body?"

C (puts hands on stomach just below the belly button): "It is a huge hot pressure in my stomach."

ETP: "What you are feeling is a blockage in your energy system. Put your attention there, gently massage it with your hands whilst you are focussing on this. Now, where does this energy want to go, where does it need to go, where should it be going?"

C: "It seems to want to go downwards but there is like a cork there, it is stuck and swirling around."

ETP: "Ah there's your energy blockage. Soften it, stroke it with your attention and your intention and let it flow away."

C: "Dissolve the cork?"

ETP: "It isn't actually a cork, it is energy that has become blocked up and stuck and works like a cork now. Intention and energy are of the same realm and they are designed to work with each other – just give that blockage permission to resolve now, melt like an ice cube."

C: "Ok, it is getting softer round the edges. Oh, oh, I can feel the first of that hot stuff from my stomach starting to flow down, it is going straight down and round, up my back!"

ETP: "That's brilliant, it is finding the channel through which this energy needs to move! Where is it going?"

C: "Up my spine, no there's two, either side of my spine. Going up, into my neck. And into my shoulders, down my arms! I can feel it coming out of my fingertips – like electricity. This is so weird!" (starts to laugh)

ETP: "You are doing really well! Now, how is that blockage, that cork?"

C: "It is dissolving, like it is melting with that hot stuff coming out."

ETP: "And how does your stomach feel now?"

C: "Oh much, much better. Not so hot and nowhere near so bloated but there's still loads in there.

ETP: "Yes well it's been storing up in there for a long time, let's give it all a chance to flow out and through ..."

(About five minutes later)

ETP: "So when you think back to that anger you had in your stomach, and about that person, what do you feel now?"

C (inward looking and thoughtful, then looks up surprised and smiles): "I really can't believe this but it is gone. No pain. No anger. I'm remembering a lot of things my psychologists used to say to me about why they might have done it but even that is – like it isn't important anymore. It happened and it was, and now – it's just not important anymore. I have a life to live!" (Client laughs out loud and claps hands in delight).

In this example, metaphors and labels were used just enough so that both knew they could talk about what was happening in the client's body; yet even then the ETP reminded both that they were working **only with energy** and not with issues, memories, judgements, decisions or even ice cubes, corks and fire.

It is exactly that direct approach which makes EmoTrance treatments so surprising, so healing, so effective and so very practical.

Please be on your guard when you learn to do EmoTrance for yourself or you do with others; it is very easy to slide into metaphor or conscious computations and remind yourself again and again: **"It is ONLY an energy."**

As soon as you do this, you can begin to influence this energy with your mind and intention directly and experience **immediate** results, even in moments of high crisis and disturbance.

Client Centred, Led By Physiology

As an aside to counsellors and therapists, but also to anyone who is a client or interested in psychology, I would point out that the ETP practitioners in our examples are NOT suggesting anything at all beyond stating that what the client is feeling is an energy.

All the rest is absolutely happening with, in and by the client – they are saying where it hurts, they are giving constant feedback on what is really happening in their awareness, they are **feeling directly** where the energy is moving to and from.

All the ETP does is to ask for feedback and assists the client in keeping focussed on **moving the energy**.

This is actually very important in many different respects as we will discuss more in depth later on in this manual; for now I would simply like to point out that this simple method avoids transference problems, false memory syndrome, totally validates the client's individual experiences, does not demand any knowledge from the ETP regarding psychology or even energy bodies AT ALL and is with all of that, incredibly effective.

Energy States & Energy Manifestations

Working with energy directly has more benefits, apart from the fact that it is instantly responsive to intention and thought, pure magic, indeed.

One of the really important aspects of dealing with energy and physiological sensations as opposed to dealing with metaphors or "anger and hatred" is that these are neutral and natural things which are outside of the usual "good and bad" judgements we people make quite habitually.

To put it simply, it is very difficult to get judgemental or angry about energy, energy blockages, or energetic injuries.

It is difficult even getting emotional about the whole process of energy flow and exchanges.

Even with colours, we accept and reject and make judgements – some people don't like pink and they love blue, for example.

This rejection or acceptance or even stronger, desire perhaps, need, want etc. clouds our judgement and it directly affects the energetic realities in question and how we process them in our energy bodies.

If we don't like pink and reject pink, that energy is being kept away from us and for all we know, it might well cause scurvy conditions in our energy bodies.

If we consider the pink energy as simply an energy, we no longer have a reason to reject it and it can flow naturally in, through and out once again.

This basic principle applies to everything we might have judged as desirable vs. undesirable in the past. I will speak of this in more detail later; but please keep in mind that **whatever** comes your way, when we turn our point of view towards the energetic realities of anything at all, we see that there is actually nothing that can hurt us **if our energy**

bodies are fully functioning and that there is nothing that we cannot derive nourishment from.

Energy & Water

We don't really have what I would call "proper language" yet to talk about the quantum ways of the energy body. For this reason, talking about energy is difficult and in order to conceptualise energy at all I have chosen to use the metaphor of water in its various manifestations.

So, energy can exist in a state like you would find it on a clear blue autumn day – it is there, in the air, but so fine you cannot even see it and it can get just anywhere in that fine state.

Then it becomes denser and becomes a cloud, fog and then crystallises into fine rain. This fine light water becomes more dense if more pressure is exerted. Energy becomes compressed and as it does so, becomes slower and thicker, and thicker still until it ceases and doesn't move at all any longer. As the energy flows less and less and becomes more and more compressed, denser and denser, it bridges the threshold into the sensation systems and you can begin to feel it physically – then we experience what we call emotions and sensations, i.e. physiological responses that do not seem to have a "hard" effect causing this. If conditions don't change, energy can become denser still and when it has become "as hard as rock", it is at that point that the real damage to the physicality is done as the energy system has come to a virtual stand still and the physicality is forced to follow suit.

This is my supposition and experience as to how it happens that energy disturbances eventually manifest in physical illness, with that in-between step of emotional/cognitive disturbances.

Now, it is important to remember that we are still talking about energy. Even though I talk about "rock hard" or "an ice cube" or "it flows like water", it is still energy we are describing and that is very important.

Energy lives in the quantum spaces, and there, different laws of nature apply.

That is the reason why it is possible – even easy – to take an ancient energetic injury or a burden that someone might have had for fifty years or more, that has become "hard as rock" and as painful a shard inside their physiologies, and we can simply soften it and make it rise like mist but for the asking.

In the quantum spaces of energy, there is no time. Time is no healer here but our intention, our thoughts, can go to work and make the most inordinate changes now, quickly, instantly – and it is easy to do so, so easy that a child can do it. Also, and because energy "wants" to flow – it is designed to do this, it is in its nature – the systemics of unblocking energy and letting it flow are in our favour; you could think of it as going with gravity, rather than against it. Our conscious minds, our unconscious minds, our body minds all agree that it is a good idea and rather than doing this being any kind of struggle or difficult to learn, we are going with the flow ourselves when we do this, and that is probably exactly why it is so easy.

Dense Energy & Energy Manifestations

Think of energy as being able to manifest in different states:

> **fine and invisible, the lightest mist**
>
> **flowing freely like light water**
>
> **flowing slowly like heavy water**
>
> **flowing very thickly and very slowly like syrup**
>
> **setting into density like wax**
>
> **hard as ice**
>
> **ancient hard ice like a glacier**
>
> **0 Kelvin – all movement has stopped.**

The "denser" it becomes, the more it becomes noticeable in emotional and then in physical symptoms.

EmoTrance As A Physical Skill

At the end of the day, EmoTrance is not a therapeutic tool as such but indeed, a physical skill for people of all ages and persuasions to re-learn to do as nature intended.

The basic steps of EmoTrance – 1. Notice a blockage; 2. Place your intention there. 3. Soften and flow it through its rightful channels, through and out – are something that **once your totality has re-learned to do** can happen automatically and restore balance, flow, equilibrium and in turn, **health** to your energy system no matter what the environment will throw at you – there and then.

Indeed, EmoTrance is designed and was deliberately designed by me in that way, to make **future visits to a therapist unnecessary**.

It is really important to note that I am not joking when I talk about this being a physical skill such as touch typing or learning to waltz. When this 1-2-3 movement has become habitual and unconscious (again), it doesn't matter where you go or what you do – your energy system will be able to fluently and **instantly** handle any form of incoming energy. People can shout the worst abuse at you; you may find yourself in terrifying situations or unbearably sad ones and you will be able to experience these situations without damaging yourself or your energy system AND you can expect to actually benefit from having experienced such human experiences.

This does not, by the way, mean at all that you will feel nothing. In the contrary. The passing of these many different energies does create emotions and sensations – but these are of a very, very different order than the negative emotions of pain and distress we are so very used to experiencing.

Some of these emotions you will experience when you move these energies as they should have always flown through you by design and by nature will have you in awe and many of these don't even have labels yet. You will feel things – and I'm afraid labels such as love, devotion, compassion et al are but the palest hint of the sunrise to come – that you never thought you could possibly feel.

A really fully functioning energy system is a miracle in and of itself, and we can have one now, every one of us. Do not underestimate the use of the simple physical skill of re-learning how to channel energies through our systems once again. It is indeed my belief and presupposition that this will bring about change of a nature and of an order none of us have actually even thought to hope for, tied up as we were in simply praying for symptom cessation and nothing much beyond.

Please remember this as you begin to use EmoTrance to make emergency repairs to your own energy body and that of others that this is NOT where we are heading and that this is only a very first step towards proactive change of a totally different order.

EmoTrance Self Help

I've heard it say numerous times now that practitioner assisted ET is more effective than ET in self help. In general, it is so that two people pulling on a string create more of a pull than one and to have a second viewpoint and a steadying other is always helpful, of course.

However, Self Help is perfectly possible and perfectly effective – providing:

1. You speak your concerns out loud.

This is one of the major reasons that people **think** other-assisted ET is so much more powerful – of course, you are **speaking** out loud about your sensations to the other.

When you do that, your focus is near enough complete, most of your neurology engaged and your intention and attention both exactly where they MUST be for the treatment of your energy system to be smooth and easy.

If you don't speak aloud but just **think** inside your own head, all sorts of thoughts run all over the place and you are most likely to get distracted or fall into thoughts and conscious content of one kind or another, rather than remaining focussed on the energy that creates the physiological sensation. But also, there are certain processes of your neurology that are not engaged and are not taking part in the process which have proven to be extremely helpful – remember for example, that magic spells NEED to be spoken out aloud to make them become REAL rather than just a musing thought or a passing fancy.

This is one of these "universal laws" you will have heard about before and it is most helpful to take note and speak aloud – if you have problems with that, find the place in your body where this problem resides and remove it before starting to do self help with ET on other issues.

2. USE Your Healing Hands.

Just like the speaking, touching the place/s where the energy is stuck, and then following the energy as it moves through your system and finds it's channels of release, has much more depth and meaning than just retaining your focus clearly on what's happening and where you are at any point in the process.

Your hands are **healing hands** not just for others but also for yourself.

They help tremendously to smooth and gentle the passage of the energies, repairing and preparing pathways that may not have been used for many years and they bridge your physiology back to your energy self, reconnecting yourself with yourself in the most beautiful and profound way possible.

NB: If the energy is moving through channels or in parts of your body that you cannot physically reach to touch, use the "Hands Of Ghost" technique instead.

3. Practise Makes Perfect

EmoTrance works best when it is not used only for old problem removal and emergency work under duress but indeed, if you do it a lot and with subtle sensations as much as with big traumatic emotions.

It is worthwhile to remember that EmoTrance is indeed a practical, physical skill to re-learn, and that it is our aim and outcome to have this process happen completely automatically in immediate response to the environment and without having to think about it at all.

Therefore, I strongly suggest you practise EmoTrance whenever you become aware of an emotional sensation or a feeling in the day, whenever you notice that there is a disturbance. You can do this whilst driving, if you are getting frustrated with the traffic or with other drivers, for example; you can do it whilst waiting in bank lines, at airports, at supermarket checkouts. A very good place to practise is whilst watching movies and TV because these are of course designed to bring up emotions – be it soap operas, talk shows, scary movies, "romantic movies" or current affairs programmes, each one is a perfect opportunity to sooth your energy system and have it run that much better, that much smoother in the process.

Having EmoTrance on "automatic pilot" and fully learned changes your days profoundly and gives you much, much more energy to get what you really want out of life.

Riding The Lightning

Let's talk a moment about emotions.

If you remember, the "discovery statement" of EmoTrance says that **ALL emotions are JUST and NOTHING MORE than feedback devices on the existing conditions in the energy body**, just like pain and pleasure are to the physical body.

A very strong emotion is a very strong pain that says that something is **VERY WRONG** with the way some kind of energy – self generated or coming to you from the environment or a loop response between the two.

This has some very extraordinary repercussions on many, many aspects of our lives and we really need to change our thinking fundamentally to make as much use of this as is inherent in this discovery.

We – as a human race – have a strong tradition of the idea that there is nobility in failing to handle our energy system, or, in other words, bursting out into tears, temper tantrums, jumping off bridges "because the pain's just too much" and writing heartrending poetry in these moments of failure.

This "nobility of failure" is counteracted by an equally strong tradition, once again absolutely cross culturally and across the ages, to look down upon those given to emotional tantrums as being weak and inferior and all cultures have a thing going on by various means to stop this from happening.

For example, the "strong, silent type" is definitely the way to be in many cultures that exist today, if not in all of them.

I put forth the proposition that the outcome – i.e. a person who doesn't stomp their feet and bursts out into tears – is actually and perfectly correct and the way it should be (in a fully functioning adult).

However, the way this is being attempted to achieve is very counter-productive.

Even if you have only begun your explorations of our energy systems and energy bodies, you will clearly know and understand that suppressing emotions or pretending not to have them, to disassociate from them or to push them away is extraordinarily damaging to the entire system and produces in effect, physical and psychological cripples rather than outstanding, shining human beings.

What we need to learn to do and absolutely learn to want to do, is to "ride the lightning" correctly.

I put forth the proposition that ANY form of energy charge, even the most profound and previously thought to be damaging kind and including the most severe trauma, bereavement, loss, disappointment and heartbreak **CAN BE CHANNELLED, CAN BE HANDLED and in handling it, will strengthen us even further.**

I cannot know at this point in space and time what a person, a human, who was no longer afraid to love and live because they not only know absolutely that they can handle the energies thus raised, but become more, stronger, farther ranging and more powerfully human in return.

Truly, I can't imagine what a world would be like where we would stop being enmeshed and immersed in our own emotional ongoings, addictions, repetitive pay-off patterns of drama, trauma, success, love and loss and so forth. Where one would look at TV soap operas and just sigh briefly at these **children's games** played out by people who had simply not learned to handle energies as they were always designed to handle them.

Where children would indeed be protected properly from too intense charges and learned much faster and more profoundly to build the systems required to handle them, to grow these systems ecologically and as they were designed to grow and develop.

This would be a world with whole new stories – new songs, new plays, new shows, new movies altogether because all the ones we have based on emotions, conflict, war and such have become outdated, outmoded and such an old hat that only human historians would be fascinated by watching these crazy things being played out in their museums.

Now, and this is centrally important, this is NOT a world without feelings at all – just completely different classes of experiences and feelings, challenges we have never been given the opportunity to face ourselves before (and by we, I mean **the entire human race** across all the ages!).

When you do EmoTrance, you will know and notice that you experience sensations you've never felt before, from little empowering shivers that go through your entire system to huge rushes of energy that makes you feel as though you could just lift off and fly.

Even if we want to keep unnecessary emotional contortions for now **because we simply haven't experienced the new classes and states of being yet** which would render them pale, insignificant and downright useless in comparison, I want you to clearly take this thought away with you from this section, namely that it **is** possible to change things that have been the same for 25,000 years and more.

It **is** possible because you can feel, know and experience for yourself how **different** the world becomes all of a sudden when you just begin to handle a few choice energies differently – opening yourself to a bit of praise, for example; dropping shields on a few minor criticisms, running through a few old stuck fears.

Remember and always retain the knowledge that the energies we're currently dealing with are in the "shallow beginners, non-swimmers" end of a pool that has so much depth, it takes your breath away.

As we are getting better at handling simple, easy energies we are opening ourselves up to beginning first to suspect, then actually tingle with the awareness of **other forms of energy**, the kind you've heard about in old legends, such as the power to make a song and castle walls cannot help but tumble.

These energies exist.

They are unbelievably powerful and grandiose.

We ARE designed to know them and to handle them, understand them, evoke them, channel them, make them our own, and dance with them in a universe that is brimming with raw untameable power which calls to us if only we would begin now to open up, drop shields and reconnect.

PART 2 - THE CONCEPT OF ENERGY NUTRITION

In the absence of a better model and in light of the fact that we know literally nothing about the finer points and requirements of the energy body, I have chosen, for now, to simply imagine that the energy body was similar in certain basic requirements to the physical body.

When I first began to investigate this, I asked myself the question, "Let us look at the basics here. What are the most basic, the most simple requirements for a functioning physical body?"

The answer to this was a stable range of environments and constantly renewing incoming nutrition - water and food.

It stands to reason to make that bridge and to consider that the energy body too has these basic needs. Energy needs to flow and just as physicality flows in its very own way (please see "Quantum Healing" by Deepak Chopra for more on this flow), if we expend energy then we need sources of replenishing it.

Human beings are designed as social creatures – we are structurally social mammals.

Therefore, a part of our energetic requirements naturally are emanations from our fellow social mammals and these come in a very wide range of manifestations, from "Romeo & Juliet" type love energies to what happens between a first class torturer and his victim on the 7th day in the dungeons or a murderous rage that seeks only to destroy being directed at you personally.

Just in human interaction, there exists **naturally** this extraordinary wide and broad range of energies of which we generally allow ourselves to experience on the tiniest narrow band – we arrange our lives with great care so that we need never experience any of the extremes if at all possible. This of course is because no-one ever taught us how to handle or channel these extreme energies.

Little boys are told not to cry but they are not told how to not cry or what to do instead when the pressure of energies builds up inside of them that naturally seeks release through tears. So they are left to their own devices and most of them either fail completely and do burst out into tears, leaving them to think of themselves as weak and powerless and then spend a lifetime avoiding situations which might cause a recurrence; others may find that if you exert enough will power, you can stop these rising energies that are seeking expression and force them back down the channels they came from, compacting them down and end up with hearts of stone.

But be this as it may, the fact is that as a result we have created a situation where all of us live in malnutrition circumstances just with people energy alone. Firstly this happens as we try and control what energies are being generated in the first place – heading off criticism AND praise both at the pass, organising our lives so we will never have to experience fear, or bereavement, or sadness, or jealousy or anger and so forth.

Next, we also build shields to protect us from what's left in the way of incoming energy that may damage us which is an important topic in itself and all of this is simply a result of not knowing how to handle these energies in our systems.

Now, you might consider it a very radical thought that "negative energies" we have been so afraid of all our lives, have seen our parents and role models be so afraid of all of theirs, are actually beneficial and needed to balance and to develop our energy bodies.

But you know, the indicators are there.

People who have been in wars and even in concentration camps, people who have really loved and lost will often say surprisingly that it was important to them to have been there, that it changed them for the better.

If offered the choice of never having experienced what they did and lead a "normal" bland life where nothing untoward ever happened to them and to trade this for how things are now, even with many practical problems arising from their experiences, they will NOT give them up for the world.

It is my supposition that experiences are designed to change us; that we must indeed change to develop into a true adult form of mind and possibly body too, and that the handling of these incoming energies in a holistic and systemic way is exactly what allows us to do this, namely to learn from our experiences in a whole new way, to be changed for the better by these experiences and not be broken by them in the process.

Saying YES To Energy Flow

One of the reasons that people in the First World often turn to pets for energy suppliers is that the barriers against love, affection and attention from other people are not in place and the energies can flow freely.

There is, of course, the other side of the coin. Animals do not have barriers as a rule to **incoming** energies and they will actually accept attention **from** humans who are bursting to give these - but cannot find any fellow human recipients for their energies, only barriers upon barriers where their contributions bounce out flatly too.

The problems with energy exchanges and energy flow are that they are either not received at all (shielded out) which happens when we consciously say "NO!" to an incoming energy form; get stuck in blockages when we say "NO!" halfway through a process (or, "Reverse, reverse!" if you will); or resist the process of letting the energy flow out by shouting, "No, I'm not letting that go!" and trying to hold on to it.

Apart from people and human energies which are not received because we have said "NO!" to that particular energy at some point there are a great many other types which then are no longer available for the essential nutrition and widely varied energy diets our Energy Bodies require for full functioning.

Weather is a good example of this. Storms, rainy weather and cold weathers are **tremendous** energy providers - if one would open up to this. Current group consensus in the First World, however, is that anything other than a sunny, warm day with a cloudless sky is "bad weather" and must be avoided, bemoaned, and shielded against in every way possible.

The very act of saying "NO!" to "bad weather" in and of itself reverses and disables parts of the energy system and this leads to people who hold these views to becoming more acutely affected by cold or rainy weather in return - with mental depression or psychosomatic flare-ups, for example.

EmoTrance & Breathing

Breathing is probably our most direct and profound personal experience of energy exchanges with the universe directly. Breathing in and out is how we determine if someone is alive or not – it is that fundamental.

How we breathe has to do with our existing mind-body totality states at the time; when people are afraid or awaiting something, they will naturally hold their breath. Breathing is used for all kinds of human activities in order to control state in people – singing together brings everyone in a congregation into rapport, as does laughing together at the same time; when you breathe together, you enter the same state automatically. This is also used in psychotherapy and related fields in order to create rapport; and another aspect of this state correlation is that the deeper we breathe, the more "connected" to our physicality we become.

We could think in our context of the act of holding the breath or breathing very shallow to be versions of saying NO to an incoming energy form; breathing something in deeply also states that we are allowing the energy of it to enter us profoundly and into every cell of our bodies.

In the basic EmoTrance process, breathing in deeply when trying to make contact with any form of energy makes the physiological responses more noticeable; you may use this to help pin point where your blockages are located.

Breathing in deeply and with focus on the existing energy blockage may help dissolve this blockage as further energy is directed to this erea. I would make the point that breathing into an overly dense erea will make the feelings worse and so this becomes a valuable feedback device in its own right.

Breathing out, on the other hand, is very helpful when you are the "soften and flow" stage and the energy is beginning to move. I often think in the terms of, "I want to sigh it all away, sigh it away and let it go ..." when I do this; I find it helps release the energies in question.

Lastly, disruptions in breathing patterns are an absolute indication of a disturbance in the energy body. When you think about something and find that your breathing becomes shallow, irregular, unusually deep or even gasping or sob like, you can be sure there is something that needs attention paying to it immediately.

Breath is an excellent indicator of the Even Flow.

There are many other naturally existing energies that are blocked by individuals. Many people have strong colour preferences - someone might say, "Orange is not my colour." or, "I don't like the colour orange." which is the equivalent of saying, "NO! to orange."

Thus instructed, the energy body deflects that particular vibration and we are very literally, in scurvy conditions.

It is important to note that the processes which have been described here are not an addition or a new invention, but simply represent an observation about naturally occurring exchanges in reality.

It is impossible to repair a person's self esteem, for example, who hold it to be the truth that they are worthless, with counter-examples or by sending them (telling them, showing them, demonstrating to them) that this is a false decision **IF** this person is **INCAPABLE** of receiving the energies associated with this sentiment.

Thus it is possible that the most beautiful model on Earth is in tears because she is convinced that she is ugly; the most beloved person who has innumerable family members and friends who all care deeply about them is entirely convinced that "No-body loves me."; and the most talented and gifted people can state with absolute conviction that, "I am worthless."

It needs to be clearly understood that it is not the **meanings** of such words or phrases which will heal and put a great many things to rights, but the **energies** these words and phrases contain and carry.

These energies go to the energy body and there, fulfill tasks of repair, of healing, of renewal. In doing so, they correct at the underlying energetic level what is wrong which then becomes reflected in psychological and physiological changes too.

In the case of psychological changes, as a person "takes readings" of their internal energetic landscapes, this translates directly into self concept understandings and realities.

In this context it is also important to note that we do actually have a great deal of influence over our energy systems and we always did. Allergies, for example, come about when the body-mind flags a substance as being a danger and puts the entire energy system into full out reversal (see Sandi Radomski's "Allergy Antidotes").

People also have severe allergies to certain energy forms which translates into strong and irrational feelings about things that really should not cause such responses, such as a particular section of species we share this planet with, the aforementioned colours and weather states, but also things such as smells, music, tastes, words, sights – all kinds.

Working with EmoTrance to return to the energetic source of these disturbances makes a huge difference in the actual experience of these occurrences on the visible behavioural and physical levels.

A Personal Experience With Saying Yes To An Energy Form

For this exercise, choose a form of music you particularly despise and indeed, have never liked for whatever reason.

Find an example of this music on a radio station or on TV, play it and now begin to consider this as "just an energy" – where does this hurt you or where do you feel it in your body?

Run the basic EmoTrance technique on this energy occurrence until the energy of that music flows freely throughout you.

Sit with the new experience and the new thoughts and insights this has generated for you for a while before you return to your normal activities.

I cannot stress enough how very wide ranging this simple movement of saying "Yes!" to any type of incoming or surrounding energy form in your environment actually is.

One lady I know used this on a train in response to getting very annoyed with two small children who were clamouring and screaming. Five seconds of EmoTrance later and she noticed to her utter amazement that she actually felt both energised by the contact with these children, as well as truly compassionate to their frustration and boredom. Other ETPs report incidents like finding the taste of raw lemon extraordinarily invigorating after a small shift and even allowing themselves to be "infected with the party spirit" in a rowdy bar and feeling quite at home with what was happening around them.

One gentleman used EmoTrance to remove all barriers between himself and a new language he had to learn and allowed himself to have it "just flow in"; the result was first of all that the language lessons were no longer dreaded and depressing, which in and of itself would have to be considered a blessing, but also that he learned the language easily and right from the start used it at home to make little comments that his wife could not understand which he thought was entirely hilarious.

I have a story mailed to me by a holistic therapist who opened herself to the "energy of the high street" where she lived – nothing but concrete, exhaust fumes and kebab shop smells which had previously left her with a strong feeling of negativity and depletion. She felt herself entirely rushed by fast, powerful energy and made the comment of having a sense of "awakening" in that unlikely environment.

Time and time again people express true astonishment how even life long beliefs and experiences can change from bad to good with nothing more than a small internal adjustment at the energy levels – I can only invite you to be without fear and give it a try.

It is well worth doing.

Having The World – And Eating It ...

Some years ago I noted that I was buying lamps rather compulsively.

Table lamps, to be more specific.

Round table lamps, preferably made of a single piece of glass or a seamless round shade over the bulb inside – I have dozens of them, all over the place and it never really struck me as being unusual until one Christmas, I was in a super shopping mall which was stuffed full of jewellery, consumer goods of all possible kinds, clothes, stereos, books, gifts, toys – everything a bored First World Westerner might like to spend their hard earned cash on to improve their fates in some shape or form, if only for a moment.

And the only thing for all the hours I spend there with my children that day which made my interest truly flare up for a moment was – yes, you've guessed it. Basically a crystal ball with a light beneath it in a shop that sold novelty table lamps.

It was then I recognised there was something amiss. What exactly was I trying to buy? I already have more than enough of the things to know that buying yet another one won't do the trick, won't fill that strange need I had to bring exactly what? into my house?

I thought about this on and off over the Christmas Holidays, and at one point was in my office when the low winter sun just moved over the tops of the houses opposite my garden and I saw it burst brightly through the windows, flooding the room and I understood that what I was trying to buy was not a lamp, but the lamp was a metaphor for something else – an energy source like the sun.

I was seeking and craving **a form of energy** that was in short supply in my life – and which clearly could not be fulfilled by buying it in the metaphorical form of table lamps.

At the time, I then went on to simply imagine a sunrise in my mind whenever I was in dire danger of yet again purchasing a crystal ball lamp and the craving receded.

Now we have talked about Energy Nutrition and in this context, there are other options to help someone who has a shortfall of a particular energy in their systems and needs it to heal or grow or become more balanced, feel happier and more at home on this planet.

Becoming An Energy Vampire

Whenever I explain the concept of taking energy out of anything at all to satisfy your own needs and hungers, people don't quite get it just how many situations this covers, how much this entails.

Placing my hand, for example, on or near a lamp in a shop that I really feel I **need** to have, buy, own, take home, **make it mine** and make it become a part of me, and allowing this energy to come to me, resolving any blockages that stand between me and that object's energy, satisfies a hunger and a need a hundred times more profoundly than buying the object.

The applications of this one simple principle are truly and literally endless – and they are endlessly satisfying and intensely healing, too.

In the olden days, tribes used to eat their ancestors and their warrior enemy's bodies in order to obtain their wisdom, strength and spirit.

Now, we look upon this with raised eyebrows, for although we understand what they were trying to do, we might have a notion that this might not be achievable in that way alone.

And yet, how is this different from eating a vanilla ice cream because that just **somehow** evokes the energies of a long gone childhood happiness that got tied into the sense, taste and experience of vanilla ice cream?

How is it different from someone trying to feel love, feel more worthwhile, more strong within themselves by **eating anything at all**?

I have stood in a supermarket, watching a friend who put just such things on the "energy of vanilla ice cream" holding out her arms quite literally to the ice cream freezer and beginning to tremble, cry and then find a whole new balance, a whole new joy that was absolutely real and left her with a deep sense of appreciation for the "energy of vanilla ice cream" and what, if it was let right into her starving systems, could do for her in reality.

It was pretty extraordinary to see from the outside.

But that is nothing to how extraordinary it feels when you are actually doing this yourself.

In this way, you can become a true energy vampire and feed on just about everything and anything – and in the process you are healing yourself and nourishing yourself so profoundly, you have to experience this to understand what I am talking about.

Hugging trees, for example, or simply dissolving the blocks in your energy body and your wider systems to really and truly partaking of "Father Earth & Mother Sky", is logical and obvious to most.

But there's so much more, it makes my head spin sometimes.

Consider this, for example – the very real and very difficult concepts of Jealousy & Envy.

Jealousy & Envy

Lazaris defines these two in the following way which I like and would like to share with you: "Jealousy is when someone has something you don't have; but envy is if they have something but **YOU know YOU will NEVER have that**."

These are very particular pains and pointers to deep wounds in our energy system that are virtually impossible to repair from the outside in; they are also dangerous energies to evoke in others.

Someone who is jealous and envious will in turn, try to provoke these energies from others in order to re-balance a system that feeds endlessly upon itself. No amount of holy thinking can overcome this; think of the root causes of both jealousy and envy as open sores and then someone sticks a needle into that sore – no amount of meditation can overcome the instant and very real pain this would cause in an instant.

Quite spontaneously, whilst out in Victoria Station with a friend, the topic arose of "being jealous of the good looking people walking by". We argued for a while if this was jealousy or far more likely, the deeper bitter envy instead but that really doesn't matter – who cares about labels when the pain is real enough?

This friend was particularly focussing on big men with broad shoulders and bulging muscles, nicely displayed on this hot summer's day because many were wearing short and cut off T-Shirts. Just for fun, we thought about trying to allow him to "eat these energies" instead of looking at these men with pain of envy and feelings of inadequacy.

As usual, there were big, big shields to allowing this energy of being well built and muscular to enter my friends systems; but once he dissolved them and allowed himself to experience this, the **envy dissolved as if by magic** and instead of hating the owners of these physical attributes, he began to admire them instead – and then began to look at other people too and made a comment about the amazing varieties and shapes of humans in general.

I will admit that I had contortions in my energy systems about "blondes" – as I'm not cheerleader material and have dark brown hair, I have harboured jealousy on that score which I have manfully try to suppress for as long as I can remember.

On this day, I dropped shields and allowed myself to interact with the "blonde energy"; after all my friend had been brave and I felt I should be able to do the same.

Imagine my surprise when something very similar happened to me. It was no big deal, no revelation or enlightenment shift, but something did shift because where these "blondes" had been a preferred focus of envious attention and negative thoughts all these years before, as soon as I did allow this energy to come into me and pass on through, they just became **people** and I too was free to notice all the other many shapes and sizes that walked by the cafe' in Victoria Station in their thousands.

We then went on to try some more features and attributes – attitude, for example. There was a group of very well dressed business men, highly focussed and discussing their important business of the day. Their energy was amazing to experience because it was so very unlike what I am used to or even used to wanting to have in my life.

Later, out on the roads in London, we "took in" the energy of statues. Of very expensive cars. Of old buildings. Of ethnic foods and music. It was truly overwhelming and a most fantastic experience – and what a difference to all those other times when I have hastened through the streets of London in a constant state of rejection, denial and wishing bitterly I was elsewhere.

These energy experiences are really quite amazing. Many ETPs report that once they began to drop shields they were absolutely astonished how **alive** everything was, the people, the landscapes, even the buildings and how much buzzing energy was all around them. They further report that they felt as though they were on a strange and amazing planet they had never visited before and that was extremely invigorating in its own way.

So, what might life be like if you became an energy vampire?

It is truly extraordinary, that is for sure. There is **nothing** that you cannot have to be with you, in you, through you, **of you**, fully experienced and then released.

It is the most empowering sensation.

I had been poor my entire life and at one point, I was beginning to earn some real money and had for the first time a large amount of money in the bank that was not immediately earmarked for urgent payments here and there. I remember collecting the bank statement and as I walked through the town, having this really strange thought – namely that there probably wasn't a single item in **any** of those shops that lined the road that I couldn't afford to buy on this day.

I had to stop and collect myself, and the world appeared different from that day on and this has not changed since then.

EmoTrance is even more profound than that; it is not just objects you can have, you can "have" any attribute, any vibration, any person, any song - anything at all and you can have it now.

All you have to do is to find out where your shields and blockages are, dissolve them and open yourself completely to the energies inherent, let them flow through you and the needs and wants are filled, old pains and aches soothed and your world becomes a different place.

Energy Nutrition In Brief

Energy is all around us.

We need to absorb energy from:

a) Energy from sun, moon, stars, weather, planet itself, etc.

b) Plants, rocks and other animal life.

c) Energy from others of our own species including:

- **Personal and physical contact**

- **Emotional Emanations**

- **Energy Emanations**

- **Transferred Emanations (Works including Works of Art)**

Energy can NOT be ingested by:

- **eating an item/person**

- **owning an item/person**

- **buying an item/person**

- **surrounding ourselves with items/person**

Energy is ingested ONLY

by taking the ENERGY of the item into our systems.

Making Room For New Energy

When people begin to work with their worst energy blockages and let this finally begin to soften and flow, that is of course not the end of the story. It doesn't just flow that one time only.

Now a flow has been re-established, this part of the energy system will draw to itself energies once more on a regular basis and flow on a regular basis, as and when. At least this part of the energy system is "open for business" once more, if you will.

That is actually a very important point when we come to consider different kinds of energies in human interaction and our responses to them.

Of course, trauma, insult and injury, which is where we started and the focus of much if not all personal development constantly lies are something we are perfectly happy to "flow away" and have it return to the Oceans of Energy from whence it came; but now, let us consider the matter of incoming "positive" energies.

I have put the word "positive" in inverted commas for of course, energy is energy and there really are no good or bad energies, as there are no good or bad clouds, raindrops or atoms in the universe.

However, we have been entrained to consider some things as positive and some things as negatives; you could say we have been falsely polarised like electric plates to draw something towards us and reject other things altogether. This entrainment sets our energy system to do this kind of thing for us automatically and below the level of our conscious awareness; and this is actually a good metaphor because of course a polarised metal plate cannot **let go** of what it has been set to attract either.

Here is an example which demonstrate this particular side of the energy exchanges coin:

ETP: "Now listen carefully. Are you ready? YOU ARE BEAUTIFUL."

C (takes a deep breath, puts one hand to his heart): "Oh, that feels wonderfully warm in my heart area, really glowing, amazing."

ETP: "Ok, it is just an energy. Let it flow."

C (instantly and with conviction): "No chance! I haven't felt that good in years, possibly not ever. I'm gonna keep that right there!"

You can see pretty much right away how we are talking once again about a serious energy blockage. Sure, this time around it isn't an energy that manifests as hurt or pain and causes **those** kinds of sensations but one that feels all warm and fuzzy; and yet let us remember that energy is energy and the principles are **exactly the same**.

This is particularly important in the context of this section, namely that energy flow, once it has been re-established, allows the possibility of more of the same energy to be received.

It is true that people who hold on particularly tightly to a particular experience, often quite an old one, actually preclude more and future occurrences from taking place – there is no place for new energy to go to in that person's system.

Moreover, these energies get stale and hard over time and are no longer useful or beneficial and of course they no longer nourish the system. But there is one more repercussion which is probably the most damaging by far.

When these incoming energies pass through the channels designed to take them, they actually **change the system** as they pass on through.

Like the hand that writes on the clay tablet in passing and thus changes the blank slate forever, in the exchange with the energies and the energy channels, the energetic organs and set ups in the energy body create a transformation – the energy body becomes new, it becomes **other** than what it was before this energy passed through.

ETP: "Look. It's just an energy. Do me a favour and just let it go through and out. If you don't like what that feels like, I can simply call you beautiful again like I did before and you can hold onto that one instead."

C (reluctantly): "Oh alright then. I'll give it a go."

ETP: "Ok, so where does it want to go?"

C: "Well it seems to want to go deeper inside me, like into my lungs? Oh my god – it is spreading from there all over my body! What an extraordinary sensation! I can feel that same warmth everywhere and now it is coming out of all the pores of my skin."

ETP: "And does that feel good, does it feel right?"

C (takes a deep breath, runs his hands through his hair, looks up and smiles): "Yeah. Yeah it does. It feels wonderful. Thank you."

ETP (smiles back): "You are welcome. So what are you thinking or feeling now?"

C (reflectively): "Ah it is strange. Good. Unusual. Like beauty was not something that was ever a part of me at all, like it was over there somewhere and I was here. Now, its like – in me? a part of me? That is a very, very strange thought to be having. I have never thought of myself in that way, never thought I had anything to do with beautiful. That was for other people, not for me."

This same gentleman also went on to make the comment that following his experience with this particular energy being allowed to pass through his systems that his idea and concept of beauty had changed completely. He stated that before the "energy experience" with beauty he had thought of it like a kind of plastic beauty, the kind you see on TV, models, actors, shiny cars, sculpted hedges and such. After the energy experience, he thought of beauty in a different sense altogether – in his own words, "a true beauty that isn't anything like that, it is wilder and much more powerful, much more real, nearly frightening in its intensity."

This is a good example of the benefits one derives from not holding on to energies but to let them pass. This gentleman's change of heart if you will from plastic template beauty to this wild, powerful and amazing definition of beauty is something that is sometimes said to be acquired by experience, and it is called wisdom. To have a personal understanding, contact and definition with the concept of "beauty" in this way is quite an extraordinary change with many repercussions along the way; and as the client said, it makes the world more real and more exciting to live in. Now, this young man is open to seeing and receiving the energies of beauty every day – and wherever he goes because this energy like all the others is an integral aspect and part of the Oceans of Energy in which we live.

To learn to not have to hold on to "positive" energies, whatever they may be, structurally opens the way for more of the same, to open our systems to these energies and to experience whole new realms of these energies.

Contrary to public opinion, the results of this are not to make someone big headed.

The young gentleman in the example did not walk away strutting like a peacock and declaring himself to be the most beautiful person in the world to all who would stand and listen – in the contrary. With his new and different definition of what beauty means and how he has a right to this simply by being a part of this world in the first place, the whole topic simply **becomes resolved to a higher level**, a different state of being.

Thus it is also with other forms of energy that people have been taught they must keep away, else it would make them big headed, arrogant, unbearable or people would stop loving them.

Energies such as creativity, intelligence, logic, the aforementioned beauty – there are many of these. Should you personally feel like the young man did that there are some of these who "are outside of me and have nothing to do with me", here is an EmoTrance reminder that they need not be if you invite them in and then allow them to complete their journey through you and out again, changing you in the process in the most beneficial and holistic way imaginable.

Now it is time to ...

Play EmoTrance With A Friend!

I highly recommend to you that you find a friend and you play the EmoTrance game with them. This is how EmoTrance came into being in the first place. A friend of mine had been severely insulted and was smarting after the fact, feeling real pain and telling me about this when it occurred to me that there was no physical cause for this pain and it had to be nothing but the equivalent of an energetic boot print on her chest if you will.

I asked her to deal with this energetic occurrence by placing her attention on it and have it dissolve away and literally seconds later, all her heartache was gone and we were both laughing and giggling.

It is important to me to have you know that EmoTrance is NOT some dour, boring ritual or meditation – it is a dance with energy. Light, easy, powerfully refreshing and basically, entirely delightful.

Have fun with this!

Allow yourself to have fun with this, because it really is enormous fun if you do it with the right mind set.

Explain the basics to a friend or lend them this book, then get together and play.

Shout insults at each other – stuff from way back when you were teased at school and that still smarts when you think of it: "Look here comes Miss Piggy!" – "Stupid Sally is a Wally!" or whatever the kids or adolescents used to throw at you and you had nothing to defend yourselves from that at the time.

Criticise each others bodies, mental abilities, motives, ethics, abilities to make things work, attitude in the ringing tones your parents and teachers used to use and that still makes you cringe in pain today when you even think of it.

Play with calling each other names, and also calling each other **by** name in the same tone of voice your mothers used to or your fathers when they called you up for punishment or to complain about something.

You know what sets you off – use it.

Use the basic EmoTrance routine to find the place where it hurts in your body, remind each other of the mantra: "It's only an energy!", move it through and out and do it again until you are just laughing delightedly when your friend shouts at you, "You are the most useless piece of *** in the Universe!"

Then turn it around and go for the opposites which are just as difficult, just as hard and some of them even "harder to swallow" than the negatives: "You are beautiful." – "You are desirable." – "You are wealthy." – "You are worthy." – whatever comes to mind and indeed, **whatever you want or want more of**.

Take turns on saying to each other with meaning, "I love you" – "I like you" – "I want you to be a part of my world" – "You delight me" and take a note where it hurts and gets stuck in the **giving as well as the receiving**.

As you do this, make sure neither of you slip off and begin to intellectualise reasons as to why you can't be beautiful or wealthy, that you cannot love or allow yourself to be loved, why it would be bad or dangerous for you to believe anything like that, etc. etc. etc. ...

"It's ONLY AN ENERGY!"

Remind yourselves, focus on it, find the channels and let the energies flow then swish fast and powerfully.

Have FUN with this – it is meant to be exciting, invigorating; a dance for you to dance with your own energy system, as was always meant to be the case.

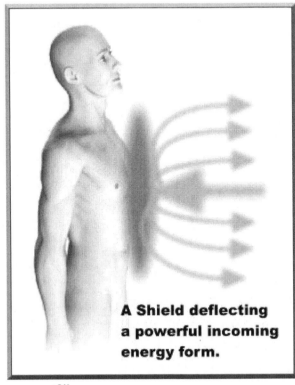

A Shield deflecting a powerful incoming energy form.

As soon as we begin to talk about taking in energies and moving them through the requisite channels of our energy bodies, we immediately encounter the energetic reality of "shields".

Here is an example:

ETP: "You are intelligent."

C: "I don't feel anything at all, it is as though that doesn't even touch me."

ETP: "So when I say, You are intelligent, how close to you does that get?"

C: "No closer than that." (indicates with outstretched arm, palm flat towards ETP, about 2 feet from his body).

ETP: "That is a shield, just like they have on the starship Enterprise, designed to keep that kind of energy out because your system thinks it might be dangerous. How would you feel if we made just a tiny pinprick hole into that shield, so just a very small amount of energy can come in, get a taste of what it would do to you, what it would be like?"

C: "Ok but it would have to be a very small hole."

ETP: "Yes, like with a pinprick laser. Can you allow that hole and I say the sentence again?"

C: "Ok. I'm ready."

ETP: "You are intelligent."

C (looks reflective)

ETP: "What happened?"

C: "Well it kind of came in fast, then it went into my chest (indicates area just between his nipples). It felt strange."

ETP: "Shall we do it again and this time, let that energy find its requisite channels?"

C: "Ok."

ETP: "You are intelligent."

C (takes a deep breath literally in time with the sentence): "Right, its gone in there and it seems to be making its way straight through, into my back and spine and then I'm losing it."

ETP: "Its just such a small amount, I guess it fizzles out. Do you feel like making the hole a little bit bigger, let a bit more energy in?

C: "Yeah, ok, it's now the size of a coin. Do it again."

ETP: "You are intelligent."

C: "Alright, it goes in, through to the back, up my spine and out the top of my head. Feels strange, electric."

ETP: "What do you want to do now?"

C: "I would like to try making the hole bigger."

ETP: "If you are sure? Alright, here it comes again: You are intelligent."

C (breathes in deeply and starts to smile): "That is not bad, not bad at all. Electric but good. It feels good. Can I get rid of the shield completely?"

ETP: "Do you want to?"

C: "Yes, I think I do. Yes, I do." (smiles broadly)

Shields are energetic realities that are **outside** the physical body. You generally become aware of the presence of a shield when:

- There is a problem but instead of the normal, clearly locatable sensation in the body there is a feeling of numbness or not feeling anything at all;

- You feel detached or far away from the problem;

- There is a feeling of "pressure" across a wider or undefined area of your body;

- You feel a physical pushing sensation away from the incoming energy;

- There is a sensation of emptiness or constant hunger;

- You have the feeling there is a block or barrier to the energy coming in which is outside of you.

All of these are an indication that there is an **energetic shield OUTSIDE of the physical parameters of the body.**

The energy can't even come in and thus, causes no normal emotional response and no physical response. What you do get, however, in the presence of the energy that is being shielded out, a sensation of **pressure** across a wide and unlocalised erea as the shield is being pushed backwards.

Sometimes, shields seem to exist for no good reason at all; but much more often, they are clearly a protective device because the systems behind the shield cannot handle the influx of the specific energy that is being prevented from entering the system for a good reason.

There may be:

- Blockages in the channels which are meant to carry this form of energy through and out. If the energy came in with force and ran into these blockages, it would cause pain and probably illness.

- Energetic injuries along the channels designed to carry this energy; and this includes the wider systems which are being fed by those channels.

- The channels not being fully developed or well developed enough to handle the force of this energy. This can be simply a developmental problem, i.e. some systems may have not grown up as they should have done, become stuck in time or have failed to develop from a juvenile state into full maturity.

It is for these obvious reasons that we don't just rush in and tear down shields as a bye-the-bye, but that we take care and investigate the conditions behind the shield first in order to make the shield **naturally redundant** or prepare it for removal or dispersal.

To find out about the conditions of the energy body behind the shield, we make a **tiny pinprick hole** into the shield first to allow a minute quantity of the energy to come in and show us where the pathways are, and where the problem ereas of the pathways lie.

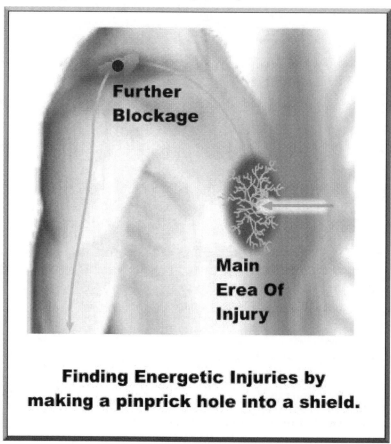

Further Blockage

Main Erea Of Injury

Finding Energetic Injuries by making a pinprick hole into a shield.

In the case of our "You are intelligent" gentleman, there seemed to be no further problems; the energy came in quite nicely and did not get stuck anywhere, found the pathways easily and it was just a question of taking the shield down to allow him to experience what the "energy of intelligence" would do to his body and his mind.

Here is an example where there was an injury behind the shield.

Here, the client has already made the tiny hole to allow herself to find out what exactly this special form of energy under investigation would do to her if it was allowed to come inside.

> ETP: "I love you."

> C: "Oh, oh that hurts. Its hurts bad, I must close the gap immediately."(clearly distressed, nearly tearful)

> ETP (gently): "Ok so now we know just why you have that shield and what its purposes are. It is obviously a protective device, protecting an injured erea. Where does it hurt the most?"

> C (puts hands over mouth and jaw area in a gesture reminiscent of someone who is deeply distressed and in shock at bad news)

> ETP: "That erea needs healing first before we can put any energy into it at all. It can't handle any energy at this point, it is too devastated. Are you ready to heal this now?"

> C (crying now): "Yes but how? It feels so terrible, it is such a mess, so much pain ..."

We will come back to energy healing at a later stage; for now it is suffice to note that shields sometimes, but not always, are callous devices directly designed to protect already damaged ereas from further pain and injury.

Luckily for all concerned, energy healing with intention especially when applied to where it belongs, namely the energy body rather than skin, muscles or bones, works extremely well, is extremely easy and extremely reliable – and once again, something even a small child can do **naturally**.

In the context of the shields, firstly we correct these problems, then allow gradually more and more energy to come through the shield until it can be resolved or dissolved entirely and the energy flows smoothly and perfectly.

With freshly restored networks and systems, we need to be careful of the quantity and intensity of the energies we are asking these to handle; in this way the shield devices can be very useful as an **active measure** to slow down energy flow for a time to give the new and fragile channels a chance to become accustomed to the energy flow and become strong enough to handle these energies directly and without any need for protective shielding.

Reluctance To Dropping A Shield

Often, people are very afraid to even consider the idea of letting a small amount of an energy into their systems from which they have hidden away all their lives.

However, this fear is of course also "only an energy" and so this may be resolved up front to clear the way to begin work with the shield.

This would work like this:

> C (shakes head, backs up in the chair): "I don't like this at all, I don't want to have anything to do with this at all."
>
> ETP: "Where do you feel this reluctance in your body?"
>
> C (puts hand to her throat): "In my throat. Hard and scratchy. And in my stomach too."
>
> ETP: "Let us deal with the throat one first. It is only an energy, remember, so let it soften and flow, that will feel better."

Once both these ereas (throat and stomach) had been released and the flow re-established, the ETP comes back to the topic of the shield.

> ETP: "Now, how do you feel about letting a small amount of energy in, just to test it out and find where there are any problems that need our attention?"
>
> C (takes a deep breath): "Yes, yes I think I'd like to do that. Only a small amount, though."
>
> ETP (smiles): "Of course. Just as small an amount as you decide. Are you ready to make a tiny little hole into the shield?"
>
> C: "Yes. I think I'll make the hole just there." (Points forward and slightly up and to the right).

I would like to repeat the note that we **never** force or try to persuade anyone, and including ourselves, to drop shields when we are not ready to do so. Unwillingness equals simply the fact that something needs to be addressed first to make everything unfold in the right order.

Shielding From "Frightening Energies"

It is absolutely fascinating to note that most shielding comes into being because the energies which are being thus stopped at the boundaries or outer layers of the energy body are being perceived as frightening or damaging when they are the opposite.

Here is a very interesting example:

> C: "I feel awful. I have a stalker and this is absolutely ruining my life."
>
> ETP: "Where do you feel this in your body?"
>
> C: "Like a pressure all around me, enclosing me like an ever shrinking egg."

The word pressure, rather than pain, and the egg description are a give-away for the fact that here are energies pressing in on a shield as opposed to being stuck in the energy body or striking an existing injury, for example.

> ETP: "Do you want to make a pinprick hole into that egg shield and let some of that energy in, find out what it would do to you?"
>
> C: "No, I really don't want to – this is nasty slimy energy and I want nothing to do with it."
>
> ETP: "Yes, I can understand that totally, I've been stalked too at one time. But when I was doing my training, they said specifically that there is no such thing as nasty energy. I wonder if we could make an even smaller hole, somewhere where it would be safe to try it out?"
>
> C: "Well I guess if we made a microscopic hole near my little finger and closed it off right away again ..."
>
> ETP: "Yeah, that sounds good to me. Shall we try it?"
>
> C: "Ok."
>
> C: "Oooh! Oh! Oh WOW!"

ETP: "What? What's happened? What's going on?"

C (excited and amazed): "That was totally weird, amazing – it went into my little finger, right into the bones and it strengthened my bones!"

ETP (amazed): "Wow, I didn't expect that ..."

C (very fast, excited): "And I got it, instantly – I've always been told I have no backbone, I'm a wimp, I never stand up to anyone – do you think this energy could give me a backbone? Strengthen my bones?"

I really find it fascinating that in this particular case, the "oppressor" energy seemed to be **exactly** what was required to bring this lady into a form of balance where she would be neither a victim, nor an oppressor but would be able to stand up to this oppressor and future attempts "with a strong backbone".

It is also interesting to note that following this session, the stalker stopped stalking, in the absence of any physical intervention or change. The client did not go to the police or behave any differently than she had before; it is my supposition based on many similar experiences, especially with children who were bullied at school that the energy shift takes the individual out of the preferred range of the oppressors – they don't "smell so tasty" on the energy levels any longer and the oppressors seem to then go and find other victims that match their preferences instead.

It is possible that this "healing with oppressor energy" could be an example of the homeopathic and also energy based principle of "curing like with like" which seems nonsensical if considered with Aristotelian logic but not when considered with Quantum Logic.

Dissolving Shields

Being a quantum energy occurrence, shields can be dissolved on a single thought command of their owner. This is usually not the most ecological of solutions though and so we dissolve them gently, step by step. The most usual procedure seems to be to make an ever increasing hole into the shield, allowing more and more energy to flow in and to keep this absolutely in step with how much of this specific energy the energy body's systems can handle as they re-adjust.

Other options are to make the shield overall less dense, more nebulous and rise away like mist; turning it into a colander which eventually breaks down altogether, or to shrink it if it is of a particular size and in a particular location.

Here is an example of the latter:

> C: "I feel there is something between me and my students when I teach – it is like I can't get through and I can't reach them." (gestures and paints a square block in the air, on a level of his eyes, about a handspan's width)

This might be a good moment to point out that **all energy manifestations** in EmoTrance can be viewed and tracked by watching a person's movements and especially their eye movements, head movements and hand gestures.

Hands especially go to the places that hurt when you ask, long before a person has worked out consciously where something hurts. Hands paint walls, shields, blockages and all sorts of other existing energetic realities into the room. Looking carefully at your own gestures and those of other people will show you time and time again where their ghosts are, where their shields are, what they duck away from, try to ward off, wave away, motion towards themselves, break through – it is absolutely fascinating.

If you can imagine these movements and gestures being directly caused by an energetic occurrence, you can begin to really **see** a person's private world and limitations; you can see where things are tense, problematic or where it hurts in their bodies and in their wider energy bodies too.

These movements are never random but in direct response to something that is there, only we can't quite see it yet.

Now, back to our gentleman who had a two foot high and three foot wide block, the width of a hand span, two handspan's out right in front of his eyes which stopped him from contacting and reaching his students. This energetic occurrence is completely defined in time and space by his hand gestures, with co-ordinates and cause and effect of its own existence; he is not imagining it but it is really there. Let's find out what happens next.

ETP: "That's like a wall. Hm. What would happen if you kind of looked over that for a moment?"

C (cranes neck in response and withdraws very rapidly, blushes and shakes his head decisively): "Oh no, I couldn't stand that, that is just ..."

ETP: "Well clearly the wall is there to protect you from feeling what you just felt. Where did you feel that, I couldn't stand that, in your body?"

C (immediately indicates his throat with one hand and half a second later, with the other hand lower down on his central chest): "I'm not sure ..."

As we have noted before, at this point it is not safe to take the wall down – there is a serious problem with the channels somewhere in this gentleman's throat and chest. This example also nicely shows something you will notice time and time again in yourself and with others – the body knows immediately but the conscious mind needs some time to figure out where it actually hurts. The longer someone takes to figure it out consciously, the more detached they have made themselves become from their own feedback devices which are designed to let you know when something is going wrong and action needs to be taken to put it right, or damage will result.

Once the healing of these channels had taken place and the energies could run in some minor quantity, it was time to make the wall smaller. This gentleman chose to have it melt from the outsides in. The very last remaining core of this energy wall was a spot, about the size of a large antique coin, right in the very center of his vision at the focus point of about two hand spans – which interestingly, happened to be exactly the distance his father preferred when shouting abuse at him whilst raising him up to his own eye-level by grabbing the child's clothing and pulling him off his feet.

Of course, for the EmoTrance process it is not necessary to know this but it is very true that cause-and-effect relationships become apparent in the course of doing EmoTrance that can have the intensity of revelations, as entire life systems all of a sudden become known and understood.

Clarity and conscious understanding which results from renewal in the energy body is something that in my opinion is one of the most profound proofs that the underlying theory of EmoTrance is entirely sound and works with the realities of human organisation across energy-neurology-physicality. This clarity and understanding is also something you can look forward to experiencing as the whys and wherefores of your own problems become revealed to you.

Here is the basic Shield Protocol once more in brief.

Shield Work Protocol

When you have discovered a shield, procede as follows:

1. **Create a small opening to allow a "taste of the energy".**
2. **Note where this energy comes into your body.**
3. **Find any blockages or sensations of the energy running into an injured erea.**
4. **"Soften and Flow" the blockage or disturbance; heal an injured erea.**
5. **Trace the path of the energy to make sure it is clear, all the way from the entry to the exit point.**
6. **Heal or repair any ereas which show up as feeling uncomfortable during this process and re-trace the channel again until you are absolutely fine and ready to let in more of the original energy.**
7. **Gently reduce the shields effect to allow more and more of the original energy to run through the restored channels. If at any point you become aware of any further discomfort anywhere in your system, stop and treat this with intention to restore the Even Flow until the energy really flows perfectly.**

When all is well, dissolve the shield entirely and let the energy rush in, through and out so you experience the "Energised End State".

Part 4 - Energy Healing With EmoTrance

Most of the time in EmoTrance interventions, with the self or with a client, nothing more is required than to soften and flow energy that has become stuck somewhere and simply assist it in passing through the natural channels and finding its proper exist point.

Once in a while, however, we find ereas in the energy body which are so damaged or blocked that nothing can flow, nothing can move and clearly, some form of major restoration will have to be undertaken before anything can find channels and go on to irrigate the ereas that lie beyond.

Skills & Abilities – I AM A Healer

We have already spoken of the energising effects of allowing comments and people energies to flow in, through and out your system, both of the so called "positive" as well as of the "negative" variety.

In the context of saying "YES!" to the flow of energy, I would like to now bring up the topic of self construct (self image) and what we are really capable of doing as human beings once we get out of our own way.

One of the practitioner training exercises is "I am a healer". Clearly, if we are teaching people to help others restore their Even Flow with EmoTrance, then it is essential that the ETPs should not have any energy blockages, reversals or basic problems with the idea that they should help another to heal to the best of their abilities.

There is plenty of evidence to suggest that people without any form of special training whatsoever can beneficially speed the healing of the physical body by such means as quantum touch, Therapeutic Touch, faith healing, laying on of hands and so forth.

There is plenty of evidence to support the idea that prayer without touch can also speed even physical renewal; so combining intention and touch when we work with the energy body rather than the physical body is of course and immediately a profound and very natural healing tool – and yet again, something so easy that a small child can do it and do it well.

Here it is particularly important for us to get out of our own way. It is quite extraordinary how very many experienced and deeply committed holistic healers still have deep reversals and blockages on the topic of their own healing abilities which of course, limit their effectivity.

Consciously, we find ideas that healing is something that only holy people can do (and I am not one of those, of course!); that it takes a great deal of talent and/or years and years of study and meditation; that if it really worked you might get burned as a witch on the stake or become totally beleaguered with sick people and your whole life would be lost and so on and so forth.

Luckily, we need not concern ourselves with such conscious contortions and quite simply consider the thought of , "I am a healer" and note where we can feel that in our bodies.

We will smooth this and gentle our disturbances until it flows freely and clearly, and then we can be ready to consider the basics of repairing the energy body **without having the faintest idea** of exactly how we are doing this.

In the section on the Energy of Learning we will make the observation that most likely, the vast majority of our complex neurology is exactly designed to read, navigate and impact the invisible complexity. What we have to learn is to really trust that we actually can repair these broken strands, connections and damaged ereas of our energy bodies (and that of others) and allow ourselves to go ahead and do it.

There are a great many things in life that get to be very difficult indeed when you pay too much attention or think about them too much; walking for example as you will know if you have ever taken a lesson in the Alexander technique. Singing is another, making love of course; relating and responding to the needs of a loved on and most certainly, energy healing.

You cannot do that with your head, you can only do with your totality and when you do, it becomes immediately effective, immediately noticeable and has wide-ranging effects.

Now please note once again that I am NOT talking about restoring the physical body; I am **only** talking about the energy body which communicates through the medium of sensations, feelings and emotions.

This is important because I have seen a great many beginning Reiki practitioners go home all enthusiastically, feeling the heat in their hands, trying to help say an aged uncle with their arthritis and nothing happens – no miracle cure. Then they go home all disappointed and conclude not that Reiki doesn't work but that they have failed somehow. Most likely, they did very well even if they were probably concentrating on the physical problem rather than the underlying energetic disturbance but to restore old, worn out physicality is not one of the fastest things to be undertaking for a newcomer.

In Reiki, a practitioner is activated by a trainer; in EmoTrance, we raise the energy of healing by clearly stating the thought, "I am a healer." and letting it flow cleanly, removing any blockages or disturbances and swishing it until it tingles in our fingertips, then we simply get to work.

Laying On Of Hands

The simplest and probably most effective technique of them all is laying on of hands. Once you know the erea which needs healing, put your hands there and let your intention to heal and restore flow through your hands into the erea.

Physically stimulating the erea by moving the hands around or gentle massaging is a very good idea and soothing to the physicality; when we do this we also bridge back from the physicality end into the energy system via sensations, just as the energy system bridges to physicality in that way.

This works for self healing just as effectively as it does for assisting another in their restoration.

Here is a simple yet lovely example of such healing for the self.

One client who was working on prosperity issues had repeatedly all the energies get stuck, messed up and generally going into complete confusion in the jaw area.

This was not a question of one single channel in disarray, but really it seemed as though there was massive damage in that area, and I describe this as looking at a complex river network into which someone had thrown a hand grenade at some point in space and time – nothing was working as it should and everything was in chaos.

Clearly, before any form of EmoTrance could take place, major healing and repair work was in order in that area.

As this was a telephone consultation and the client in question was a Reiki healer, I advised her to cup her jaw, with the middle fingers pointing directly at the ears and the palms of her hands meeting below her chin to start the repair work in that area and set this as an interim homework task.

This is an interesting posture that I have since tried out on a number of people and have also actually done with people – it seems a very intimate thing to do and shifts energy quite powerfully.

Also, an interestingly high percentage of people who were dealing with topics related to "Love & Relationships" as well as money problems, had energy problems in the jaw on the topic of "Love and Romance".

As it is such a common problem and the EmoTrance solution is such a nice and very pleasant sensation, here is the

The Jaw Healing Posture

Take three deep breaths and put your hands together, heels of your hands touching.

Now, make a healing intention and then put your hands to your face, cupping your jaw gently and settling into a comfortable, natural position where the palms of hands meet just by or under the chin, middle finger pointing towards ear.

Warming and or healing that entire area is a very pleasant, very nice and somehow rather intimate sensation that I've just enjoyed thoroughly and I think my jaw area did too, with much yawning, popping of ears and clicking of bones in the process.

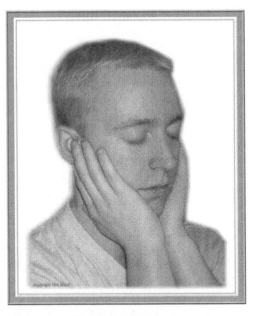

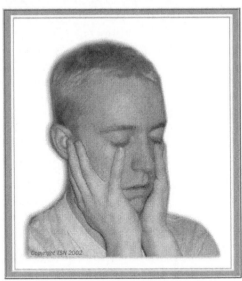

Moving the hands slightly so the little fingers are pointing towards the eye instead is also very relaxing and did that whole area the world of good - very nice all around.

This is not, as I understand it, a posture to be used with specific opening statements or any intentions other than healing and restoration. If you would like some thoughts to focus your mind upon, I'd recommend simply "Heal and Restore", "Soften and Flow", " or any thoughts that would bring about the required relaxation, release and comfort for that whole area which seems important in the overall scheme of things.

Of course, any other part of the body that requires this in-depth healing may similarly be held and restored gently.

"Hands Of Ghost"

Healing With "Hands Of Ghost"

Instead of using your physical hands, you can use what we call Hands Of Ghost instead to bring "the healing touch" to an erea of your energy body or that of another – imaginary hands to help heal disturbances, assist the movement of energy and to stroke and soothe the system overall.

Using imaginary hands transfers your healing intention in the most clearly understood fashion to the energy body

You can have **more than your two physical hands** if you need to work on more than two ereas at the same time to enable the shift. They are not just hands but arms for the holding, hugging, stroking too.

This is also particularly useful if:

- You are working on yourself and you cannot reach the erea;
- Your physical hands are not big enough to cover the entire erea;
- You are working with a client who cannot be touched;
- You are healing something that needs this energy-to-energy approach and does not want physical interference.

Hands of ghost, or as ETP practitioners have taken to call this manifestation of intent, ghosthands, are a very powerful way of restoring and stimulating the energy body.

Indeed, some people "borrow someone else's" hands of ghost if they feel that their own energy is not what is required at this time.

You can take this as far as having more than one person supplying the ghosthands, angelic ones and including allowing your unconscious energy-aware mind to create them entirely for your use and maximum benefit in whatever form or shape they may arise.

Working With Healing Energy - Adding Energy

Adding energy – with intention, with your hands, with your ghosthands, with generators such as crystals - is useful in general repair and re-connection healing; to revitalise "dry channels"; to flush away a blockage; and to add a spark of life to trigger re-growth.

There is a general sense amongst people that "if you just throw enough energy at a problem, it will be cleared". This is absolutely not so and I would strongly advise you to think flow rather than warfare.

We are always seeking a gentling and refreshing of the existing conditions **in the energy body** regardless of the practical outcome.

Adding energy is NOT by any means the only option, and actually most of the time you will find it is the incorrect option as we are mostly dealing with channels and systems that have lain fallow for a long time; deep energetic injuries which have caused whole system-groups to shut down altogether, and fragile, unbalanced and unstable situations – none of which can handle huge inpourings of energies at all and that is why they are protected, shielded and switched off altogether in the first place.

When we add energy we always do it gently and we start with **minute quantities**, just like in shield work, to test the pathways and find out what happens when this energy runs in through the system.

You might have heard or even experienced the so called "healing crisis" in energy healing; Reiki initiations being particularly famous for this, but also Tachyon energy and a lot of other energy products, including crystals, directly causing allergic responses of actual physical sickness.

I believe that this is:

a) Entirely unnecessary. Energy flows smoothly and we can heal smoothly; when we apply energy with common sense and are completely aware and in tune **with the feedback from the physiology**, there simply is no healing crisis.

b) Caused by mishandling of energies. Because people can't see energy and have not yet learned properly how it works and what kinds of effects it has, they are often in the position of a deaf man who has his finger on the trigger of a machine gun and fails to notice that they are spraying the entire community with bullets. Especially beginners try way, way too hard and chuck way too much energy at the problem because they are unaware of their own strength as it were; please be careful with this.

Now that we have established that "simply chucking energy at a problem" is hardly ever the solution, let us look at other energy movements used in healing.

Removing Energy

This is amongst humans at least, one of the most healing manoeuvres you can possibly perform. As we have noted, because humans are so shielded against each others energies, it is actually very difficult to find a recipient for these energies – which is ...

- why old people in homes do not really have conversations with nursing staff, but **download** at them at a rapid rate instead;

- why people have pets so they can stroke them and tell them they love them in order to have a target for their overflowing energy systems;

- why lonely children, people stranded on lonely islands, hermits and prisoners in solitary confinement "make up" invisible friends to direct energies towards; and

- why simply sitting with a client in psychotherapy or on the other side of a confession box and saying absolutely nothing whilst a person "unburdens" themselves are so very useful and deeply appreciated by so many.

After direct damage to the energy systems, the inability to discharge natural forms of relationship energies into some form of lightning conductor which will receive and take these energies away is the most direct cause for energy blockages, build ups of stale energies, pressurising dense systems (as you would find in "depression", for example) and generally, chaos within our energy bodies.

The fact is that even if people do not know this and have come to think that you need to talk to people in order to discharge loneliness pressures, energy is energy and it can be discharged at any time, straight back to the Oceans of Energy, if permission is given.

In human interactions, we are used to waiting for permission before we are allowed to "discharge" – think of a small child hopping with excitement because they have something to tell to their parent, only the parent is on the telephone and has not yet given permission by eye contact or gesture that the discharge may begin.

Thus, intentional control is placed upon the energy system to hold these energies in **until and unless permission to discharge** has been given.

If there is no-one to give it, it cannot occur and then the pressure of unexpressed energies begins to build up.

It is essential to understand that it is one individual's own permission that is deciding whether or not to allow energies to flow, and their own belief in needing permission to do this which is stopping it.

You can see this in action when an individual circumvents the permission structure by having an imaginary friend or spirit guide, talking to an object (such as a teddy bear or the statue of a saint) which they have set up in such a way that this "other" gave them permission to release these energies to them.

Now, they can love, they can talk, they can share their doubts and fears and release.

Greeting The Day, Greeting The Night

This is a beautiful and very moving exercise that benefits you in many more ways than you might suspect just yet. Do the exercise for a week and you will begin to know just how much support and sustenance there is for us - simply by virtue of being here. It is also a training exercise to teach us about the energetic realities of giving and receiving energies and to give us practice at working equally confidently with either form of flow.

1. Greeting The Day

Step outside as soon as you have risen and open yourself to the World. Take a moment to breathe deeply and then say, "Day, I greet you."

Allow this day - rainy or bright, cold or hot, no matter what - to come to you, to bring you it's totally unique properties (for not one day is ever quite the same as the day before, nor all the days to follow).

State your intention to receive this unique energy into all your systems, and now pay attention to any physical responses you might be having to this enterprise. Any emotions, where they localised? Place your hand there and soften the sensation, until the energy there runs clearly in all ways. Any sensations of pressure, discomfort, nervousness, any sensations of rejecting this day at all, localise them and make them run smoothly.

One more time, re-state the words, "Day, I greet you."

Remain with this for just a few moments, then thank the day for it's unique lessons on this occasion and step back inside and into your ordinary life.

2. Greeting The Night

When the night has fallen, step outside.

Take a moment to look around, to get into rapport with the night and become a little more still and a little more observant, and then say, "Night, I greet you."

As before, check yourself for any physiological sensations or emotions which might denote an underlying energy blockage that stops a true exchange of energies between you and the night on this occasion.

Especially, look for any "stuck" energy that might have accumulated during the day in your dealings in The Hard and soften this, allowing the night to take away whatever is no longer needed, drawing all this up and into its endless self.

Give the night everything you need to give, really allow it to draw from you your energetic burdens, your unexpressed stale energies, anything at all – your love, your loneliness, your unfulfilled desires. The beautiful night will take it all.

Allow this process to complete - it can be as swift as a thought, that is entirely up to you.

Give a sincere "Thank You" to the night for its assistance and its lessons and then return to your normal activities at this time.

These exercises take just a few moments of your time each day but in energetic terms, they are truly profound and most balancing, soothing, healing and energising.

You will notice that with even two or three repetitions, your ability to channel energy from the day and night increases dramatically as your systems and their pathways are becoming clearer and more efficient.

To begin with, you might strongly "take from the day" and "release to the night" but as time goes by you will find that indeed, for both the day and the night what is happening is a true circular exchange for you as each have their own unique lessons and energies to give, as well as assisting you in taking what is no longer needed.

It is a beautiful and very moving exercise that benefits you in many more ways than you might suspect just yet.

Do the exercise for a week and you will begin to know just how much support and sustenance there is for us - simply by virtue of being here.

Clearing Channels

With EmoTrance™ we are working purely with energy and how it is experienced/felt in the physiological body, so we know exactly where the energy is stuck. Therefore, we can use intention alone, our hands or our ghosthands to facilitate movement of any blockages thus allowing the energy to flow on freely through the appropriate pathway/s.

1. Place your intention in whatever form into your body where any energy feels hard or stuck.

2. Let it remain there until you feel the energy flowing.

3. You may move your intention in a circular movement around the edges of particularly stubborn blocks, softening it from the outside in.

4. You can also use this circular movement to help you discover where the exit channels are likely to be and help prepare these for the flow of energy as they are designed.

Repairing Broken Channels

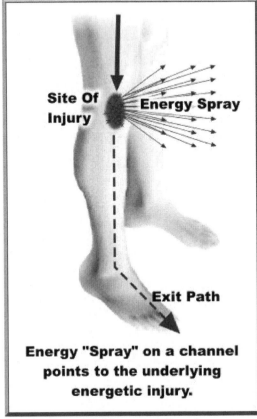

Site Of Injury

Energy Spray

Exit Path

Energy "Spray" on a channel points to the underlying energetic injury.

Sometimes, you come across a channel "spraying" the energy straight out through a part of your body where there doesn't seem to be a natural exit point.

For example, there might be an energy that goes down the hips and into the legs and on the left, exists straight out the toes, but on the right side, there is a spraying sensation as the energy just shoots out the knee as in the illustration.

Clearly, this is an indication of a broken channel, our metaphor for a damaged part of the energy body.

Here you can see why it is so important to work gently and mindfully, with minute amounts of energy at first to **test the channels** properly before undoing shields or adding in more energy; obviously if there is a big pouring in it makes it much harder to repair the underlying injury.

Gently stroke around the area of the broken channel, moving once again **from the outside in,** to repair that section, until the energy there flows freely once again and can find the correct exit route from the body.

Only then begin to test with increasing quantities of energy flow, giving these channels a chance to get used to this and bring it up until it really flows clearly and smoothly.

Tracing A Channel

Often, channels are still very sensitive and freshly healed after a major blockage has been undone. Also, there may be parts to the channels that have not been used in many years and these need gentle stimulation to "awaken" them properly.

Further, the main channels "irrigate" much wider and connected ereas of the energy body and the wider energy body; once again, these ereas may have lain fallow for a very long time and they may not be ready yet for a full flowing of the energies right away; there may also be further ereas of damage within these fallow systems we need to discover first before we turn on the flow.

Especially in the context of shield work, there is a great deal of merit in tracing the entire system with small quantities of energy first to achieve a first Even Flow to restore as well as stimulate not just the main channels but also their respective tributaries and lowland ereas.

Overall Healing With Innocent Energy

In brief, Innocent Energy is:

- not love based;
- does not require a "relationship"
- does not require "to be received"
- has no "healing intention".

The metaphor we use is that Innocent Energy is like rain, light and softly falling onto all the energy system.

Unlike all other healing energies used in EmoTrance, this energy does not come from you and it does not flow through your own body; it is an outside energy called in to assist in a very specific way.

The concept of innocent energy is particularly important in the EmoTrance system as we do absolutely not heal with "love energy" or "the light" or the usual types of energy invoked in healing.

The fact is that there are too many systems in our energy bodies, especially if we have been severely traumatised, abused, injured etc., which **simply cannot take** these types of vibrations and which will get burned and sustain further damage if a healing with these energies is attempted.

Even the idea of "universal energy" can still be interpreted as being "God's love" and indeed in this instance, taint what truly needs to be absolutely neutral, absolutely natural and absolutely **innocent** energy.

I have never found a way to explain this concept better than with a quote from In Serein, where an executioner stands in the rain and thinks the following:

> *"I have no idea where I am but wherever I am, I am alone here and this is a relief as intense as the cold rain that bathes me steadily on, never caring if it fell on me, or on a stone beyond, or on a blade of grass, or on a smouldering wet fire that, if you stirred it somewhat, would contain bones, and teeth."*

There are parts of our energy system which are so reversed, so damaged and so chaotic that they need this innocent energy which seeks no response, which makes no connection, which does not need to be channelled or processed in any way and which truly doesn't care if it fell on an executioner or on a blade of grass but cleanses them both regardless because it is entirely innocent of all such distinctions, labels or designations that may have been made about these parts of the energy system at some point or the other.

Evoking Innocent Energy

For a moment, breathe deeply and allow yourself to rise up lightly on each inbreath.

When you are ready, call upon the Innocent Energy and feel all around you and from above, the lightest, finest mist beginning to come down and enter your energy body, just like a fine, light and sparkly rain beginning now to fall.

Allow yourself to open yourself completely to this fine, light rain of innocent energy that needs you to do nothing at all, simply be there and notice, feel how it simply fills all your channels, even the smallest and even in the spaces between your channels and systems, it falls and as it does, it clears away old debris, old thoughts, old burdens you no longer need.

It falls steadily and gently, a rain throughout your energy body, doing nothing but clearing and refreshing, gentling and taking with it what it needs to take.

When you feel you are done, look up and thank the Innocent Energy, opening your eyes and feeling clear and refreshed.

Innocent Energy is used in EmoTrance for the following purposes:

1. Preparation

It is well known in all types of magic that a clearing precedes any form of magical endeavour; priests take baths before they conduct a mass for real to achieve this.

Evoking the Innocent Energy prior to a healing endeavour with EmoTrance is a clearing and very centring experience that sets up the energy system to run smoothly and freely.

2. Loosening & Softening

Innocent energy can manifest in many different guises and it is always safe to use. It can be used like a steam cleaner, a rushing waterfall, a soft mist and very importantly, with different temperatures to cool hot systems and to warm those who need this extra energetic dimension to

104

soothe it away. "Frozen" systems are especially receptive to this application.

3. Actual Healing

You will come across situations in the energy body where a simple application of the Innocent Energy will simply sooth away and wash away the blockage or accumulated debris and resolve the problem perfectly when application of intention did not; this is often the case with reversed systems or systems that have been consciously labelled as "evil" or have been rejected for whatever reason by their owners.

4. Soothing Freshly Healed Systems

Applying the Innocent Energy to any freshly healed system prior to allowing energy of whatever kind to run through it is a very ecological and enlivening experience that is much appreciated all around.

5. Overall Energy Re-Balancing

This is probably the most important use for the Innocent Energy in EmoTrance, namely to "wash the system all over" before we conclude the healing session. This settles the entire system, rejuvenates it, brightens it and washes away any remnant thoughtfields or debris. It also helps the system to find a balance in the new and changed order of being.

Make no mistake about it: although EmoTrance seems so very natural, gentle and easy, it really does create massive changes in the energy body. Without this re-balancing at the end of a session, be it with yourself or others, the transition from how it was to how it is now can be quite frightening and disconcerting when there is no need for this at all.

Healing The Fault Lines

When you have worked with EmoTrance for a while, you will notice that the same ereas in your energy system are again and again the blocking points for Even Flow.

For example, for some people everything grinds to a halt in the jaw area on many different topics and with many different emotions; some always experience **any** emotion in a certain part of their bodies **first** and regardless of where the specific blockage resides or what the topic or problem may.

We have called these places the "fault lines" because what we have here are very highly damaged ereas that are simply hyper sensitive and the first to respond to stress of any kind.

Chronic emotional problems cause much confusion because of this; normally it **is** true that certain emotions are stored in certain places but when the owner of a fault line system looks up their symptoms in a Louise Hay type book to discover their meanings, it doesn't make any sense. This is because whenever there is added stress, the system will crack at the fault line first just as a piece of glass will crack where it has been scratched and NOT where the pressure is actually applied.

The Fault Line ereas of the energy body are the most damaged and devastated of all the systems; they have no tolerance or threshold at all for any form of incoming stress or indeed, any form of incoming energy whether it is regarded to be beneficial or otherwise. **Any** pressure on these ereas causes immediate and intense flare up of emotional pain (and often also severe physiological responses) which seems entirely disproportionate to the stimuli which caused them. Think of the equivalent of a deep and weeping sore that is infected. Even the lightest touch will cause extreme agony because of the state of the wound.

In some people, there are ereas in their energy bodies which are like a complex river network into which a nuclear bomb has been thrown – all is in disarray, the pathways destroyed, others are wrongly connected, many more reversed, many more fallow.

These ereas need deep healing and careful restoration before **any** outside energy can enter here without causing even further pain and damage; for this reason they are very heavily shielded. But even the pressure of the shields being touched is still painful; so we know we have to procede with great gentleness and care. However, when these Fault Line ereas have been healed and restored, the person in question will feel an inordinate relief and increase of energy through a wide variety of symptoms and problems. So the Fault Line work is at the center of healing with EmoTrance™ and indeed, a **prerequisite** in many cases for bringing the automatic systems which flow energy and nourish us from deep within on line in the first place.

Healing Fault Lines

Firstly, become aware of your own Fault Line ereas. Where in your body are they? Which parts of your energy body are giving you physiological feedback most strongly, or which are totally numb which is another way of trying to live on in spite of important systems being in an agony of disarray?

1. Before you start, make a healing declaration, preferably out aloud so that all of you can hear this and understand that this is your will and your purpose today: "I want to heal this part of my energy body, deeply and in all ways. I want to restore the Even Flow."

2. Place your hands on the erea and begin to align yourself with your intention to restore, repair and put back in place what once there was and will be again. Don't try too hard, your conscious mind doesn't know how to do this but there are other parts of you that know **exactly** what to do and in which order and sequence and will begin the process of restoration as soon as your intention has declared it should be so.

3. Start from the outside and gently work your way inwards from there. As you slowly move in closer on the core injury around which the entire Fault Line system has grown, and PLEASE do not do this any faster than the feedback from your body and your emotions will tell you, the healing work begins to ripple into more and more of the damaged systems. It is important you should not hurry this stage.

4. Stop when you have head enough and conclude the session with an overall soothing (see below).

Notes On Fault Line Healing

- Although we know that we are working in quantum space where there is no time at all, and that EmoTrance™ can let blockages disappear in an instant, just for the asking, there is all the merit in the world to be very, very gentle with the Fault Line ereas and with yourself.

- We are complex beings and what we don't need is for ourselves to "do healing with a brick bat" and try and force things if it hurts. For this reason, you may consider healing your own Fault Line ereas in stages and over time; a little more each day for a week and until all has been restored and is bright and fresh once again, at last.

- Allow yourself to be guided by your own sensations and intuition in this work exclusively. There is no "should, must, have to" here – this is a truly co-operative venture between your intention to heal yourself now and the Universe supplying the necessary energy. If your responses are becoming too intense or you are getting stressed, back off and take it easy. Move in on the erea slowly and steadily and keep at a distance that feels comfortable and soothing because this tells you exactly that you are healing in the true sense of the word.

- As you move in closer to the core parts of the energetic injury, you will find pathways leading to and from this damaged erea which are also in need of repair – the injury cannot heal successfully and remain in perfect functioning if there are no pathways to both supply energy to it, as well as draw energy from it as they should. Finding and repairing these pathways is a most important part of the healing process so trace the channels as we have discussed before to be sure they are fully restored and running cleanly, in and out.

- Stop when you feel you have had enough. That is also an extremely important feedback device for you and as there is no other healer present, only you, you will have to take **full responsibility** for your own states of being. You know when you have had enough when:

- Your attention starts to wander;

- you feel tired or in need of sleep;
- nothing further seems to be happening;
- you get an indication (voice, picture, sensation) that it is time to stop and let the changes settle for today.

Concluding A Fault Line Session

Moving energy, and most especially in these old fault line ereas, causes extremely wide ranging changes which need to settle. There is much merit, especially when working with a Fault Line erea, to conclude the session with a hands on self healing and overall soothing.

Simply place your own hands on the erea to cover as much as you can, take a deep breath and make these concluding healing intention statements:

- that the changes you have made will continue to propagate and ripple on, leading to further restoration and rejuvenation of the erea;
- that you are deeply satisfied with how much you have already achieved;
- and to thank yourself for the intention of healing you have given and received today, and the Universe for supporting you in this endeavour.
- Then, call in "the innocent energy" for an overall systems clearing and re-balancing.

This concludes any form of self healing most satisfactorily and will leave you in a relaxed and balanced state, knowing you did very well and ready to do some more, as and when required.

Healing & Resting

It is very beneficial to take the time to rest after a Fault Line session. Unlike ordinary EmoTrance™ work, which leaves you in a highly energised and buzzing state, here we are dealing with an unfolding reconvalescense that is affecting very many systems of the entire energy being you are.

Especially when you are healing a large or particularly damaged erea in stages spread out over time, please make time to rest or sleep **immediately** after your session; you might also find it helpful to align yourself with the acts of ongoing regeneration which happen automatically when we sleep and rest deeply. This is achieved by remaining in the state of mind of healing yourself and supporting all of your totality with your conscious attention as you lay down to rest.

Rather than beginning to think about other matters which may or may not be urgent or interesting, turn your mind to remembering a particularly healing landscape where you can lay and rest, where the natural energies are just right to help with your regeneration, your rest and your re-charge. This does not only call directly on these forms of universal energy and raise them to support you, but also keeps you in the healing mind and makes it much easier for the rest of your totality to work with focus and without disruptions on this important task.

Natural Healing - While You Sleep ...

Sleep, rest and restoration play a key part in all health and well being - everybody knows that.

Yet, when you are feeling under the weather it is often difficult to get to sleep at all; at other times, you worry yourself into exhaustion and this not a good approach to set what goes on in your dreaming mind, in your physical AND your energy body in the night.

Here is a seemingly simple technique that combines lessons from advanced hypnotherapy, the quantum energy spaces and the new energy healing approaches to make bed time a time of true R&R for all parts of your mind and your body.

Natural Environments, Natural Healing

Stressed out city folk will go outside their concrete walls every so often to "soak up nature" - just to stand outside in a landscape with rocks and trees, the sky above and the wind in your hair is absolutely healing and restoring, soothing and gentling to both body and mind.

There are special places in nature which are so healing in their energy and in their vibrations, people have build temples there since the dawn of humanity and the sick and suffering would go there, just simple be there, and become eased and well.

As human beings, we all have the unique ability to "raise these energies" simply by thinking about them.

Stop for a moment and consider a landscape that would be just right for you, right now - what might it be?

Would you sigh with bliss if you were by a slow ocean at dusk, soft sand still warm from the day beneath your feet, the evening wind gentle and cooling on your skin?

Would your cares simply drift away if you were to sit on some dry, soft leaves in a grove of ancient trees, sun flecked sparkles dancing in the breeze?

Would your body soak up with delight a morning in a dry place, perhaps by an oasis, the sun golden and strong above and the water crisp and turquoise green?

Just thinking about such things and allowing yourself to really experience being there makes you calmer, easier - this is the original nature cure, healing by the clean and innocent vibrations of natural environments in many, many different states of being.

This night, before you go to sleep, turn your mind to a landscape and a time of day that is just right for you, for which you might well hunger in ways that cannot be fulfilled in any ordinary sense.

Simply be there for a while, wonder what you would see, what you would hear and what you would feel. Let yourself be drawn to a comfortable place and here, you will first sit down, then lie down in comfort and begin to rest. Allow yourself to take in the energies of this place and have them run cleanly and soothingly through your systems, gentling away any blockages or disturbances that may interfere with its path and destination.

As you are resting there, you might think about beginning to dream. You can dream of anything you like, but if your mind is overactive and still way too alert, you might dream a dream of a beautiful, soothing and supporting landscape and a time of day that feels just right. You can be there for a while, wander about and find the perfect place to sit a while and just relax in those energies of nature. Should you get drowsy, you can snuggle up in comfort there and simply, let yourself drift off to sleep.

This process is both soothing and healing; with very little practise you will be able to step into "that kind of energy" you would need to re-charge yourself and balance your body and your mind at any time of the day, not just before going to sleep.

So I bid you many a good night and hope you will have wonderful dreams of healing and of restoration - at any time you need them.

Healing Shame

Shame is a very strange sensation. I won't even call it an emotion because it is firstly and foremostly, a sensation, a real feeling of energy rushing hot and dark and spiralling you into a place of powerlessness, undeservedness – a horrible draining of power, of thought, of individuality.

The sensation of shame is an underlying driver to many other emotions that are layered over the top of it so one hopefully need never experience this again; the original injury that causes this particular response sensation in the first place is clearly something that, if it was healed, would allow a great many other "emotional problems" to simply cease to exist.

I would like to share with you a story of a young lady who had been self mutilating since a multiple rape and abduction event, five years previous to the time of our meeting. She would cut her arms and legs in moments of intense disturbance, had attempted to commit suicide numerous times and suffered from many different symptoms and including anxiety attacks, paranoia and delusions which had rendered her housebound.

In spite of all the many very pressing problems, she was no longer visiting with therapists and healers because they had never really allowed her to express her opinions or feelings and she had never felt they understood her at all.

Shame was something she had never even considered as a major concern, until her unconscious mind one day had her simply speak the words quite conversationally, as her right hand made a slicing movement exactly in parallel with the many scars on her arm, "Well, of course, shame cuts a certain way ..."

We both stopped and stared at her hand, frozen in mid-movement in that cutting motion across her arm and she flushed violently, instantly and said, "Bloody hell and I never knew THAT is what that was all about ..."

We discussed the repercussions of this insight and agreed to "heal the past self" who was a mess, broken and entirely shamed, lying there before us.

So far, nothing out of the ordinary.

But when we turned to face "the mess" with a view to healing it, we realised in an instant that **it was not the past self who needed the healing** but it was the young lady herself, who experienced violent emotions of all kinds as a direct result of allowing herself for the first time in consciousness to directly come face to face with "the mess".

And that was when with my help the lady began to trance these emotions of fury, rage, anger, hatred, guilt, shame, and then emotions that had no labels at all, such as "I'm so terribly sorry," – "How could I do this to me?" and others of such kind.

One by one, these emotions began to recede as they were running clearly through their channels and pathways.

One by one and energy by energy, the now-lady began to change as she looked at "the mess" and **healed her own feelings and injuries**.

Even halfway through, the previous "mess" turned into a person who was just that, and not even pity or compassion was in order for that past self – **ONLY HEALING FOR THE NOW SELF** was required and happening.

Automatically, and systemically, without any kind of direction from me, that past self became more and more of the same system as the now-lady was herself until there was no more distinction between one and the other, and all sense of shame and anger had gone entirely. It was a most extraordinary process indeed, a classic EmoTrance process that took on a life and direction of its own, taking the session and what happened into a direction I had never expected and which was, in hindsight, the perfect resolution and **only** possible resolution to the problems.

I would make the comment that it was not only that young lady who left the session with no longer being terrified of her own shame. I don't think anyone who would have been there and witnessed this extraordinary healing would have been able to come away and not have a huge burden of fear at their own emotions simply melt away. I really don't know if we can overestimate the power of dealing with all human emotions and sensations in this systemic fashion which is so non-judgemental and where words that were previously so frightening – like shame, for example – become nothing more than a procedural cause and effect that simply "happens" and not something that denotes lack of character, being inferior or something one would have to be "ashamed of ".

True Forgiveness – Finally Healing The Oldest Wounds

Most if not all psychology and spiritual treatments constantly exhort the necessity of "forgiving" those who caused you injury in order to be free of the past.

What they don't tell you is how you are supposed to do that.

Forgiveness is not a process but an end result, a statement of "health regained", an effect but not a cause.

To seek to be in this state is healthy - but how can you forgive when you are still in daily pain because of what happened, what someone did to you, what you did to yourself?

The simple answer is that we are asking the impossible.

To ask someone who is still hurting to forgive those who hurt them is like telling a man with broken legs to walk and then climb to the top of a magic mountain where his broken legs will finally be healed.

It is impossible, it is cruel and it will hurt him even more in the process.

What we need to do is to talk about healing first, and when we do, we find that forgiveness follows suit swiftly, sweetly and completely, without any further heartache, headache or need for therapy.

The first question asked is always, how come that time hasn't healed the pain? Why is it that the body regrew new skin and new tissue, and now you can't tell that once this child had broken bones from the daily beatings, that once that woman was raw and bleeding from her rape if you just looked at their outside appearance?

What is it that has remained **unhealed** for all this time, is still raw and sore just as it was back then - what is it that causes the constant pain that simply makes "forgiveness" an impossibility?

Of course, we know the answer – the energy body has not been healed because it lives in that timeless space where fifty years ago is the same as today; that is why time cannot heal the energy body.

Ordinary medicine does not heal the energy body and that is why the wounds from the attack closed all that time ago with the physical treatment that was given and the physical bodies own powers of restoration and growth through time is now no longer visible, or has become a faint scar as the years have passed, yet the energy body remains unhealed and sends its signals of pain through the medium of emotions and sensations that seem to have no rhyme or reason, no cause or effect in this consensus reality of ours which simply ignores all that cannot be seen to be measured.

To heal the invisible scars of the past, we must heal the injuries of the energy body. Then the pain will stop and our minds and spirits return to a place of quiet, of tranquillity and peace where we understand perfectly what happened and why it happened, even understand the perpetrators and why they did what they did - but it is now really in the past where it so rightfully belongs, has belonged all this time in truth.

At the most simple of all the levels, an awareness that such healing needs to take place is the very first step towards a true recovery process - recovering your balance, your power and your equilibrium, re-gaining a state we call the Even Flow where all is as it was designed to be.

As usual, we first localise the erea of injury - we find the old wound.

This does not entail guesswork or intuition. People will hold their middles, put their hands before their eyes, clasp them to their heart, cup their jaw or hold their head in their hands in response. Of course they know where it hurts! That is where the injury is, plain for all to know and all to see.

And once we know **where** the injury is located, we can begin to heal it with the techniques and methods from EmoTrance.

It is simply so that no-one seems to remember to heal the energy body too at the time of accidents and incidence and all healing intention at the time seems so totally focussed on the physical alone - it is understandable.

But the fact remains that we now have the means at our disposal to really heal the past, and when we do, forgiveness too comes into being naturally and as a direct result of having restored The Even Flow.

Indeed, I would strongly recommend to turn it around and actively use any areas of your life where you know you can't and won't forgive to show you exactly where your old energetic injuries are located, using your "unforgiving" as a crucial diagnostic tool to show you the way to true and real freedom from the past, real and true peace of mind at last.

Proxy Work

ET Proxy work is very useful for distance work, work with animals and also geopathic work, spiritual release work, and parts work. Based on the shamanistic principles of "becoming the other" in order to understand and heal the disturbances in question, this simple form of question is used: **"Where do YOU feel PETER'S SADNESS in YOUR BODY?"**

The first time I used this was in response to working with a telephone partner, a therapist who were worried about one of their clients. It wasn't 100% straightforward at first because the therapist was very enmeshed with THEIR own various fears but I repeated the question clearly a few more times until they finally sighed and gave a location. Interestingly, after "Peter's sadness" had been cleared, there was then revealed further and seemingly related aspects such as Peter's disappointment (very big) and Peter's anger which was a very big explosive thing which the therapist reflexively tried to push down but then stopped and noticed with surprise that it needed to go the other way - upward and then it exploded upwards and out.

Proxy work is often not considered to be scientifically sound and it is true that we cannot be sure **whose** anger, disappointment and sadness was being treated here and if the treatment had any repercussions on "Peter", whom I had never met and knew nothing about his problems.

I tend to view proxy work very **limited**; I force myself to that because of the dangers of slipping into theosophist style delusions which is all too easily done. I contain myself with the thought that I am working with "a part of the person who is" instead of with the real distant person, animal, object themselves and in doing that, seek only to find **relief** for that person I'm working with and **NOT** the proxy target of the intervention. I am however happy to accept that there is a possibility of quantum interlinkages and interactions which **might** influence someone or some thing at the distance; however I do at this point keep it as an "icing on the cake" side effect that may or may not happen and an open mind as to further evidence on the theories and actualities of these processes. I would mention that ET Proxy Work is **incredibly useful** for disassociative states or "parts of the self" which seem to have become functionally detached and for relationship work of every kind, including Inner Child healing protocols.

PART 5 - EMOTRANCE AS A HEALING TUTOR

EmoTrance Contra-Indications

Interestingly enough, confidence is **everything** in healing as it is just as well as it is everything in singing, in relationships, public speaking or even driving a car successfully, day in and day out, and regardless of whether or not you were involved in an accident at some point.

There is a simple principle which if it applied rigorously will make the addition of EmoTrance to an existing practitioner's repertoire 100% positive in all ways, namely to know when you should not be using this system but to be doing something else with the client instead.

There are people who will reject EmoTrance; there is no one healing system in the world that can cure everyone and there are people out there who are even allergic to penicillin or aspirin.

This is in no way a shortcoming of the system itself; we have already observed numerous times that the truth is a pathless land and so, even as systemic as EmoTrance is, you can't please everyone all the time.

In my experience, people reject the idea of moving energy for the following major reasons.

1. Energy Body Disassociation

There are an estimated 5 – 15% of the population who do not respond to energy treatments of whatever kind. These will say, "I feel nothing" when a healer floats their hands over them; they do not respond to the Meridian based energy psychology treatments such as EFT, TFT, TAT etc. and usually will not "get anything" out of other mind-body treatments such as hypnosis, guided imagining, Reiki etc.

A part of this population can learn or re-learn to access the systems they need to get back in touch with their energy bodies by doing regular energy drills, such as prescribed in Donna Eden's "Energy Medicine" or by taking up martial arts, yoga or chi gung. I have also heard that some of these people have achieved breakthroughs in their situation by swimming with dolphins (which is also used for autistic children).

Another part of this group may be able to do EmoTrance and then, all the energy approaches as well if their problem has arisen because of strong shields to all and any form of energy, especially from humans (which may explain why dolphins get through when psychologists don't). If such a person is willing to consider this or it sounds "right" to them or they have other indicators that this may indeed be the case, shield work with an experienced ETP can present a true turning point for such an individual. These indicators could be that they talk about a distance or a wall between them and other people or use phrases such as "not being able to break through" their detachment.

If someone insists that they "feel nothing" and they are getting resistant or distressed, do not labour the point and either switch into a different modality of healing or simply ask them what they would prefer to do instead of EmoTrance – perhaps they would just like to talk. This advice is essential really for any practitioner; it is my absolute opinion that a client who is not actively and forwardly engaged in the co-joint processes of healing will not derive any benefits from their sessions, and neither will their practitioner, no matter what the modality and no matter how much money was received.

The second major reason why some people reject EmoTrance is because it is:

2. Too Easy, Too Effective

Some people really cannot handle the fact that a problem that has been with them for what seems like an eternity can simply disappear, just like that. They do not like the idea at all and will, as soon as they have some notion of what we are attempting to do, go into flat out, full out reversal to the treatment, the technique, the ideas behind the technique – basically, just NO!

This is not a disaster but simply feedback to switch techniques immediately and do something else instead. I would make the note that Munchausen clients, i.e. those who use therapy for attention energy on a regular basis, will resist EmoTrance profoundly as soon as they discover that it really does resolve their problems and can get quite angry when a problem which has served them to this end for many years is no longer there.

This effect can also happen when someone did do the EmoTrance procedure quite willingly, never believing for a single instant that it would do anything at all to change the existing problem set up. This may seem strange but it does happen; so especially as a beginner, be a little careful just who you offer this system to and for any professionals, I highly recommend to take a licensed EmoTrance Practitioner training to get some hands on experience and more detailed information on working with clients.

3. Religious Rejection

Under that heading, I group all rejections based on the problem and conflict that, if EmoTrance was real and it really worked, it would mean (something) which would be in serious conflict with life long beliefs of one kind or the other. Religious fundamentalists sometimes raise the objection that we are here to suffer and full of sin and to alleviate this condition is to work against the will of God, or because there is no distinction between good and evil energies; scientist fundamentalists might reject EmoTrance because "there is no energy system and it is all unproven hocus pocus". There are many other forms of such clashes between various belief systems and EmoTrance and if they are severe, then simply don't talk about it any longer and do something else the person would find easier to accept.

So, and to sum up, when it works it really works and when the client rejects it, we do something else instead. In this way, all clients are happy and the relationship with the practitioner remains perfectly balanced.

Now, let us turn to the remaining 75% of clients who find EmoTrance a real blessing in its ease of use and effects and find out why I consider this system outstanding as "a healing tutor".

Intuition VS. Feedback

One of the greatest challenges for anyone at all who begins to study magic, ESP, healing, religion, or any of the arts related to working with the "invisible" para-realities is to know the difference between "knowing when it is real and when I am just imagining it."

This is also at the very root core of so many perfectly sensible people rejecting the para-realities and dismissing all of the many manifestations as nonsense.

The plain fact is that it is **incredibly difficult** to really know if something is your problem, someone else's problem, a repressed memory of your own, or indeed an image that has come to you as a direct guidance to what happens inside a client.

Let us face it – we don't even know about ourselves half the time if we are really "seeing" something or if we are just imagining it; and if we have really seen something, are we interpreting it correctly?

I often tell a teaching story to illustrate this point. A client came to me in a state of deep upset because they had attended a psychic healer meeting where the healer had said that they could see "maggots in her uterus", left there by all her many and varied abusers and rapists over the years.

She had been entirely unable to sleep since and was near hysterical – and it is true that I cannot blame her in the least. She had enough problems already without being told that, of all things.

Now the psychic may have indeed seen **something** in her uterus which we would call one or more ereas that we would simply dissolve away as we don't do what had caused the lady so much distress – we do not name or label the erea beyond noting that it is there and enquiring as to its nature and where it needs to go, what needs to be done to correct the situation.

I did explain this to the lady, we resolved the ereas and she was incredibly relieved and grateful.

This psychic healer had a great deal of experience in what they were doing and they were confident in their declaration; but how many people who "dabble in healing" ever get to that state of confidence?

Indeed, having someone **know exactly** what is going on in someone else's energy systems takes schooling, practise and at the core, it takes a personal feedback system that is reliable.

The hardest task of them all in teaching and training healers is to help each one develop just exactly that reliable feedback system so they really know when they are hallucinating and when they are reading an existing energetic reality correctly.

I have been aware of this problem for myself and for my students for many years and I am happy to say that the practice of EmoTrance is designed to develop any person's feedback system simply, directly and incontrovertibly over just a few weeks to the point where they will have the exact same confidence of that psychic healer with 35 years experience – and a lot more sense in explaining to the client what is wrong with them, at that!

This is how it works.

EmoTrance, even practitioner assisted EmoTrance, and even when conducted by the very best and most experienced trainers and including myself, does not rely on the ETPs intuition and is specifically designed that it would not so that the ETP **can not** start to hallucinate or begin to treat their own problems rather than those of the client.

No matter how exulted an energy magician the ETP may be otherwise, they will always, and only, ask the client directly the two questions of, "What is the problem?" and "Where do you feel that in your body?"

Practitioners who wish to develop their abilities of correctly reading energy systems and then correctly interpreting their readings make a silent "guess" before the client has a chance to answer or to show with their gestures where the problem is located.

The client then says where it **really** is and shows this, at which point the ETP will have received **instant and immediate feedback** as to whether they were warm, hot or cold.

There exist subtle difference in the experience of a real reading and making a hallucination or having just some prejudiced thought because the last client with that same problem had it stuck in the chest, or because those sort of problems are "always associated with the Governing Vessel", or because the client's problem lit up the ETPs own problems which happen to be in that particular area, etc, etc, etc.

It is indeed a subtle difference and the entire "development of intuition" or, as I prefer to call it, getting better at understanding how exactly we get the information we glean from reading energy systems, rests on the individual learning what these differences are for themselves, because they are idiosyncratic. Reading and interpreting an energy system causes a fine state shift which is experienced primarily differently by people – some feel it tingling in their body, some have a sense of rising or the lights getting brighter all of a sudden, some get a very particular sensation in their head or hands – it matters not as long as **you know to tell the difference**.

As the client is moving the energy, the ETP can at any point make further guesses as to what the energy might be doing next, and each time the client will give immediate feedback as to what **really** happened. Immediate (instant) feedback is the way by which all our systems of body and mind learn the fastest and most profound; if you see clients every day then you will notice an inordinate increase in "hits" as opposed to "misses" or "near misses" if you play this learning game with every one of them.

To learn about what intuition is for you and how you handle, receive, process and deal with the information you are getting through your **extra sensory perception** is in my opinion the greatest healing apprenticeship anyone could do; not only do your guesses become more and more accurate over a very short period of time but also you will get to notice just what causes your misses, as well. This too is entirely individual; some people notice they miss more if they try too hard or think too much; others miss more when they are distracted and not paying enough attention; and everyone notices that you have to be in a particular state in order to become near enough infallible in reading the conditions and movements of energy in a person's body.

As is always the case with states, the more often you access them the easier they become to access; and the more profound the experiences become.

Self Healing For The Healer

Every client represents a superb self healing opportunity for an ETP and this is not confined only to those who cause such a strong resonance with their own problems that it overpowers the ETPs intuition as their own energy system begins to scream as well.

Essentially, the ETP has a lot of time on their hands in sessions where they really do not have to do an awful lot. Compared with most other forms of therapy, they do not have to shoulder the burdens of having to be the expert alone because of course, the client is the expert on their own problems and energy systems.

They do not have to become detectives and look for minute clues with focussed concentration because the client just tells them where it hurts; and the treatment itself is so simple that once the client has been familiarised with the idea of moving energy, very little is required of the ETP other than asking for feedback, giving a little encouragement and guidance, and helping out with their intention when the client gets stuck somewhere.

This leaves a lot of time and a lot of room for the ETP to be doing EmoTrance for themselves throughout the session on everything and anything they experience in response to the client and their problems.

In case you think this is unfair because the client has paid for the session and "deserves our undivided attention" I would point out that firstly, for an experienced ETP the EmoTrance process is either automatic or very fast by now and also, consider how it would be for you if you were to see a practitioner of any kind and they were to instantly upon meeting you for the first time, be able to drop all prejudices, prior learnings, contortions, transferences and their own problems relating to people of your sex, age, race, body type and dress and instead, receive you with delight and an absolutely open mind?

Now you know, I would pay a hundred dollars just for the experience of that initial handshake!

Healing Beyond "Conscious Contortions"

One of the most profoundly beautiful aspects of EmoTrance is the fact that we are working in a system "above and beyond" conscious contortions, parts, aspects and beliefs, values and attitudes.

For example, in one treatment session a client had something stuck in their throat and there was both some crying involved as well as some reluctance to let it go.

So I say at this point:

"I would just remind you here that we are only dealing with an energy blockage, a damage spot in your energy system.

"Energy must always flow and there cannot be ANY exceptions.

"Having this energy stuck there in your throat doesn't do anyone any good – not your family, not your friends, not your pets, not the Universe at large and most of all, not yourself and your plans and desires for the future. It doesn't have any benefits or any purposes at all and so you can just let this go now, return that part of your energy system to the Even Flow and everyone will be much the happier for it."

Time and time again, people are simply amazed of how EASY it is to allow healing to take place when you take the thinking mind out of the equation, which comes up with a thousand and one reasons of why it is good to be in pain and remain in pain, indecision and emotional ill health.

This makes "healing" **incredibly** easy in comparison to talking therapies and other interventions, where resistance to change and parts conflicts are the rule, all sorts of contortions arise for all sorts of reasons. There is no primary or secondary gain considerations. There is only Even Flow or a stuck, contorted energy system that causes the owner pain to choose from – and for even the most downtrodden and masochistic individuals, put like that the choice of health over the status quo is truly easy to make.

In order to be able to do this, it is essential to direct our own AND the client's attention, like in the example above, to consider ONLY the energy system and not slide off into the old emotions resulting from the state of the energy system, then label them in some shape or form, then bring up all kinds of memories relating to this, and all kinds of previous decisions and interpretations, post hypnotic suggestions from all and sundry, all of which are in and of themselves, further disturbances in the Even Flow that underlies both mind and body and stops it from working in perfect harmony as it was always designed to.

In retaining this high and exclusive focus on the **systemic nature** of the energy system, we get to learn a great many things first hand and by experience that simply override all the many false learnings, erroneous theories and false cause-and-effect equivalencies that were there in the first place.

In this way, for an ETP conducting these sessions with self and others becomes a first hand experience of the energy systems as they really are and if you wanted to do this, you could begin to draw your own maps, organise these learnings into a new book that might be same or structurally different from what the Yellow Emperor said all those many years ago.

Comparing your personal findings with existing materials in the field is another outstanding way to really increase conscious and unconscious understanding of the human energy body and its systems to a point of mastery.

Ecology & Aspects

The way EmoTrance handles ecology is nothing short of wonderful. Now I don't want to take credit for this because it's simply natural and something that occurred spontaneously but I must say I simply love it.

When an issue is presented and the relative disturbance in the energy body picked up and translated through the physiological interface devices, i.e. physical sensations, and thus brought to the person's attention, the first thing they feel is blatantly the FIRST disturbance that needs to be treated and resolved. The next time the same issue is re-presented, a different body sensation may arise – you could call that "an aspect" if you wanted to, borrowing terminology from Thought Field Therapy for a structurally related energetic injury or blockage that is systemically linked to the presenting problem and makes up a part or aspect of the problem group.

Following the order and sequence of the body sensations **as and when** they are being presented is so simple and so structurally sound, it just makes me laugh with joy.

Once again, in the personal, direct experience of the **reality** of aspects, how they work together and how their order and sequence contributes to the resolution of the problem/s teaches more about the dynamic, systemic nature of these systems than reading a hundred thousand books could ever achieve.

"Infallible Healing"

What we have then here, simply by following the route clearly and undeniably laid out by the client's own sensations and experiences, is complete ecology and aspect tidy up, **in the right order and sequence** even, and it is near enough impossible to make **any** mistakes at all in it, no matter how complex, long standing or multi-issue the original problem gestalt might have ever been.

Infallibility as a therapist. How wonderful is that?

What does that do for a therapist's or healer's confidence, relaxation and ability to say, "YES!" to their role in the resolving of the client's problems? It is truly beautiful in its logic and simplicity – and of course, then so are the results.

PART 6 - ENLIGHTENING COGNITION

We have already touched on the idea that the movement of energy through the energy body changes cognition and affects beliefs, values and attitudes.

I also made the comment that this is one of the tests of the underlying theory as far as I am concerned that EmoTrance makes real, structural changes to a persons totality, and very importantly, to their neurology.

The EmoTrance process changes beliefs, values, attitudes and impacts cognition directly; one of the most fascinating aspects of this is the enlightenment insights people report during and sometimes after an EmoTrance experience.

The neurology and the cause-and-effects of someone's personality, problem groups and interlinkages, past and present are absolutely not Aristotelian in nature, but instead a multidimensional matrix with layers and levels so complex that the greatest supercomputer could not begin to unravel.

People's neurology, on the other hand, is exactly designed to compute this multi-dimensional complexity. This is exactly why we have "more neurons in our brains than there are stars in the visible sky and the connections between them, are to all intents and purposes, infinite".

We really do not need such brains and systems for computing n-complexity in order to poke at anthills with sticks in monkey fashion; and the simple reason that we only "use 5%" of our brain capacity is because most of the rest of it is there for computing multi-ordinate, n-complexity systemics in the Oceans of Energy.

That is a natural ability with which everyone is born and everyone can do this, if they want to – and if their energy systems are flowing freely because these energies do not just carry "life energy" and "nutrients" but indeed, they carry **information** of such density and complexity, it is breathtaking and entirely un-imaginable in terms of data storage in mechanical systems we are familiar with.

We have already observed how five minutes of EmoTrance gave people understandings of how their problems originated in a fantastically logical fashion that they most likely would have taken many years in therapy to arrive at – if they had been able to arrive at these insights at all, using 1-2-3 linear talk and the flat limited logic that we have all been entrained into since birth.

You might recall the lady who had been stalked and found a "backbone" through the aggressive energy – but more so, she completely understood why she had been the target and victim of bullying and stalking her entire life, what the nature of this victimhood was and how to change this.

That is a very, very complicated cause-and-effect set and yet, everyone who reads this case story or hears about it, just like the ETP who was present and the lady herself, "understands it perfectly" even if it is very difficult to explain in words exactly how that all works, how it all hangs together across the time and space of not only her totality, but that of all her aggressors as well.

There was also the gentleman who had build a wall between his students and himself. The **original kernel** around which the wall grew was a defensive device against his father, a survival device designed to stop his young and developing neurology from burning out under the onslaught of fierce energies that his young systems were incapable of channelling safely.

But the kinds of "quantum insights" that can be arrived at with the EmoTrance process are sometimes even more extraordinary. Always completely logical with hindsight, it is truly an awesome experience when something profound and very basic becomes revealed and the person in question (and their ETP!) learn something important about themselves.

Here is an example of such a profound insight.

This client was seeking weight reduction for health purposes and was working on a sensation of strong hunger which would arise spontaneously and then she would have to eat large amounts of bulky (starchy) foods in order to make those hunger pangs go away.

As many other EmoTrance clients, she had already received much therapy, counselling and coaching which had not impacted the problem.

We pick up the story just after the ETP has asked where in her body she feels these hunger pangs.

C (puts hands on large stomach, fingers spread wide apart): "I feel it right here. It really is painful."

ETP: "Well, let us consider the energy there. Where does it want to go?"

C: "There is an upward pressure."

ETP: "Let it flow and gently encourage it to go upward, tell me what's happening as you do it, please."

C: "It is going up my chest, between my breasts, into my throat and ... oh ... oh I don't believe it ...oh no ..." (starts to cry softly)

ETP: "What happened?"

C (crying silently): "I know what the hunger is, the emptiness I'm trying to fill. There should be babies in there."

This client was truly shocked and absolutely at a loss to explain why she never even thought of this before; she had three grown children and consciously, never once expected to be wanting any more. The session developed into an understanding that when this lady had felt her babies move inside her stomach during pregnancy, she had felt "not alone" for the only time in her life and now, when she felt alone, "the hunger pangs" would arrive.

What is so fascinating about this process and the cognitive repercussions is that with hindsight, it is totally logical and absolutely understandable – yet would never have been discovered by "talking with the head" at all because in her head, she was absolutely congruent that she didn't want any more children and really didn't even want the ones she'd had.

The fact simply is that we cannot solve all our problems with the kind of communication we are used to – not between each other and not within ourselves. Talking with linear language and thinking linear thoughts gets us not very far in the realms of a totality that is made of energy, of physicality and of conscious thought that can affect the very fabric of reality.

The breakthrough cognitions that go with EmoTrance make a **re-connection** between all parts of the totality and that is a very important aspect of working with EmoTrance.

For example, in this lady's case now there is compassion for the parts of her that suggest a solution to the problem of "being alone"; her eating behaviours make total sense and there is no longer a war between the various parts of consciousness, neurology and physiology. Even if the problem of "energy collapse due to loneliness" had not been tackled in the session afterwards and resolved, a very different state of understanding and congruency in self would have been achieved.

To have the correct information about occurrences in the Oceans of Energy is of course, a prime requisite of being able to function successfully, to survive without damage and to be able to take action in response to the environment that will work. Fighting loneliness with calorie counting doesn't work; it doesn't bring the correct results, it really is as simple as that. It leads to chaos and even more disturbances. Relieving the energetic blockages that create the sensation of loneliness, on the other hand, brings about immediate cessation of both that **as well as** ending the well-meaning yet futile attempts to replace babies with carbohydrates to create a similar body sensation.

The aspect of **energy as a carrier for information** is probably one of the most exciting and most fascinating aspects of the EmoTrance process once we get beyond mere emergency treatments.

Learning "With The Heart"

The Yellow Emperor notes that "You learn with your heart and you process with the head."

I am sure I don't have to tell you how the 1st World learning and teaching methods have that particular rat hanging upside down by the tail entirely – you have been to school, you know what it is like when you are sitting there and try to stuff dusty nonsense into your head with your heart yearning to be elsewhere.

That is systemically so appalling that words truly fail me.

There are even suggestions that "if you can make the material interesting, the student's retention rate increases significantly".

Dear oh dear. Wake up "the heart" just a little and a little is learned; learn with "the heart" directly and all is learned, then we can process in the head afterwards.

Strangely, I know this of course and so does just about every teacher who does not have a giant energetic wall between themselves and their students. For years, I have been structuring workshops to say virtually nothing past, "Good morning, my name is Silvia and I will be your instructor for the next three days ..." and to go straight into an exercise. I did this on the grounds that if someone has an experience of something, then we have something to talk about and not before and you will notice that all my books are structured in that way as well – straight into the material and the explanations come later because I am too well aware what happens when people try to discuss something they have **no experience** of.

When you open yourself to the world and take in the energy of a thing, you learn about the thing in a whole new way.

So, for example, if you wish to become a geologist, energetically speaking the right approach would be to spend time with rocks, open yourself to these rocks and let their energy flow into you, bringing with it all you need to know about the **nature** of rocks. When you have done **that** and not before, you can begin what the First World wrongly terms "study", which is looking at the head stuff – chemical composition, maps of where they occur, formation and such.

That way around, you will be a first class geologist who will contribute significantly to the collection of human head knowledge about rocks; chances are you will be able to add some very surprising findings about rocks that "came from nowhere" and they will hail you as a genius in geologist circles.

The same applies for every field of human endeavour – there are levels of learning, of knowing, of understanding which are way, way above and beyond book learning.

When you begin to work with "the energy of learning" for yourself and in this way, you will probably encounter energy blockages on the topic of learning that have arisen because of the wrongful ways learning is being handled systemically and the terrible experiences we have all had, leading to totally damaged self constructs believing that they are stupid, that they cannot learn, that they cannot learn to understand because they have failed to arrange two dimensional symbols in the "correct" order and linear sequence.

Here is an exercise you can do for yourself or try it with a handy child and simply note, like a true scientist and explorer what happens when you do.

1. Find a rock. Most will head straight for a meaningful crystal at this point but I would suggest you go outside and find a little stone in the street as all the "learnings" you have programmed into your head about crystals will cause more contortions and blockages in your energy system than would normally already be present and we don't need that at all for this beginning exercise.

2. Put the rock on a table and sit, looking at it. Relax.

3. Where can you feel that rock in your body? Show me with your hands.

4. Where does the energy from the rock want to go? Allow it to come in and find the requisite channels.

5. Allow the rock energy to flow into you, through you and out.

6. Keep it up until you have a steady flow between you and the rock that needs no further conscious attention but runs naturally by itself.

7. When you have learned, thank the rock and put it back where you found it.

This is the basic move of "learning with energy".

You might come away from this exercise a little disappointed because it might have felt nice but when you look for "real information" about the atomic weight of the molecules in the rock, there seems nothing new there – that is NOT the kind of learning we are doing here. That is kid's stuff – this form of learning has been reserved for shamans, priests, healers and their apprentices throughout the ages, the very best people of the tribe.

A hundred thousand years ago it may have been so that only the very best people **could** learn that way – now, we all have the neurology to just that. It is time that custom got in sync with genetic evolution and tribal habits caught up with reality – and that reality is that we can **all** learn to understand not just rocks but trees, animals and **even other people** on that level.

Opening To True Learning

Now, go out and learn. All it needs is to firstly, consciously becoming aware of any blockages, shields, barriers to receiving the energy from (the tree, the cat, the plant, the grass, the earth, the sky, the night, the moon, etc etc etc) and to dissolve them so that the energy may flow freely through the requisite pathways and enter our energy bodies. In doing so, these energies will be like "the hand that passes across the clay tablet" and the learnings will become yours, a part of you absolutely – they can never be forgotten, they cannot be undone and no-one can ever take them away from you.

I cannot tell you what that feels like nor what that does for you as a person; you will have to go out and experience it for yourself.

Keep doing it, and remember that the true object of the EmoTrance exercise is **to put this whole happening on automatic pilot** so that you don't have to think about it any longer. So that when you are in the presence of something you want to know better and feel more connected with, **understand** on a visceral level of having **true experience** of it, your energy system automatically corrects the blockages to this energy because it has learned **that is what you want and need** it to do.

Once you have found the courage and conviction to be doing this consciously, we can move on to the PhD of energy learning – learning from people.

The Clear Blue Field And The Problem Of Erosion

The so called "pyramid of human learning" which refers to book learning or head learning rather than **experience** which is what learning with energy straight into our energy bodies could be called has through the millennia (and still does today on a massive scale!) suffered from the Chinese Whispers problem.

I have much experience (yes, indeed, experience!) with the evolution of a field beyond the person who originated it in the first place.

What happens regular as clockwork is that a person discovers or develops something that brings about truly amazing results **when they do it**. Students flock to them in order to learn how to do the same; but they don't and what was a "clear blue field" of something or other that was amazingly effective becomes eroded with every teaching and learning generation away from the originator until, within a few short years, it becomes entirely unrecognisable as what it used to be and muddy, diluted, and basically ineffective.

It is my supposition that this happens because the students don't allow the energy from the teacher to become a part of them and to change them so that they may learn to do the same as the teacher did.

It is my further supposition that this occurs primarily because of the "silverback" principle – some form of genetic and culturally enshrined monkey behaviour by which there is one silverback who commands the tribe and although the young wannabes watch him with envious eyes, they need to be **better** than him and when it is their turn on the throne, must overthrow anything that would remind anyone and including themselves that there ever was another silverback before them.

Plato and Aristotle, if you will. A dynamic which condemned the lot of us to spend over 2000 years in the dark ages and they are not over yet, not by a long shot.

When I put forth the proposition that in order to really, really **learn** from any teacher, one would have to open up entirely to them and allow their energy to run into you and change you, people simply freak out. But – would we not be poisoned by them and all their shortcomings? Would we not become their slaves? Fall in love with them? Never have another original thought of our own? Inherit their limitations and make the same mistakes?

Well, what can I say.

Try it if you dare, and if you dare, you might just find that what happens and what you learn from this is as different from your expectations as the before and after definitions of that young gentleman we met earlier of "Beauty".

For what its worth, whenever I have done it, I have come away loving the person indeed. I have understood them in a way that I cannot explain in words, and I have been completely aware of their limitations and disturbances as a result, allowing me to move **their** explorations on without having to destroy them or thinking of myself as being better as they are. I also understood **their** materials and explanations perfectly and moreover, what they were teaching and how they were trying to teach it **made perfect sense to me**.

All The World Your Teacher

I have met many people who were seeking a or even THE teacher, the one who would bring them to enlightenment and who would show them the way out of their own personal darkness into paradise.

I used to look down upon these, especially the ones who would stick themselves to a one who would hold out that kind of promise like a limpet and then, when it didn't work out yet again, turn poisonous against their previous teacher and still then set off for their next victim.

I understand now that they were nearly on the right track – and nearly there (dicht daneben ist auch vorbei!) can be more frustrating by far than just not even being anywhere near this idea at all.

The thing is that if you consider the forms of learning we have been talking about, it would be madness to put the burden of developing you into enlightenment on the frail shoulders of a single human.

To learn about the universe, of course we need to learn about all the universe – including humble rock, the clouds and sand. People can teach us but not just one person – all of them.

Everyone can be your teacher in that way, and the more you open yourself to that without fear and nothing but desire to learn (and because it is such an amazing experience that **feels so good!**) the more you learn and the more **experienced** you become.

If you dare to learn, you can learn the most amazing things from a tramp in the street, from that annoying little old lady who is holding up the queue in the supermarket because she is trying to have a conversation with the bored check out assistant, from that droning, boring politician, from that low class urban layabout petty criminal, from that redneck army sergeant, from the downtrodden, worn out mother-of-five – from everyone.

What you will be learning is not just about their limitations but about **the human condition**. You could say that each and every person has **something** to teach you that you didn't know about yet, that you might have never expected to know at all.

However, I appreciate that this is advanced people learning. You might want to start by just dropping all remaining barriers to your favourite teacher, someone you feel comfortable with and who has inspired you. You can evoke them by playing a video tape, an audio tape, bring out a book they wrote or look at a picture of the person.

Then, it is only a matter of the basic EmoTrance process and for you open yourself wide and say, "Teach me."

And perhaps the thought, deep in the back of your mind, that ...

"My heart is as open as the sky."

The Doors Of Perception ...

"If the doors of perception were cleansed, everything
would appear to man as it is, infinite." - William Blake

There are things, I'm sure you know, between heaven and earth and beyond that do not come in the shape or form of a tree, a cat, a cloud or a person.

There are other realities from which we may learn energetically and where knowledge and cognition may reside that could truly take your breath away. ESP – extra sensory perception – what is that but learning just in that way we have been talking about across the last chapters? The future is there to be read like a book in the quantum spaces where here is now, yesterday and a million years ago are happy next door neighbours and space is not an issue, either. Reading other people's minds, predicting events and even influencing the very fabric of time and space at will are all possible from the basic presuppositions of the universe where EmoTrance comes from.

Are you ready to cleanse your doors of perception?

Just for interest and perhaps to wonder, where are my "doors of perception" or if they're not doors, what would they be? and where? and where do I feel that special fear at the thought of clearing my "doors" of perception? or what would happen if I really started to perceive things as they really are?

What would we "see"? Dead people?

Are there really aliens, demons, angels, ghosts?

Are there really spirits in the trees, in the rocks, in the ground?

Is there a God?

We might best be speaking about the "shields to perception" and of course, that's a plural and it may be very, very interesting to have a little feel around for those, have a little wonder of what would happen if ...

Perhaps a pinprick hole at first might be in order ...

I leave you with this thought and the tantalising possibilities that reside in this entire notion.

PART 7 – PATTERNS FOR HEALING & TRANSFORMATION

To say that there is **a lot** you can do with the basic EmoTrance technique would be a serious under-estimation.

In this section I have brought together some interesting patterns, uses and approaches we have come across so far.

By all means, try them out, find out what you can do with these to make **your** life more interesting and exciting than it has previously been.

Eating With Love

You might be familiar with the concept to bestow an energetic blessing on food prior to consuming it as a means by which to make it even more nutritious and healthy than it already is.

This following pattern is more about "making friends with food" which is something a great many people really need to do.

Just about every food item is "bad" in some way; we have been told scare stories about genetically engineered foods, crop spraying, impoverished soils and artificial fertilisers and then of course, the terrible effects especially on one's fatness (aka ability to attract love and livelihood) - food has become a threat rather than a wonderful class of living beings which enable us to be around to enjoy this incarnation at all.

So let us consider the energetic dimension of eating something - anything at all and let us also consider what happens when we consciously reverse and block up energy flows between us and the food which after all, will absolutely become a part of us in all ways as soon as it is beginning its journey towards our stomachs.

In the light of this, try the following:

1. Get any kind of food item, it matters not what type, and hold it in your hand.

2. Look at the item and say to yourself, "THAT is actually only an energy. Hm, where do I feel THAT item in my body?"

3. Do EmoTrance on the resulting body sensations.

4. Now, eat the item. As you do so, keep focussed on the idea that this is a welcome energy which will keep you alive; and that if it is absolutely welcome in a fully Even Flow situation, will do you the world of good in every sense and on every layer - and definitely including the level of the physicality.

5. If you become aware of any reversals, blockages or other unhelpful sensations as you bite off, chew and swallow the item, remove them in the usual fashion.

6. After consuming the item, wait for a little while and consider what might have changed and what different ideas, thoughts etc. are coming

to you. If there are strong fears of any kind or other forms of strong emotions as the result of this first exercise in "eating with love", be sure to treat those as well to make the every day experience of consuming food into a whole new experience.

As a side remark, I might make the note that by changing your response to a great many things, physical responses also change. I have evidence of at least two people who, following an EmoTrance session, no longer suffer from hangovers following alcohol "abuse", for example and very many more who have used the change in the flow of energy in their bodies in order to suddenly no longer have "cravings" or "withdrawal symptoms" to all manner of substances. Allergic responses can also change quite dramatically.

EmoTrance is a very new modality and as I have said numerous times before, we do not treat for physical symptoms and any change in the **physical conditions** of the body are only side effects and not the point of an EmoTrance treatment.

Although we may have in the back of our minds the thought that if we change the energy relationship with food, we'll "lose weight" and then become lovable etc., in my opinion even going into these "eating with love" exercises from that point of view of that is not the right attitude.

The energy body and our relationships in the Oceans of Energy deserve our full attention and commitment entirely regardless of the benefits or outcomes, the secondary gains or the pats on the back from others. Indeed, you cannot abuse these systems for if you try them from the wrong standpoint or for the wrong reasons, they simply bog themselves down altogether and the disturbances get worse, rather than better.

Unconditional regard for the energetic realities – and including our own energy bodies – is the only way forward towards true health and benefits which might follow.

Now, Where Do You Feel THAT In Your Body?

Very early on in the development of EmoTrance, we found a particularly enlivening application.

Try this with another:

1. Lightly place one fingertip on their skin at any given place.

2. Ask them, "Can you feel this?"

3. Have them let this "energy" find its requisite channels and circuits - all the way in, around, through and out.

4. As they move the energy, make tiny circular movements to stimulate the sensation.

5. Continue until they have reached the Energised End State

There are clearly a great many usages for this particular pattern and the therapeutic applications are by no means the ones with the most impact, nor with the most fun being had. Two (or possibly even more!) people being able to do EmoTrance doing this as a partner exercise and at the same time create experiences and sensations which would leave Tantra practitioners gasping with envy - and without the need for much practise, at that.

Raising Sexual Energy

One of the most powerful energy systems in the body, if the sexual energy related ereas are not functioning as they should you can absolutely guarantee ill health and misery in mind, in body and in spirit.

Even those who do not wish to actually have sex and want to raise these energies for different reasons must appreciate that unless these energies run smoothly and clearly, they are useless for any endeavour, no matter how good the intentions or how holy the pursuit.

The "touch" protocol from above will come in useful to track disturbances and to begin a healing process in this area of your energy body and all the related systems; working with affirmations such as , "I am a sexual being" - "Sexual energy is innocent energy." - "Sexual energy is power for my life." etc. is extremely useful too.

People who have had bad experiences with human sexual exchanges, may they have been physical or non-physical in nature will need healing before they can start trancing. Depending on how much damage exists in the fabric of the energy body, this might require both self healing and then to seek a capable assistant.

The 360' Field Clearer

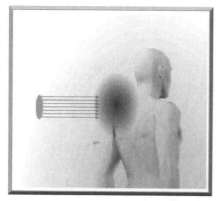

This is a more advanced EmoTrance exercises that is very useful under many different circumstances. For this, we need a steady energy source that comes from one direction.

Examples of these energy sources could be the sun, the moon, a person, an object such as a photograph or a generator such as a crystal or a tachyon cell.

You can also create a steady energy field by **making it**, for example to have a horizontal waterfall of a particular energy source coming towards you.

Once you have established your energy source, procede as follows:

1. Stand facing the energy source squarely on and open yourself to the energy. If you need to work on your shieldings and any damaged or blocked ereas, do so until the energy flows smoothly.

2. Now, slowly – I mean very slowly! – begin to turn and allow the energy to flow into you as you do so from the different angles as you move all the way through 360' degrees.

3. If at any time you become aware of further responses which would indicate a disturbance, stop there and trance it through until there is no longer a problem.

4. Once you have completed an entire circuit, do it again, a little faster this time, to make sure that your energy body is entirely clear all the way around.

5. You may do it once again and really go for the energised end state on this occasion.

The reason and purpose for this exercise is to become aware of systems disturbances that are **behind our conscious awareness**.

We have a tendency to store things that would be too troublesome to have within our field of awareness behind us (as is, for example, indicated in the common phrase of, "I have put the past behind me.")

But out of sight is not out of existence and indeed, some of the most profound disturbances and energetic burdens can be found on "the dark side of the moon", including injuries you are not normally aware of and also, displaced and disconnected ereas including attachments (energetic systems not derived from or produced by yourself).

This is also something to be considered for practitioner assisted sessions and one of the reasons why some ETP interventions are best done in a standing position.

The Fairy Wish

I have been working with the underlying structures of goal setting and the process of making something "come true in the Hard" for many years.

In general, and although this is a deep oversimplification, how likely any given thought, idea or desire manifests in the Hard is strongly linked to how congruent a person can be when they aim themselves towards this goal.

Fears, doubts and internal conflicts undermine the endeavour of reality creation at every step of the way.

The Fairy Wish is an EmoTrance clearing pattern to be able to **wish for something** with all your heart, if you will.

The Fairy Wish Pattern

- As with affirmations, in self help this pattern is best performed in front of a mirror so you can make the wish to yourself.

- In partner work, one partner makes the wish and the other becomes the "fairy godmother" who will grant the wish.

- Pick something you have always wanted but cannot imagine ever having unless there is a miracle of some kind.

- State the wish **out loud** (that is **very** important) to the witness – yourself in the mirror or your partner.

- Note where the disturbances occur in your body as usual.

- Treat the disturbances in the order of the biggest one first, as usual.

- Re-state the wish.

- If necessary, perform further healing and clearing until your energies run clearly and powerfully, and the act of stating the wish has a powerful sense of **creating reality** about it.

- Your practise partner or you to your mirror image would say, "Your wish has been granted." to conclude the Fairy Wish pattern.

Giving & Receiving Gifts

This is a partner exercise you can also do with yourself in the mirror. It is particularly popular with young children and truly wonderful fun; indeed, if performed at Christmas it might well bring back the idea of the Christmas Spirit as a reality.

Look at the person in front of you and think of a gift to give them. This gift will be an energy form; in order to transfer the gift we will have to package it into metaphorical form so the conscious mind can take part in the game.

As we are transferring an energy form, there is no limit as to what may be given; you could give, for example:

Direct objects such as a diamond, a golden crown, a beautiful sculpture, a warm coat etc. If you for a moment allow yourself to tune into these four energies, one at a time, you will notice that they are all very very different indeed and even quite specific; if you were to notice how they feel in your body and then consider them as energies alone, you understand how the transfer is being achieved.

You can also give:

Qualities. We have already mentioned this, but you can think of yourself as a real life fairy godmother and bestow intelligence, luck, fame, fortune, beauty, logic, joy, peace – anything at all.

Colours;

Music;

Animals. The energy of animals is something that many people deeply crave and every species has an energy all of its own. I would make the note that phobias of animals may be cleared in this easy, natural and ecological way.

People. This is interesting and can be a very powerful process to give someone a mother, a father, a child, a lover, a guide, a friend, a teacher, a protector. Remember that we are only dealing with energy here and the ability of the recipient to be able to run these energies cleanly and to be free of injuries and disturbances on the topic.

Landscapes and natural manifestations. This includes anything from a single small plant in a pot to an entire ocean, a desert under a moonlit sky, a tropical jungle and further out to giving a sun, many suns, the night sky, the universe and everything in between.

Symbols. Symbols are things we might often not really understand but which carry a lot of energy. Be it a pentagram or a cross, anything that is not simple Even Flow is an indication of a disturbance; we should not fear or worship either for they are only symbols for existing forms of energy. Other symbols include, for example, the tree of life and of course, the entire Tarot deck.

Mysteries & Magic. This would include generic and open ended answers and questions, understanding and learning, higher energies, higher beings and the Akashic records; and more mundane things such as astral travel, ESP, clairvoyance and telepathy.

The Gift Protocol

1. First person to raise the energy by considering a gift for the other (or the self if done in mirror work).

2. Once the gift has been found, you speak out clearly, "I give you the gift of (...)" and hand over the gift, making an appropriate gesture of giving with both hands.

3. The recipient notes where they feel this energy in their bodies and makes the necessary adjustments with the help of the first person.

4. The gift is repeated until it is received entirely and runs through the system clearly. Make sure the recipient does not hold on to this energy anywhere, no matter what – re-assure them if necessary that it will feel **even better still** once the Even Flow is fully established, even if they cannot imagine it just yet.

5. Share any insights and then switch the giver/receiver positions.

NB. The giver should also take some note as to what it feels like to raise and give this energy. Sometimes, it can be even more powerful an experience to create the Even Flow from that perspective, rather than as the recipient.

The Energy Of Money

Quite a few of the EmoTrance patterns in this section revolve around the simple process of making peace and finding a peaceful, Even Flow resolution to painful energetic relationships.

Money and the energy of money and people are forms of energetic occurrences in the Oceans of Energy who need some serious relationship counselling.

Here are a few basic patterns to work with this energetic relationship.

1. A Penny Saved ...

Simply hold a penny (or the smallest coin in your denomination) in your hand and look at it. Work with the energy until it rushes through you freely. Notice how your thinking, decisions, ideas and feelings towards this smallest representative of the idea of money changes when you have cleared your disturbances.

2. The Concept of Money

Where do you feel "money" in your body? Do you have any shields to money? Any places where you are holding on to that energy form? Clear it all and establish Even Flow on the idea or concept of money.

3. The Past, The Present & The Future

Consider your (and your families, if appropriate) money history and treat what needs to be treated. Then, consider your money present and your money future. On this particular topic, you might be wanting to take a look at the time/money connection too and where that would be noticeable in your body.

4. Accepting Being Rich

Choose a representation of rich. No, not just that sort of rich – I mean, **really** rich. Sultan of Brunei rich; Sun King of France rich, Citizen Kane rich.

A picture of a palace, the Hope diamond or the vaults of Fort Knox might be useful in order to raise this energy so that you can work with your response to this.

As No. 3 brings in the time connection, this brings in the power connection and this particular exercise is an essential pre-requisite to being able to conceive of owning and handling large amounts of money cleanly, easily and without putting your energy system into reversals.

5. Partner Exercises

Partner exercises in sending and receiving all and any forms of money, abundance, wealth etc energies are extremely useful to bring awareness of problems in the giving-receiving energy systems and to allow you both to clear these successfully.

Especially in the context of money, being able to give and receive without holding on or trying to impede the natural flow (or even to speed it up unnaturally!) is absolutely essential for really understanding how money works, as well as being absolutely confident and comfortable with this energy form in all ways.

Prejudice Removal

This is one of the most fascinating exercises with EmoTrance you can undertake. Very simply, the aim is to remove prejudices about people from your energy system.

People automatically create templates and cause-and-effect relationships between energetic injuries and the people who caused them, just as they make these cause-and-effect relationships between positive experiences and people.

People, however, are not templates and just because a man happens to have curly brown hair does not mean he will be just as nice or just as horrible as "that other man from way back when who had curly brown hair".

Templating is a dangerous thing either way around; it can lead people to be drawn to certain templates or types without finding out what they are really like just as well as it can lead them to reject certain types because of the same reason. Whether it is too much trust or too much rejection, either way is not very useful and can lead to a great deal of totally unnecessary trouble in relationships.

Further, templating strongly interferes with our natural abilities to "read another person" because simply put, when we template we just don't.

That little grey haired woman becomes instead "my mother" and not only do we never get to find out just who this person really is, nor get to find out if indeed she has important new learnings for us or what the possibilities of a relationship, no matter how fleeting.

This is a very dangerous state of affairs; someone could easily let a homicidal maniac trustingly into their house because "he reminded me of my dear old uncle Bob" when if this template had not been in the way they would have been able to read that murderers true intentions and would have been able to protect themselves.

So now that we have established that it is safer, better and generally sounder to meet people directly and without prejudices, here is the Removing Prejudices exercise.

This exercise is extremely powerful and the more you do this, the more amazing it becomes in its repercussions on you and your reality.

Very simply, upon meeting or seeing a stranger, we ask ourselves, "Where do I feel that person in my body?" and then resolve the blockages and disturbances, "good or bad" it matters not, until your are running completely cleanly on that person.

You will find two things. Firstly, you will notice things about this person as though your eyes had been opened to all manner of qualities and aspects (good or bad!) about this person you didn't see before.

Secondly, you will notice a real increase in your desire to learn more from and about this person. This does NOT mean that you have to spend time with any of these people or make them be your friends. You don't have to listen to them or talk to them at all; just being able to "receive" people without blockages gives you a great deal more information than a year's surveillance by the CIA could assemble.

I would also like to re-assure you that in opening yourself to people, one at a time, will not make you unhappy, depressed or vulnerable; if you are afraid or have a strong negative response to this idea on whatever grounds, please treat this first and as a high priority. Energy relationships are blessed in the fact that they do not have to carry the burdens and contortions of responsibility for the other over time and space; all the "hard" problems and difficulties are suspended and they really no longer apply.

If you have the will and the courage, this is probably the most transformational energy exercise you could ever wish to undertake.

Mirror, Mirror, On The Wall ...

Talking of "transformational exercises", what would happen if you were to stand in front of a mirror and ask yourself where you feel THAT person in your body?

You might do the totality or concentrate on aspects – your hair, your wrinkles, your eye colour that is so uncannily like your father's ...

You might do this with your clothes on or off, in front of a full length mirror or in the bathroom under neon lights and run your response energies until you begin to have some kind of idea developing that you are not what you always thought you were.

Energy Dancing

Music, movement and dance are flow personified; when we combine this with energy clearing, we create extremely powerful and moving experiences that are as deeply pleasant as they are healthful and transformative.

Music raises powerful energies and produces powerful emotional responses in people.

You know how some songs and some kinds of music affect you; to do EmoTrance by yourself and dancing the movements of the energy in your body through and into a full out energised end state is literally ecstatic.

An ETP once went to a festival where two hundred drummers were performing; when she opened herself fully of the sounds, sensations and energies this produced she said she nearly fainted with the power of it.

We can use the power of music to touch our energy systems to bring out into the open things that might need resolution but we would never be able to express in words or even understand consciously quite what they might be about.

Music also circumvents our defences, such as cynicism, anger and denial and it just catches us out and brings us face to face with our pain, loneliness and the realities of our feelings.

This being so, learning to run these energies with the aid of music to help evoke them in the first place is an extraordinary self healing tool with tremendous transformative power.

Once again I would re-assure you that working with music in this way does by no means turn it flat or meaningless or makes a song that you really loved (but it always makes you cry!) into something unimportant.

EmoTrance does not work that way.

You will be able to experience these energies differently once they do not hurt any longer and the true beauty and meaning for you personally will become revealed.

It is truly worth doing for that alone.

PART 8 - RAISING ENERGY FOR MAGIC, FOR HEALING & FOR LIFE

Give a moments thought and grace that possibly out of all and any species on this planet we **can raise our own energies** through the application of consciousness and free will at any point and **regardless of external circumstances**.

That is a pretty neat trick if you learn how to do it and the fact is that once you are in a position (as we now are) to undo our contortions in the energy body on the topic, it is incredibly easy.

We have already touched on the aspect of raising energy in the "I am a healer" movement prior to healing someone; we are literally conjuring up the concept of The Healer and then running it into our own energy bodies, easing out any blockages and letting that particular energy setting the tone and state from which we operate.

What a wonderful advancement on those poor efforts of having someone stand in front of a mirror and helplessly with a quaking voice saying, "Grr, grr, I am a tiger ...."

Contrary to public opinion and the much preached delusion, affirmations do not work at all **if the person who says them** is reversed or energetically blocked on those topics.

A person with a seriously disturbed energy system on that very topic (if it was working, why?? do affirmations in the first place??!) will cause themselves pain every single time they raise that form of energy. It may be that they get used to the pain and it may be that by accident or good fortune things start to shake loose and sort themselves out, but it is just as likely that the affirmation will make the already existing chaos and confusion in the energy system even worse and the person gets even less of what it is they are after – be it the tiger energy, being successful, loved, beautiful, in tune with the universe and all the rest.

Here is the basic process to raising all and any kind of energy form you might ever require and, more importantly, make sure that those energies flow smoothly in, through and out to the extent that you will **never** have to speak another affirmation to raise them because they are simply there and have totally become **a part of you** in the long run.

1. Choose your energy.

The world's your oyster – beauty, enlightenment, prosperity, abundance, wealth (yes they are all quite different), love, tiger energy, dolphin energy, cloud energy, creativity, angelicness, brutality (you might need it one day so don't go into a reversal on me here!), it is all here but for the thinking of it.

2. Make the statement that will raise the energy.

When you are working by yourself, obviously the "I am" phrasing will be of the most use to you. "I am a tiger" – "I am wealthy" – "I am beautiful" is one form of version; I suggest you try something a little more radical such as, "I am beauty" – "I am wealth" – "I am health" which is an interesting way of really stating your intent that you wish to no longer make a distinction between you and these qualities and become them absolutely.

3. Speak the statement and run the basic EmoTrance protocol.

Where do you feel that in your body? Follow the basic EmoTrance protocol until the energy truly rushes and sparkles and you are having a real experience of what it feels to be that, to be in this state. If you cannot quite reach this on your first try, do what you can and then the next day, do some more until all blockages have successfully been resolved, all ereas pertaining to this have been healed, and even the postman notices that something very important has fundamentally changed about you.

I must really put it to you that this form of using EmoTrance with "affirmations" is one of the most powerful personal development techniques I have ever encountered. If you cannot think of what kind of energy you would like to raise and make your own, you can buy books on affirmations in every bookstore. Just look at the standard suggested affirmations there and you will probably find things that you didn't even know (consciously) you always wanted to have, to be, to do, or to experience.

Performing Powerful Blessings

It seems to me that one raises energies for a purpose and not just because they are there, although that too can have its merits as you will find out for yourself.

Mostly however, we raise energy in order to do something with it. The "I'm a tiger" guy is probably wanting something very specific, for example being successful in a sales conference or asking his boss for a raise.

We raise the "healer" energy prior to healing.

As we have noted, unexpressed energies are a huge problem in our energy systems and when you raise energies, especially very powerful ones, then they have to go somewhere – holding on to these energies is strictly not an option.

One thing we can do with these energies is to perform blessings.

Try the following exercise.

Find any household object, place it before you and raise the energy of "security" in a phrasing that pleases you – "I am secure" or perhaps, "I am security" if you will. I have chosen this particular energy for a purpose and because it is not commonly raised in our society, if at all so you will be having a fresh experience.

Raise the energy until you are really feeling it and now, turn to the household object, hold out your hands towards it and let this "security" energy flow from you and into the object in question.

Do this until the accumulated energy from the raising has flown out of you and your systems are at a well balanced level which is running smoothly and normally, then stop.

You have just performed one of the very oldest religious acts – that of blessing an object.

This is a simple skill which is virtually never used as it should be used, as it could be used. Sometimes parents of children do this unconsciously when they stroke a coat, for example, and think, "I hope this will keep you warm and protected." Lovers do this when they kiss the letter prior to sealing the envelope but these things are truly a pale comparison to

159

blessing objects deliberately, with intent and from a state of a free-flowing energy system.

There are, once again, so many practical applications that I could fill book upon book with just this one simple energetic movement of raising energy for blessings.

Here are some very few ideas for you to really start playing with.

1. Healing Water

Water is **incredibly** responsive to energetic imprinting and raising energies and putting them into water which can then be taken, drunk or bathed in by yourself or any other is of course very useful. Small pretty bottles of water labelled, "Health", "Happiness", "Joy" or "Prosperity" also make a very attractive low cost gift for any occasion which is mostly received with much good humour even by the unwitting.

2. Imprinting Crystals & Dedicating Stones

Instead of having music playing on the CD, you can have energies playing on a small stone in the corner of your room. I am very serious about this; try it. It is good fun. It is also enormously therapeutic and something that small children (of all ages) really kick into – making your own small guardians, dream catchers, dream generators, protectors and much much more by raising the energy and then imprinting it into an object that remains is excellent fun as well as being most effective.

3. Blessing & Dedicating Rooms & Environments

The energy of "Harmony" is an example of something that would do well to exist all around a family's dining table and main living areas.

Depending on the family, it might require regular renewal. "Tranquillity" does a lot for children's bedrooms as does "Love" and "Productivity" is a good energy for work environments.

These powerful energetic manifestations raised and placed by someone who knows what they are doing also drive out energetic gremlins and stale ereas of all kinds; they can also counteract and completely alleviate unfortunate environmental energies and all kinds of other environmental energy toxins.

The same applies for outside areas, gardens, homes, entrances – you can really do a lot when you get into energetic home improvements and decide where you place what kind of energetic manifestation and for what purpose.

4. Blessing People

It is unfortunate but I would probably advise to do this quietly and to keep it very quiet. Also, chances are that your blessings will run into some powerful shields and then they are rejected and fruitless, no matter how good your intentions might have been, or how desperately in need of these energies the intended recipient might have been.

One of my favourite people blessing occurrences is for small babies at christenings or shortly after birth, to give a real blessing gift just like the fairy godmothers do.

Performing blessings in practise groups or with friends who are also re-learning to accept such extraordinary and valuable gifts is at this point the most widely used application; I look forward to the day when many more people will be able to confidently bestow and receive blessings as a matter of course.

Curses

The flip side of blessings are obviously curses which might best be defined as designed to increase chaos rather than to alleviate it in a directional fashion.

A great many holistic people try to close their ears, eyes and minds to the fact that we can injure just as successfully as we can heal and that we may curse just as well as we may bless; it is at the end of a day a simple fact of nature and ignoring this does no-one any good at all.

Ad nocendum potentes sumus – We have the power to harm.

A healer who doesn't understand that or doesn't want to know about it is a danger to themselves or others. You don't get to pick the weather and especially with large systemic reversals in place, the more powerful a healer you become, the more powerful a harmer you become too. That's just one of those things and one of the reasons that many of us keep ourselves bridled and not moving forward as we could indeed.

Curses have their own interesting set ups and occurrences in the energy system.

Many people cannot accept the fact that they can heal because that would mean power and responsibility which they feel they cannot handle – and perhaps they are absolutely right in that assessment as things stand in the prevalent conditions of their energy bodies.

To raise the energies required for curses is even more difficult because not only do we have the same power issues again, but this time we also have the weight of thousands of years of entrainment that it is bad to do this, that it is incredibly dangerous, that it will condemn you to hell and that it backfires to seriously contort the process.

Until and unless you are absolutely clear of all these thoughtforms and reversals entirely, it is indeed extremely dangerous to use these energy forms for the purposes of cursing, just as it is extremely dangerous to use pure love energy if your channels aren't sufficiently developed to handle this.

Purely energetically speaking, the process itself burns you up if you are not ready and of course is bound to go badly wrong when conducted from an incongruent state full of reversals, swirling chaos of doubts, fears, anxiety and thoughts of evil and repercussion.

As tempting as it may seem to start taking revenge right away using the EmoTrance processes, I strongly suggest you leave these forms of energies for a time when you are not only a great deal more ready, but also have a great deal more experience and wisdom in the ways of the energy laws of the universe.

Thoughtfields & Reality Creation

Another very useful use for raising energies is the direct and conscious act of creating thoughtfields.

Thoughtfields are dense ereas of energy which become more and more "real", the more attention and intention goes into their creation and into their maintenance.

A very good example of such a dense thoughtfield would be the imaginary friend of a small child which is, to all intents and purposes, entirely real to the child AND can be picked up and described quite perfectly by psychics who have never met the child before.

Mostly, people don't even know they are actively creating thoughtfields of one kind or another all the time. Most are wispy and just blow away in the breeze, but others can become so dense and real that they bridge into felt reality and are with the person in question all the time.

Standard personal development goal setting strategies try to achieve exactly that – to make a goal so real that it simply steps across into reality and "becomes".

Where this tends to go wrong, as it does with the standard affirmations, is that the energy of the whole process is not being considered.

Goal setting does not work simply by visualising something every night before you go to sleep and wanting your heart out as you look at it. I can really assure you that this has been tried to no avail by many hundreds of thousands of people, maybe millions, who have purchased personal development products where this basic strategy is being told and taught, time and time and time again.

First of all, let us be clear what we are doing with this process of reality creation.

Rightly, we have to start with an idea. That's where it goes wrong right away, because people make an idea of a house, or a boat, or a car, or a preferred lover and **think they are going to create the object itself** and not the energy that object represents in metaphorical form.

There is a well known sales adage which goes, "You don't sell the product, you sell the feelings."

What that means is that salesmen know that people don't buy a house for a house but for the hope that they will feel good when they live there.

If we think back on how "good feelings" come to be – well of course, they are an indicator of the underlying conditions in the energy body. And the energy body doesn't want a house – it wants energy, of course.

Now, this makes me laugh. The energy body wants a particular form of energy as represented by a particular house in solid metaphorical form in order to create a state of affairs where the physical body notices the change and starts to feel good. First question – when does it want this energy? In forty years from now upon retirement? Answer, no of course not. It needs this energy form right now. We can't have any idea of what the energy body might require in forty years from now, but chances are it will be something very different indeed.

And this sad misunderstanding causes people to "chase their dream" their entire life long, whilst putting their entire life on hold until they "have their dream". Then they move in and it is such a disappointment, they die not long after. Citizen Kane is a really good example of this process in action.

Second question: if you pull up the metaphor of the dream house and sit there with longing and heartache, does that make it manifest any quicker? Answer: it is highly dubious. What is not dubious however is that to cause these hunger states and to use them to motivate desperate action by the totality to alleviate them is as archaic and out of fashion as is starving the slaves in the mines constantly in the belief it will make them work harder.

It might do for a while but they die faster too and don't work anywhere near as efficiently as their well fed counterparts (and you can get serious revolts and bloody revolutions if they really had enough).

It is completely unecological from the energetic standpoint to try and motivate someone towards a goal by having them be hungrily wanting it, especially over long periods of time, years, decades or even longer still.

The good news is however that we need not be hungry for our "goals" any longer.

You can have all that energy and you can have it right now – if you need a fast car (or so you think), try soaking into yourself the energy of the fastest, most expensive car in a luxury dealership and just notice what happens to your hunger and so called goal as a result.

If you have had for a long time an image in your mind of a house or a landscape you think you need to be happy, call up the image ("raise that energy") and allow yourself to let this energy flow into you, soften and gentle any blockages, repair what needs to be repaired and notice, once again, what happened to that idea that you needed to physically live there for you to be happy.

This is a truly extraordinary process and side effect of the basic pre-suppositions behind the EmoTrance system of energy nutrition.

You can create **exactly** the right thoughtfields that provide **exactly** the right energy your energy needs and is calling for, right now – and it won't cost you a single dime.

How cool is that?

Do you feel any fear that you might not know what to do with yourself once you have "eaten all your dreams"? If you do, locate the corresponding body sensation and of course, you know what to do by now.

What happens when you actually do that?

Well the very first thing that happens is that houses become houses once more, and not the answer to your prayers, the solution to all your problems, or some kind of guarantee of bliss everlasting.

That can only be a very, very good thing because it really must be such a horrible shock to have discovered after 65 years or more of constant slavery and self mutilation that the big house doesn't make you happy at all – and you sacrificed everything for this, your health, your relationships, your life and all the experiences you could have had but didn't because you were too busy running after your dream.

This is very much the same process as with anything else anyone might think they need to be happy – a special person, that special relationship, that once-in-a-lifetime event that validates everything.

Now, I am not here to destroy anyone's dreams. That is not the purpose of what I do. What I do hope sincerely though is that when you and I are on our respective deathbeds, we will have lived and we will have no regrets about wasting our lives on a false dream.

A Different Dream – Goal Setting To State

So now we have established that houses and people don't make you happy.

But then, what does?

The answer to that is of course, experiences.

That is the core of the sales slogan, "You are not selling products, you are selling feelings." You could also re-phrase that and say instead, "You are selling certain energy states that produce the sensation of extraordinary feelings."

Now, in our society we have a general consensus as to where extraordinary feelings can be had and where they come from.

The first group entails loving relationships and family relationships which are said to make you blissfully happy (but generally don't, or not very often from what I have observed so far); the second group revolves around **unusual** experiences such as high drama in war, natural catastrophe, seeing a spaceship land, sky diving, or something you do on holiday but don't get to experience when you stay at home.

You may or may not be familiar with "Guiding Stars", my work on high moments of magical, mystical experiences of love and connection and the effects these anti-traumas have on providing guidance structure for a person's life.

Either way, I have found in my research that "magic moments" of amazing power have the disconcerting habit of happening just anywhere, just any time, with just about anybody – and the truth is that you don't get to have them because there are certain people there, because you are in a certain landscape or because there are certain special circumstance such as it being Christmas, but simply because for an instant, an opening occurred in the individual **who was actively having these experiences** to allow them to see and feel a state of being that is actually there all the time, wherever they go.

If you have ever felt truly alive, truly connected, truly in awe of another person or of the universe itself in any manifestation at all – then you have your goal.

THAT is what you want more of, namely to feel like that and better than that again, more often, more predictably and more reliably.

So in EmoTrance, the goal is not one of the many components that were present during an amazing experience but simply to learn to **shift into that magical state of being** where you all of a sudden awaken to the beauty of the universe, to the possibilities of connection between you and everything around you and not least of all, awaken to yourself at last. When we can even come close that goal, you can put us literally anywhere, including in a concentration camp, and we will still be glad to be alive.

Now, isn't that something worth having?

Isn't that a goal worth attaining – reaching a state of being where we are always in love with the universe, no matter what, no matter where?

That is something that once you have achieved it, can never be taken from you and is absolutely independent of any and all occurrences that can befall us here in our lives. It is independent of bereavement or pain, of riches or lack thereof, of aging or losing limbs – because it is a state of being. How do we reach this?

I think you might have figured it out already – we reach these states of enlightenment for this is what they truly are by repairing our energy bodies and have them fully functioning, fully connected and fully in the flow of all-there-is once again.

I cannot guarantee you enlightenment if you take up EmoTrance and really apply it with volition; but I can guarantee you that it will give you experiences of feelings and sensations you have never had before, even at the very first beginners levels. When you have had your first experience of this, you will know that I am absolutely right in my idea that the ultimate goal is enlightenment. We can make steps towards this, and even our baby steps are worth a hundred expensive villas, fur coats and sailing yachts rolled into one. What do you think we can learn to feel, learn to be and learn to do given just a little more time and a little more adjustments towards Even Flow?

I will leave you with this thought on the topic of goals and life achievements.

A Developmental Model Of The Energy Body

I would like to now introduce the concept of the energy body as a developing, growing entity that has not yet reached its adult form.

If we go back to the archaic maps of the energy system once more, what we find is a particular state snapshot that is considered the ideal, in spite of much talk about Kundalini rising.

You could think of the Kundalini rising idea as a transition of the energy body into a different state of being which would resonate closely with our previous concepts of thus having entirely different experiences then we have become accustomed to having, even though our external circumstances have not changed (see the old "Before enlightenment, chop wood, carry water. After enlightenment chop wood, carry water." slogan, probably designed to put as many people as possible off the idea of seeking enlightenment.)

However, what we do not have at all are maps of what the energy system is supposed to look like "after enlightenment" and of course, we have already discussed at length how unhelpful the idealised representations of the human energy body actually are and how likely to be flawed, considering where they came from and what purposes they served.

Krishnamurti, who was a very respected thinker on such matters, said, "The truth is a pathless land and you cannot reach it by any organisation which in itself becomes a cage which stops an individual from being totally and unconditionally free."

I would translate this across to our concerns and say, "The energy body is a pathless land. You cannot develop it by trying to put it into a pre-shaped corset and hope for enlightenment that way; the corset itself becomes the cage which stops an individual to finding their own path which is what they need to do."

Energy bodies develop (or at least try to, as they groan and chafe against the constant strain and pressure of societal corsets of one kind or the other) all the time.

They never stop and just as our bodies keep on developing from birth to death in a natural progression, energy bodies too grow, shift and change. It is their purpose and their design to be doing so as they become changed by the experiences and encounters with new forms of energy.

There is never a perfect adult, never a perfect child, never a perfect old person – we are looking at a sliding scale with infinite subdivisions here as is always the case in naturally unfolding systems.

Enlightenment does not suddenly burst upon you from out of the blue – there are precursors, warning signs if you will. There is one experience on time, then a long time later another. I suspect that enlightenment would be a perfectly natural progression if left to its own devices, with some teething pains here and there but other than that, quite smooth and predictable.

The only reason that this isn't so is because our energy bodies have not developed as they should and have sustained grave injuries which were not repaired properly at the time. They have been seriously mismanaged in every way imaginable and have been misdirected so much by our conscious activities that a serious breach in trust and communication has occurred which now leads us to be talking about "conscious" vs. "unconscious" minds which are in conflict with each other and then with the "body mind" on top of it.

This would all be seriously depressing if it wasn't for the one true saving grace – namely the **instant** response of energetic systems in the quantum realms to conscious thought and well managed intention.

So I would propose that we should firstly, heal the sores of the metaphorically terribly mistreated children our energy bodies are; allow their worst injuries to be healed; give them good food in a reasonable quantity and most importantly, give them lots of attention and find out what it is that need from us so they may shake off the past and now, begin to grow and develop into these amazing adults that have gifts for us of an order and a value we cannot even conceive of just yet.

Managing Major Life Shifts

I have written many books on a variety of personal healing modalities but this is the first time that I felt the need to include a section entitled, "Managing Major Life Shifts".

It is true that in the development of this system I was indeed looking for something that was not just a quick fix for our niggling little problems so we could go on just the same as we were before, just a bit more comfortably so.

I was looking for a tool for transformation and I got it.

What do you think happens when someone who has lived for twenty or thirty years in a certain way really releases one of their most core problems or disturbances?

They change.

They change not just a little bit but to the extend that they will say things like, "I am a changed woman." – "I feel like a totally different person." – "I look back and I don't recognise who I used to be."

Now it would be nice to think that such a change which is always and absolutely clearly for the better for the individual in question (cessation of fear, shame, guilt, anger, sadness, depression, desperation, loneliness, low self esteem etc) would be applauded and celebrated with joy by their "loved ones" and their communities.

Sadly, this is not always the case.

Someone might be in a partnership which was begun under the contract of "You are submissive and I am dominant." If one of these partners change, the dynamic of the relationship falls apart and if there is not enough will or love left, this relationship will die and there is no going back.

Someone may have applied for and be given a job because they were always quiet and never spoke up for themselves – that was the contract of that employment. Now, they do express an opinion or suggest changes and this contract will have been broken; they may get fired or decide to leave.

170

These are just two examples of serious life changes which can come about as a result of using EmoTrance and especially at the beginning, they can be frightening.

A long time ago I conducted an EFT (Emotional Freedom Techniques) treatment with a lady who had been seriously phobic of a particular representation her entire life. When we tested the treatment by having her walk towards what had been the object and focus of the most intense panic attacks imaginable, her steps faltered and she hesitated, looking very scared.

I mistakenly thought that the phobia had not been entirely removed and asked her what was wrong; but she was not at all afraid of the object any longer.

She said, and I quote, "I have never not been afraid of this and I just don't know what I should think, how I should feel – I don't know anything at all and I am afraid."

You can imagine that this particular moment was a watershed for this lady.

It was like she could make a decision here – go back and simply have the phobia again and her life would procede as before, predictable, safe, with all possible occurrences planned for and practised many times, possibly an entire life path right into retirement and death planned out already.

Or, she could go forward into the unknown – into a life that was completely new in all ways, with whole new sets of challenges, unpredictable outcomes where not even goals were known yet. That is the Tarot Card numbered 0 and called, the Fool but without whose step into the abyss none of the others – The Magician, The High Priestess, The Emperor, The Star – could **ever come into being**.

I sometimes wonder when I think about that particular lady what would have happened if I had not been there to encourage her to go forward in that moment; and further I have wondered if these watershed moments do not actually arrive far more often and regularly in our lives than I had previously suspected, and we make the decision of "No, I'll turn around, keep it as it is." many times, indeed, time and time again?

If this becomes an issue for you or any of your clients, the answer is to firstly be clear in yourself if you are really willing to grow or if you want to give up and turn back. Most people find that they do not want to turn back once the question is out in the open and some, including myself, find they cannot even if they wanted – they had already come too far.

Once we have made the decision to go forward, it is best not think about the details of what might or might not happen too much (as we simply cannot know!) and to treat this very fear of the unknown with EmoTrance, take it right to the energised end state and have the fear of the unknown turn into a true excitement and sense of freedom about the future instead.

As with many things EmoTrance related, I cannot tell you here what that actually feels like, to make that decision and step out into the void of the newly unfolding you, but just to give you a flavour, here is a message I received from someone who found the courage to say "Yes!" to a completely new life.

I went to the Cirque de Soleil show yesterday at the Albert Hall.

There was an incredibly powerful image when a woman was swinging on a single trapeze hundreds of feet up in the huge dome of the hall. She was on her own, performing incredibly beautiful feats with a very thin safety wire attached which didn't detract at all from her grace or power or daring.

It made me understand I may have/had a safety wire attached but it doesn't take away or negate anything I have done, soaring high, seeing everything and everyone from a different angle, feeling the rush of flying high on my own.

It was incredible, reclaiming my achievements, the overwhelming feeling and the realisation made me weep.

EmoTrance does not take your emotions away – in the contrary, it shows you whole new realms of experiences you would never have believed could have been possible.

I know this and I have experienced this too; I also know that change can be frightening and people get very upset when you change before their eyes.

However, and this is a great comfort and allows for a great deal more courage all around, EmoTrance can help with the fallout and repercussions of change just as much as it can and does engender them in the first place and I would say from my own experiences that it wasn't easy, but it was nowhere near as hard or terrifying to change than I had always thought and feared it would be.

This does not mean that you will not have your own moments.

EmoTrance is a superb tool and it really works but the truth is, we have been doing certain things in certain ways for a very long time for the most part and there certainly is entrainment in the energy body, as well as state anchors everywhere in our environments.

We also have a whole lot of work to do if we want to bring out energy bodies back on line and fully functioning and one thing that does happen is that as you clear the top layers of shields and contortions, the deeper stuff will come to your attention at last.

EmoTrance does powerfully re-connect us to our bodies and many of us have lived for a very long time with that feedback device turned down or turned off altogether.

I am not going to promise you that by reading this book and learning the base technique your life will be one of instant bliss from this moment forth.

We have good days and we have bad days. When you are having a bad moment – you know, one of those when there really isn't any Ocean of Energy and you have forgotten just about everything that could be used to help you out at that time! – it isn't going to be any more pleasant than it ever was; so once it has passed (as they always do), please note the following:

- You will find that these "moments" do not last as long;
- They are not as overwhelming as they once were;
- That you move back into a state of balance more smoothly and faster;
- You will notice that they are further apart;
- That it takes a great deal more to trigger them than it used to.

That is one scale by which to measure progress, rather than the childish thought of, "Are we there yet??" when we have only just put on the seatbelts.

Another scale of measuring progress and to keep some form of clarity as to what is happening **over time** is to make a mental note of indicators of positive changes, no matter how small these may be.

Here are some examples of such "small indicators" of change; what they have in common is that they were unexpected, surprising, and usually experienced for the first time.

Angela: "I was walking through the town center, feeling displaced and nervous as I usually do and something really strange happened – it was as though a part of me slowed down and, I don't really know how to describe this properly, it came back and it was like sitting right down inside myself. Like coming into sync with myself. It was really strange but what a difference that made. Walking was lighter, easier. I was breathing easier. The lights were brighter and the colours and the people didn't frighten me anymore, it was just so – comfortable, that is the best way I can explain it. The feeling lasted all the way back to the car park and I can get it back when I think about slowing down and sitting down inside myself. This is totally new to me, I have never felt like that before and it feels right – and people even used to say that I am always getting ahead of myself."

Victoria: "I was at a railway station, it was cold, I had masses of time to wait (totally misjudged the time needed to walk there and get a ticket) so I headed for the warmth of the ballroom-like toilets downstairs. I was feeling pretty nervous, taking a trip I really wasn't looking forward to but thought no more of it, when you're in a weird situation it's ok to feel weird, so left it at that. However, on the way back up the stairs, and I must admit by that time I was feeling quite hot and bothered, I all of a sudden heard quite distinctly - Let me through, I'm only an energy - and felt this enormous whooshing up through my entire body and out, it literally felt like a crowd had parted to let it through. I smiled briefly as I opened the door shaking my head slightly at the wonder of it all and just got on with a particularly difficult day as it turned out."

Dan: "I find that I can just go into this strange space of – do you know that thing in American Beauty where the girl asks, why are you filming a dead pigeon, and the guy with the camera says, because it is beautiful? I don't want to sound naff but I do this. Sometimes it just happens and I can bring it on – it is like I shift inside myself, tune to a different wave band, and there it is. Beauty. The world. And the best thing, it is getting easier to do it all the time. The other day, for the first time, something new happened that really blew me away. I didn't shift out of it to normal awareness but there was this strand of the other space that came with me, it was there. I could still do the work and even have dinner with the in-laws – with an underlying silver strand of beauty. It was unbelievable. Now I never expected that."

Look out for such energy occurrences and remember these when you are having a moment of doubt. These are new things, new experiences and they are amazing; what is getting you down still isn't like that, it is just the same old stuff you have struggled with for so long and no more.

It is the new experiences which hold both promise and proof that you are indeed going in the right direction and it is the learnings from these new experiences that make the old storms seem less important than once they were.

So be patient with yourself and do the best you can with what you have got; don't try to push yourself too hard, be kind to yourself and allow yourself to be human as you are shifting in and out, from the old to the new and back again, a swing movement that will take you a little further into the new each time.

ADDENDUM 1 – THE ROAD TO EMOTRANCE

The following is an annotated transcript of the first time EmoTrance was presented to an audience of MET peers at the European Energy Therapies Conference, August 4th, 2002, Lady Margaret Hall, Oxford University, by Silvia Hartmann, PhD.

This lecture outlines the developmental history of EmoTrance and how the underlying principles and pre-suppositions were arrived at.

EmoTrance – The Developmental History

You might have heard a few things about EmoTrance by now, and so what I want to do is to make you familiar with the theoretical underpinnings and the developmental history of the therapy form I have called EmoTrance or ET for short.

In order to understand what ET is, what it is for and how it works, we have to back up to 1988. Now it is important to understand that I am not a teacher or a healer, but my mission is to learn and find out more about the universe. I see things and if I find them fascinating, I will explore them with single-minded intention. When I understand something new, I might write about it.

EmoTrance is a completed segment of a jig-saw puzzle I have been working on for as long as I know. It's a fantastic healing tool, a superb intuition trainer and a lot more besides, depending on how you want to use it or what you want to use it for.

In 1988, I was working with the patterns of animal behaviour. We were studying the drivers for attention seeking behaviour disorders in social mammals at that time and I certainly wasn't swimming with the dolphins back then. We were studying things like the effects of certain food colorants on the behaviour of Cocker Spaniels, doing statistics and actual research, collecting data and such.

But our story begins as we started researching the Attention Seeking Behaviour Disorder (ASBD) patterns – and I must point out that this particular disorder spans a vast range of problem behaviours and can manifest in extreme and bizarre problems. Attention seeking behaviour can escalate into aggression, withdrawal, self mutilation, autism and rage attacks, trance behaviours, in fact all the really serious behaviour problems in social animal behaviour not directly caused by environmental circumstance are attention seeking behaviour related.

Now, this was the very first time that I personally came across the idea that there was something invisible at work, that there was something a social creature needs, and if they don't get this invisible and un-measurable something, the creature will get sick. First, it gets stressed out, then it gets psychotic, gets skin diseases, the body breaks down and in the end, it will die.

We tried to find what this might be, find alternatives – pheromones, chemicals, practical, hard causative reasons for this but in the end, we just had to throw up our hands in horror and admit that there was, indeed, something invisible at work – a kind of **energy exchange** that happens when one social creature requests attention from another and if it doesn't receive it, there is a of **shortfall** in their systems and they are reacting to this with panic.

There are old studies that prove that babies will die if they don't receive social attention, even though their physical bodies were being cared for. It is true that variants on the old "attention seeking disorders" probably account for 85% of all human illness, mental and physical alike. That's why people die in old people's homes and women whose children leave home become depressed or hysterical as a result.

But be this as it may, what we have here is that energy is being requested from another creature, usually of the same species. This energy needs to be sent, and then it needs to be received by the one who requested it. Lastly, they need to be able to process it. There is something beneficial, nutritious about this energy which social creatures need to function and actually, even to survive.

This was my first ever contact with the "energetic nutrition system", and it was profound. Now when the energetic nutrition system breaks down, as is the case in autism for example, when the creature will seek attention but when it is given – sent – but they cannot receive or process it, very serious problems arise.

In 1993 I published my research findings and the resulting conclusions I drew from it in a paper called The Harmony Program which explains and deals with the problems relating to this systemic energy exchange that is absolutely structural and just the same in people as it is in dolphins, monkeys or poodles.

So, as I said, this was my first brush with the energy system and the understanding that we as people have energetic nutritional requirements. From then on, I began to tentatively investigate these invisible occurrences that had such amazing impacts on the physical well-being and an individuals abilities to deal with life at all.

In 1993 I began the study of General Semantics after coming into contact with this most extraordinary of fields through NLP, and for the next years I would continue to work on my "universal map" every day, and in many different ways. Always I was careful and kept myself strictly focussed on directly observable, provable **behavioural** results as the final test for any of the very many modalities, approaches and disciplines I explored during this time.

In 1998, I discovered EFT. I found it deeply fascinating and took the leap of faith and ordered the tapes. And when I started to look into it, I began to see that there was something special going on – this was not just hypnosis, not just a pattern interrupt, not just some weird ritual. There was an **extra component** that fascinated me and the effects of the basic EFT sequence on people's minds and bodies. And still, I was not thinking or talking about "energy bodies" or any such thing, for what, pray tell, **is** energy?

When asked for a scientific explanation, these days I shrug my shoulders and say, "Energy is something invisible that we can't see and can't measure, but that must be there else certain things wouldn't be happening at all."

Like a hologram or a pebble you throw into the pond and you can't see the pebble anymore, but the ripples are there and clearly visible, and ergo there must have been **something** to have caused these ripples even though I can't see it now.

Therefore, and still to this day, I don't seek to find or look at energy. What I do is to look at the **results**.

And the first question I always ask is, "Could this result have been caused by something else? Something that might seem like energy but it isn't?" Low level pheromones, hearing things at the far edge of your perception and you're not even consciously aware that you might have heard it at all, substances in the environment, other factors explicable by current science, and so on.

See if you take all of that away, then you are left with the real magic. I want to be absolutely ruthless about that, strip it right back and always check and test, not fall into delusion at the first opportunity. Strip it right down and there it is – real magic, and boy do I want to find this.

Now, I have a very, very low boredom threshold and a very short attention span – unless I'm really interested. Do you know, I spent 4 years doing EFT. Four years! 20 hours a day, doing it, teaching it, researching it, thinking about it, talking about it. And not variants of EFT either, in the vein of, "Let's tap all the points backwards and hey look! I have a new therapy!" but the classic protocol exactly as it comes.

I wanted to really learn about EFT, so I stuck firmly with Gary Craig's original design and did that, and nothing else, over and over and over, so many people, so many opening statements, so many problems, so many different circumstances. Until after 4 years of this, I finally got to the point where I thought, I'm beginning to get a hang of what this might be and what this might mean.

It was only after this had happened that I allowed myself to learn about the other Meridian Energy Therapies like BSFF, TAT, TFT and so forth, because that basic EFT sequence, as simple as it might appear, has so much depth to it and represents such an extraordinary opportunity to learn about how people really work, it is simply fascinating. And I won't begin to say that I know everything about it now, I think you could spend a lifetime with it, just enough so I feel I have some appreciation of what EFT can teach us about people.

Amongst the most important things that EFT taught me was about the relationship between the energy system and emotions. The EFT discovery statement says that a negative emotion is caused by a disruption in the energy system. Everyone knows this, everyone reads this but few people actually sit right down and really think about what that actually means.

And if you were to take it to its final degree, what it does mean is **that emotions are to the energy body as pain is to the physical body.**

Emotions		*Feelings*
------------------	=	---------------------
Energy Body		**Physical Body**

Now in physical medicine and care, it's been a while since people only tried to treat pain and make it disappear – "Oh the pain is gone, that must mean the problem's over." Sure, some horse trainers still do it. The horse tears a ligament and you numb the whole leg with a powerful painkiller so it can still run the race. Ok, so you have to shoot it afterwards but at least you've got that one last trophy.

Medicine used to be liked that, but isn't anymore. When you come with a pain, they won't just give you a painkiller but instead they ask you, what could that be a symptom of?

Thus is the deal with emotions and the energy body just as well.

But we'll come back to that in a little while.

During my time with EFT, I was developing various therapeutic patterns based on the insights derived from working with energy, emotions, memories and people's various manifestations of their totality.

One of the breakthrough patterns was what would eventually become a paper called Guiding Stars.

EFT treatments showed me how limited the existing psychological models were we were dealing with prior to the advent of energy psychology as a whole, and they were limited because they were basically all trauma based. The idea was that we get born more or less alright, then something horrible happens that messes us up. This, however, isn't true all by itself because there is this whole other realm of outstanding emotions which are non-trauma in nature, positive if you want to call it, numinous experiences that mess us up just as well. Because it's not the pain of an experience that causes the changes, the cascading neurological shifts at all but instead, what does it is the intensity of the emotions, and this is regardless of whether they are "good" or "bad".

If the emotional intensity is high enough, it causes cascading shifts in the neurology. It creates new life patterns and overwrites what went before and from then, new patterns of behaviours are established and these are entirely regardless of whether they end up being damaging or have any shred of sanity about them at all.

As an example you might like to consider a grown woman who has been in terrible relationships all her life. Is she a deranged masochist with low self esteem? Actually, probably not. It's far more likely that in a childhood devoid of loving attention and joy, there was this one moment when her father (who also abuses her on a regular basis) stumbled home, reeling drunk and smelling of alcohol, sat her on his lap and called her "My little princess." And she felt loved for the first time. And it was such an amazing moment of joy, of transpersonal happiness that she patterned unconsciously all her relationships from thereon **on that one moment** – the lesson the neurology has learned is that if you want to feel loved, you need to find a man who structurally and practically resembles that one man who made you feel like that before, right down to the smell of alcohol on his breath as he said the magic words. That's Guiding Stars, originally from 2000.

The reason I never released this pattern properly was because when you uncovered Guiding Stars, people had such appalling abreactions, it was truly frightening.

Imagine something has gone on for 50, 60 years and find out just why it was that they have put their children into a position of being abused by one horrible man after the next, and they're now in asylums or have committed suicide for example, and they got how it was and what it was and **what they had been doing with their lives** the abreactions were so horrendous, I've never seen anything like it.

The loss of life for the sake of this one moment of happiness – I have ruined my entire life.

Especially with women who can't have children anymore, but also all over, you can't turn the clock back, can't do it differently. Whoa. It's horrendous. And the pain they had caused by following this route towards the Guiding Star to themselves and everyone around them – it was so horrendous that I didn't dare release the thing.

But now here we are getting into interesting things.

Guiding Stars made me stop and understand that it isn't the emotion that's the problem, but the energy behind the emotions and the intensity of that energy – the concept of Significant Emotional Experiences or SEEs. However, these are usually **only** applied to trauma – negative emotions, thus leaving a whole heap of drivers for people's behaviours like addictions and staying in unhappy marriages and a huge range of bizarre choices and behaviours that make no sense at all, not even to the person themselves, come into consideration. And this is when I really had to do something. For it is when someone comes to you and talks about joy and they talk about pain, we are so entrained to want to keep the joy and get rid of the pain, it is really difficult to keep a clear and scientific mind on these issues. But that is exactly what we need to do to take the next step in this progression. I need to re-name this. I can't think allow myself to think in terms of "good and bad" emotions here because it will totally compromise the whole investigation.

So I started to simply think in terms of energy.

Hence, the slogan – Energy, NOT Emotions.

Energy Not Emotions

Now once we started to do that, things were getting interesting. Well, they were pretty interesting before that, too, but you could say they were getting a great deal more interesting still – a quantum leap in interest!

Energy – NOT Emotions.

As soon as you put your mind around that, a whole lot of things just start to cascade.

You treat the sickness, NOT the pain in medicine. We need to treat the energy, not the emotions, in energy therapies. And that clicks it all into place.

You have a cut in your arm and you stare down at it and you will it to close.

Does it close immediately?

No, of course not. You can argue the point and bring out statistics that say if you stare at your arm and will the wound to close you stand a chance of it healing between 5-17% faster than if you gave it no attention at all, but generally that's a waste of time, so much energy expended for so little in the way of results and that's why no-one's doing it.

Can you in the middle of a panic attack just think, ok, I won't be having this anymore?

No, of course not.

The reason for that is that we are using a screwdriver where you need a wrench.

Intention is designed for and ONLY works with energy.

Intention moves energy – instantly, in quantum space, immediately, just for the asking as though it was just nothing.

The old magic principle states, "Where attention goes, energy flows.", and that's pretty close to the mark. To move energy is exactly what intention does and what it is for. That's how it works. Totally quantum, timeless and spaceless, you can do distance healing for someone on the other side of the planet or someone who died 15 lifetimes ago and have it be effective because in that realm there is no restriction on time or space.

Intention moves energy because it is made of that same stuff, it's of that realm.

When people do therapy and let us leave the meridian tapping out of that for a moment, they label and talk about their emotions.

Person has an emotion, like they are scared, and now we are going to label it, then we talk about it, more labels, and what this is, is an interface device like Microsoft Windows is for your computer. So the labelling becomes an interface device – and the labels we give to our emotions such as calling them a sadness or an anger are always only translation devices and you always, always loose a great amount of information in translation. There is a hell of a lot more going on in the code of a computer that runs Microsoft software than you could ever see or guess from looking at the screen.

Where this really gets complicated is that the emotion is not the problem, not at all.

The problem is of course the energy system underneath which tries to speak to us through that medium of emotions.

Now we are beginning to see why psychotherapy is so hit and miss compared to surgery, for example, namely because it is at least doubly abstracted away from what is causing the problem in the first place.

Now, back to the Harmony Programme.

In 2001, I was thinking to myself, "Ok, so we can tap on traumatic problems. And we have been tapping for four years. But we are not actually getting any major shifts in our life styles. Ok, fair enough, I want to give EFT, Gary and Roger Callahan every respect that I have. What I do does not replace EFT at all, doesn't even compete, isn't even in the same ball park. Gary Craig should get a Nobel prize for the design of it and making it so user friendly. EFT is brilliant.

And it's not that EFT doesn't work wonderfully or that it isn't quick enough. The problem is the chunking down movement to the details of the problem. It is difficult to deal with global problems with the tapping therapies, and every person who is a developer in the field is trying to address this problem in some way. I've noticed this when I was making up the AMT trainer's manual – TAT, bigger, more global, like I forgive everything. BSFF says, my God there's a million aspects, can we just go down to the root causes of them all and release them quickly, because if we have to tap for each one of these aspects, we'll be tapping until the stars are falling from the sky.

I made the SLOW EFT protocol at some point which was tapping on the bigger issues, more global nominalisations, the big interlinked gestalts like, "Mother", "Money", that kind of thing. "I" – whoa! So what I did was to make the Slow EFT protocol to tap on a single point whilst concentrating on a global nominalisation like "money" – I don't think anyone ever got through that.

Well – I called it SLOW EFT, didn't I. You take something like "money" and you tap on this one point, just one point, until the whole thing has run clear and all aspects have exhausted themselves – well it takes forever! After just one point you end up a complete wreck on the floor, and you can't possibly start on the next point until the next day, and that's why I say that to my knowledge, no-body actually ever got all the way through that protocol. But at least I get credit for trying. I was trying to do something to make EFT more useful for big, global life change issues. Which is something a lot of therapists like the sound of, real sea changes, become someone else. Not little fiddly bits like not being afraid of mice anymore.

Big stuff, like being someone who could be happy, being someone who could be loved, being someone who could be successful.

So that's what I was wanting, was working towards from every angle I could think of. I was trying all sorts of things to get these big shifts that would transform a person into a whole new state of being. And one of the things I was trying, and this is very relevant in this context, was the "Inner Child Healing Protocol" and the other was a Project Sanctuary based technique called "LoveLine".

All You Need Is Love ...?

I was still trapped in this whole George Harrison thing, all you need is love.

If you chucked enough love at people, they'd get better. Love is good for the energy system, right?

Oh – WRONG!

That is one of those strange delusions. As though love was the only form of energy existing on this planet! Worse, as though most people even knew what love was in the first place – what are they all labelling in that way? Is your love the same as my love? I have this funny feeling it probably isn't. And if we both channelled universal love if we were brave enough to touch THAT, which most people wisely don't even though they might say they do, and it flows through me, it still ends up completely different by the time it comes out than it would if it flowed through him over there.

But still, there I was, under the delusion that all you need is love.

So I thought, ok, let's do a spiral loop pattern whereby we do proxy healing for past selves and particularly on the baby you yourself once were, because a whole heap of people go round saying that they have birth trauma – after 40 years in psychiatry they are still – **still** – saying things like, "I was never meant to be here." – "My parents never wanted me." – "I shot out like a cork across the kitchen table in a flood of blood and that's why I am the psychopath I am today."

Now I've heard this so much that I thought we use a solid proxy protocol to heal the baby, with opening set ups like, "Even though the baby was never loved.", "Even though this baby was abandoned..." and so on, in order to heal the part of the person who was that baby because in quantum space this baby will grow up better than it was before; as it does so and the changes ripple through he becomes a better healer to heal even more of the injuries of the baby when you do the spiral loop pattern next time around.

A lot of people really liked it and they're still doing it today; it's a nice pattern.

However, I was disappointed with the lack of instantly observable change this produced. It was nice and holistic but not fast and furious enough for my liking.

I wanted more.

So back to our friend "love" which is said to heal all ills.

Ok, I thought. If love heals, I'm going to chuck love at the problem. We're going to generate so much love that people are going to drown in it.

I designed this excruciating pattern called LoveLine which is a Project Sanctuary/TimeLine based pattern. It would have the victim stand in the place that denoted the moment of their birth, looking ahead at a long road, stretching off into the distance. On the side of this road would materialise all the people who had ever loved this person, be it only for a split second – a stranger in the street perhaps who looked at them, really saw them and gave them their admiration, a market trader giving a small child an apple free of charge with a smile, right up to a lover who had declared their love **and had entirely meant it – at that one moment in time**.

So. There would be all these people coming to me because "no-one's ever loved me".

I would run the LoveLine pattern on them – and what would transpire?

Even the most forsaken individual had literally football stadiums full of people crowding the sides of their lives roads – thousands and thousands of incidence of love, big ones, small ones, every day, all the time.

It was truly extraordinary.

It was just as extraordinary how **shocked** the "no-one's ever loved me" people were when thus directly placed face to face with how much love there actually been in their lives. Shocked is the only word for it. They would look at me, eyes wide open, mouth open and say, "But how can this possibly be? I can see now how much love there was for me – but **why did it never feel like that**? Why do I still feel so unloved, and so lonely? What's wrong with me?"

I was beginning to seriously wonder the same thing about myself.

As I was taking people through the LoveLine pattern, of course I couldn't help but make the journey myself, time and time again and it was true, it was as though I was walking within an invisible shield and all the love and admiration, friendship and offers of support would bounce flat off and never reach the starving me who lay inside. And from this place of constant starvation, I was driven to ever more desperate attention seeking behaviour which, in turn, would produce the energy that **still** didn't reach me, no matter what.

Love autism, if you will.

And that's where EmoTrance begins to unfold. There is something wrong in humans with the way they process these incoming energies; it was then I began to understand and make the connection between the presence of energy forms (all kinds) and any given individual's ability to not just receive these energies, but to process them correctly and **derive the necessary nutrients** from it as it passes in, through and out a person's system – the Even Flow.

From being a very small child, I have been fascinated by the story around scurvy.

Ships became strong and fast enough to make very long trips across the oceans of the world and on the really long trips, the sailors would become ill with this disease called scurvy. The sailors would become ill but the officers strangely did not; this was attributed for quite some time to the fact that the officers were better bred and from wholesome stock than the low mutant class sailors. Until one day this rather intelligent doctor guy started an investigation into diet, found the Vitamin C connection and today, we don't really have to have scurvy anymore and the children in the First World get told, "You better eat your sprouts or your hair and teeth will fall out."

This is one of my favourite childhood stories; as I was doing LoveLine and considering the lessons learned there, I remembered the scurvy story and connected it with the symptoms that people were showing; but the malnutrition was not only about love. By this time I was also well aware that emotions are just feedback devices for the energy body and I knew that there was more to energy in the Universe than just love.

There is a whole wide range of energies. If the energy body is anything like the rest of the Universe, then the energy body NEEDS a huge range of incoming energies to function properly and fulfil the purposes for which it was designed.

Do you know, I can't begin to imagine what a fully functioning, fully operational, fully fed human energy body would actually look like. It wouldn't surprise me if it was a huge sun, a star that radiates out far and wide. Perhaps that's the whole deal with "stars" – people want to look like them, want to be like them, want to be close to them? Perhaps they have just 5% or so better functioning energy bodies than the rest of us.

I think we should be clear that the human energy body doesn't end at the barrier or the skin. There are people who say we have these "further" energy bodies, etheric, Auric layers and so on. It's difficult to prove or to disprove. We don't have new scientific evidence or proper measurement procedures for this kind of thing. What we do have are some very, very,

very old maps. Very old maps drawn by people who did not know how to represent 3 dimensional objects on a 2 dimensional tablet or drawing. This didn't actually come about until the middle ages, and I let you draw your own conclusions as to what that might mean about the diagrams we are using at the moment.

I am not happy and I have to be Spock under these circumstances and I would have to say, "I don't trust this map. It is better not to have a map at all and to look around yourself, take readings at regular intervals to see how much water you really have under your keel than to blindly follow a map that may or may not be completely wrong and lead you straight onto the rocks."

When I don't trust a map, I go back to direct observation. That's what I do and it has served me well. I am very lucky to have as one of my good friends Ananga Sivyer, who is a meridian specialist and researcher who works with the Chinese system but also the Ayurvedic systems which precede the Chinese energy systems maps.

We have an energy body and it is my hypotheses that the energy body has nutritional requirements. What might these requirements be? Let's start big – it could be all of it, every available form of energy on this planet. What generates energy? Once again, the answer is everything. Everything on this planet generates energy. A rat produces energy, this table has an energy body – everything emanates energy.

If we think about our energy body as the body of an alien, an entity which we know next to nothing about and which we can be pretty sure is not egg shaped like the diagrams will have you believe in most people.

Indeed, you could think that they were distorted, swirled up, with back spots and with vortices, and one thing they all are and that is they are ENTIRELY UNIQUE for each individual, for every single human on this planet, for even if they were conceived as identical twins, from the moment of conception their environments would be different as their physicalities inhabit different locations and their experiences diverge.

Everybody has a totally personalised, totally individual energy body.

That is so very, very important to understand and to know.

That is our first principle, we have to bring energy in somehow.

One of the most basic, basic tenets of the Universal Laws is that energy needs to flow.

Energy **is** FLOW and anything else is unnatural and damaging in the most profound and easily measurable ways.

So I began to devise methods to make myself and others "drop shields" and to take incoming energy into their energy systems, into their starving energy bodies, where this energy could be used to source repairs, vitality, and immune functions to help us bounce back far more swiftly and profoundly when "shit happens", as it does invariably and simply by design of living in these societies and states of being of ours.

The Storm Drains

Whilst I was trying to figure out a way to get people to drop the invisible shields that keep all the beneficial and much needed energies at bay and out of reach, something dramatic happened to me personally one night.

I saw something that caused me to "freak out completely" – a technical term, if you will, denoting an instant and profound loss of control and any common sense, any conscious input, as I was simply overwhelmed by a flood of emotions, they were so painful, they had my physically on the floor, choking and retching.

For a long time, I could do nothing but suffer this and eventually regained enough composure to start an "emergency ritual" – I'd been doing EFT for so long, it came to me as the Lord's prayer comes to a one who has counted rosary beads for years and recited it so much, it was a ritual.

This relieved the symptoms enough so I could start thinking again, and the very first thought I had was that this was all wrong. This is not the right response to an environmental happening, to be so completely disabled by what is nothing but a natural occurrence, a part of life itself. If there were still predators about, this would be a survival issue, hell, if I'd been in a car or "operating heavy machinery" when I saw what I did and it had happened there, it would clearly be a survival issue today as well.

It simply can't be right to instantly drown in a flood of emotions like that!

There **must be** existing systems to deal with that kind of occurrence – storm drains, if you will, that can spring into operation to prevent a complete systemic collapse and shutdown as had happened there to me in that moment.

I talked to a colleague and friend about this and it was there that I first began to think of emotions as **nothing but feedback devices** to the existing conditions in the energy body, and that what I had experienced were just the repercussions of an energetic happening – an incoming energy form that I had no way of dealing with, no "storm drains" to channel it through and out.

When we re-called the experience and began to look for the possibility of real pathways in the energy body which were designed to handle these energies, and handle them with ease, we made some very surprising discoveries, and EmoTrance as we know it today, was finally born into conscious awareness.

The Benefits Of "Bad" Energies!

It's a natural response to want to keep "bad" or "harmful" kinds of energy at bay – however, in nature there is no such thing.

There is **only** energy – different kinds, different flavours, different manifestations, but at the end of the day, it's just energy. Orange is no better or worse than green – it only becomes that way when people get involved and make decisions as to the merits of one over the other.

When they do so, an automatic process is initiated that seeks to protect someone from that which has been declared "bad" – it will deflect it, keep it out, hide away from it and generally do anything at all the energy system knows how to do to keep the "bad" energy away.

However, I had a very personal experience to the opposite a few months prior.

I had initiated a mailing list project about abundance and set tasks for the participants – little challenges of one kind or the other which had to be completed to prove one's dedication, else the person was removed from the list. One of these challenges led to about hundred people being removed, which caused a storm of protest, accusations and a flood of email into my inbox full of insults, curses and being called every conceivable "bad" thing under the sun – from being insane to a dictator, from arrogance to imposterism, take your pick.

At the time I got upset about it and decided to try something new – there was so much of it that I could not argue all of that away. So instead, I printed out all the emails and sat myself down in a comfortable place, read them all carefully and for every statement being made about me, I **forced myself** to consider what it would mean if it was right, if it was absolutely true.

Now, I didn't know that what I was doing was instead of deflecting the "incoming", opening myself up and to take it in instead. My unconscious mind always precedes my conscious understanding by many months, sometimes by years!

What happened that instead of sinking into deepest, darkest depression, I learned many things about myself, felt less vulnerable to criticism of all kinds, adjusted my self concept and came away from the exercise with a whole newfound sense of strength and personal power.

It also taught me something about labelling myself – I was no more the ogre than I was an angel, I was no more arrogant than full of humility, no more good than bad; instead, I began to think of myself as a human who does all these things, best they can, and sometimes it works out, and

194

sometimes it doesn't but at the end of the day, who knows but me what my intentions were.

So, and when we were beginning to search for the "storm drains", I remembered the above exercise and suggested to my friend and fellow energy magician Nicola Quinn that we should try to hurl some insults at each other, see what would happen and if we could find a system that could channel these "incoming energies" through and out, so that "words would never hurt you again" and also, so that we would learn something about the hypothetical storm drain system in the energy body.

One fine night in the spring of 2002, on the telephone, I shouted an "insult" at my friend Nicola.

She responded by saying that it was just like she'd been punched in the solar plexus with a physical fist. Intuitively, I had the notion that it might feel like that because the incoming energy had run into some kind of shield, causing these physical sensations as repercussions.

I asked her to allow the energy in (just the energy, not the insult or "it's meanings"!) and when she did, and when she found a natural pathway through which these energies travelled, and when they moved smoothly through these pathways and out of her fingertips, she ended up laughing in delight and saying, "My God, that feels so good! Hit me again, quick!"

For the next two hours, we shouted insults at each other – simple things about our physical appearances at first, then more deeply rooted, older stuff, and eventually things that we had **avoided all our lives** – things and statements we were so afraid of another **ever** possibly saying to us that we had constructed our lives around **never having to hear this being said**.

"You are a liar." – "You are an impostor." – "You are a miserable coward." – "I am so disappointed in you." – "I've never loved you and I never will." – these and many, many more were traded on that night, allowed into our energy bodies with some struggle at first, and once they had arrived and found their pathways, moving swiftly through and out, leaving us sparkling, high, feeling virtually invincible and so profoundly delighted, it is hard to convey.

Now, I really do have a wall in my house upon which I make notes of new therapy patterns and breakthrough insights. There are hundreds of patterns on that wall, and I only write up and release the most minute percentage of these. Many of these are extremely good, others a little too good for public release (as in too powerful, too frightening for the general public). The basic EmoTrance pattern joined all these others and we kept playing with it in the days that followed.

I have a number of friends who are therapists and I usually run the new patterns by them for feedback and to try them out, to get a bit more perspective and also, to help me make up my mind what is useful and what is not, and which ones to place my further attention on to develop them into a user-friendly therapy pattern or technique.

They liked this pattern a lot and as I was telling one person about it, I noticed that they didn't have the usual resistance to letting the insults come their way. I had a hunch and tried something new – when she was waiting for me to come up with a new insult, I said clearly and with volition into the telephone: "You are an extraordinary healer."

Bull's eye! She burst out into tears on the spot, and thus the next level of application had been found – energy system contortions to incoming compliments. I should have thought of this before in view of the LoveLine experiences, but here we were, in the country of firstly allowing so called "positive" energies to come in as well and moving them through and out just exactly the same as we had done with the "negative" insult statements.

The main trick with the basic EmoTrance process is to come in from the physical, i.e. the **physical sensations** that occur in the physical body as a response to an incoming energy form. Playing with insult and praise for a week or so with a number of different people had the effect on me that I began to notice the physiological real-life sensations that alerted me to the presence of stuck energy and emotions in my system, and notice these sensations in many different environments.

196

For example, I noticed a tension and pressure in response to a dubious email heading in my inbox. Noticing it and then, moving it away gave me a deep sigh of relief and set me to wondering how I had managed to go through life for 43 years and NOT notice how emotional responses were affecting me all the time, in so many different situations, all through the day and night.

I – and the other EmoTrance™ experimenters – were beginning to re-contact our physical bodies, after a lifetime of ignoring the physiology as best as we could, until it would really scream at us and could no longer be ignored. We were also becoming far more acutely aware of the actual movement of emotions, feelings and sensations in our bodies in response to our various daily lives and as extraordinarily illogical as it may be, working with the energy body in this way became very grounding, heightening our perceptions of what was going on with us and clearly showing us where we might need to stop and think, or do some more work, or change our minds entirely as to what we thought was good for us and what wasn't.

In the meantime, we were widening out the applications for the basic process of moving energies through our systems with nothing more than intention and the will to give permission for this to occur.

No longer was this confined to what people said or did to us. One of us found that **human touch** also produces a physiological response and if this was thought of as an incoming energy, a single fingertip resting lightly on the back of your hand could literally send shivers throughout your entire body as the energy from the touch travelled in and through channels we never even knew we had. A feast of kinaesthetic stimulation for bodies that were rarely touched outside of intimate relationships and a wonderful set of experiences lay all of a sudden very much "at our fingertips".

"In The Field"

As I said, I have many, many therapy patterns and techniques "on the wall". What totally convinced me of how **useful** EmoTrance actually is and made me say, "That's it. I'm going to release this one, big time, and I'll put my name to it, no holds barred!", was a personal experience at a party.

On this particular occasion, a person arrived I'd been trying to avoid for a long time. It was late, I was tired and had quite a bit to drink. A situation unfolded and they said something to me that really did create the "punched in the stomach" response – in the past, this one incident would have been enough to floor me with psychosomatic symptoms afterwards for about a week.

But there and then, immediately as it had happened, and without being in any position to give instructions or any attention at all, there occurred a softening and the sensations and feelings **simply began to flow** and moved through me, all through me and then there was peace and congruency in my body, and clarity of thought in my mind.

The Storm Drains had happened. We had woken up my energy system enough so that it **automatically** sprang into action and dealt with the "flood" – simply, instantly, profoundly and WITHOUT me having to do anything at all.

I sat at that party and truly, I couldn't believe it. That it could really be **this simple**. That my body had **really learned** how to do EmoTrance, and remembered, and just went right ahead and did it for me when I needed it and the conscious mind wasn't able to give the instructions.

I had received what I had asked for – a natural system for transforming emotional energies IN THE FIELD as a natural response to what the World presents to you.

And that night and in that moment, EmoTrance was fully born and created.

More Repercussions, More Surprises

At this point, I was a happy bunny. I had what I wanted – a response instrument, a ready made technique that with very little practise really changed the way we experienced the World around us.

Being able to NOT get upset and stressed out anymore about what people said and did to us, led absolutely directly to not being afraid of many things anymore. It was quite extraordinary. When you're not afraid of criticism anymore, you can do a whole lot more and easily so than you could before. When you're not afraid of bad press, you can publish to your heart's content. But there was more! For example, those of us who were controlled by feelings of guilt and others were using this mechanism to have us do and be all sorts of things that we didn't want to be doing or being, with the guilt "pain" gone, we found we could stand up to them and just say, "No!".

For many of us, that was about the first time in conscious memory that we were free of all kinds of fears, of doubts, of direct blockages that had stopped us from going forward and getting for ourselves what we in our hearts long knew, we deserved more fully than was ever previously given.

Also, being able to allow positive comments into our energy systems brightened us absolutely and it really did begin to change our self concepts and our ideas as to who or what we actually were.

What more can you ask for in a simple little technique?

It worked a treat on emotions, and the more you did it, the better it became, the easier, and then it went onto automatic pilot so you didn't even need to pay attention to it anymore.

I didn't give any thought at all to long term "therapeutic" applications, only to be able to deal with emotions as and when they arose – after all, there's only this now and then the next now after that, and if you can handle your emotions in the now, then you can handle them, period!

Indeed, dealing with the "now" emotions was a really important aspect of my new dream technique – to be honest, dear reader, after all these years in Personal Development I am just sick and tired of stirring around in the old messes, the old memories, the thousands of small and big incidents, remembering them all and re-living them in order to change their hold on me. I really have come to a point where I no longer care just what Daddy said to me when, or what the birth trauma was – please. It's been decades, let it be enough now. I wanted to just declare an amnesty on the past and instead, concentrate on the here-and-now as this is, truly, the only leverage point we can ever have to make the future better than what had ever gone before.

But one day, Susan Courtney interviewed me about EmoTrance and following the interview, we had a little chat during which she mentioned that she had just received the "most unflattering" photographs possible from a shoot for a national magazine and was very upset and incapable of choosing one – they were all terrible and she had thrown the lot of them into her dustbin prior to phoning me.

I suggested she retrieve the photographs and do the basic EmoTrance process whilst looking at them. I thought of this much as being very similar to doing mirror work with EmoTrance, which we had done quite a bit of by then.

Susan did as I suggested, by herself after the phone call was over. Then she rang me back to tell me, very excitedly, that her feelings about the photographs had changed entirely and she now "liked what she saw" and was even fascinated by the woman in the pictures and wanted to learn more about her – a major breakthrough one might say.

Back then, as she was telling me about her experience just a few moments after the fact, something strange came to me.

Theoretically, and if ET **only** changed the experience in the now, Susan should have been appalled every time she looked at the photos – as in: look at the photo, feel appalled, move the energy, feel better; look at the photograph, feel appalled, move energy, feel better, and so on.

But that wasn't what had happened.

Doing it just once on each photograph **changed the actual experience** of the photograph profoundly so the feelings of being appalled never came back – and that must have meant that something else was changed by the act of moving the energy the first time.

Something profound, something old and something that may have had many roots in childhood, self concept, self image and all sorts which might take **years** in therapy to even list, never mind begin to treat.

It began to dawn on me that EmoTrance was thereby not just changing the now, but was changing the very energy system itself and permanently so, AND in so doing, removing old injuries and problems that might have been there for 50 years or more!

And that is when EmoTrance all of a sudden became a "therapy tool" and we began in earnest to use it for therapeutic applications.

"Where in your body is the sadness ...?"

It is interesting isn't it.

You know what that's like. Someone comes and says to you, "YOU! are an EVIL person!" and it's like whoosh! punched in the stomach. It's a physiological reaction to someone just **saying** something. Oh and as a bye-the-by, pointing with the "naked finger" at someone is actually a form of directly sending energy at someone, and that's why little children aren't supposed to do it. We don't need magic wands - we have one. Two. Five – ten, even!

This thing with saying something to someone, telling people things, like, "You are beautiful." - "You are an idiot!" produces these responses of shields or blockages. It's a fantastic example to make energy, incoming energy, and a person's response to that not only visible to the naked eye but also feelable to the human body.

So these sorts of energies - let's find someone who doesn't think they're particularly beautiful so we can demonstrate this better? I see we still have some blank faces. Nicola would you like to be so good, because you are a responsive person.

What can I insult you with?

N: "My nose."

S: "What's wrong with it?"

N: "It's big and horrible."

S: "Ok just be relaxed have your hands loose and just respond."

S: <loudly and strongly> "You have a BIG and HORRIBLE nose!"

Now look at that. The whole woman is actually swaying away here, as though a physical force was pushing her.

S: "What IS that on your nose? Is that some sort of a lump?"

Look, she is physically turning her head away there. As I'm speaking, the energy is travelling towards her and she is moving out of the way as though it was a missile that mustn't strike her.

S: "But of course, you know your nose **is** truly horrible? Seriously now. <turns to the audience> When she came in, be honest, wasn't that the first thing you all thought? My god, how can the owner of such a nose take it out in public?"

<Nicola curled up, holding her nose in her hands to cover it up, audience is laughing>

S: "Ok, look now would you like to sort yourself out because I don't wish to hurt you in any shape or form here. Let's do the basic EmoTrance protocol. Where is this energy coming into your body? Where can you feel it, where does it hit you?"

N: "On the top of my head."

S: "Can you just let it go through and out as it should, so we can have the Even Flow established?"

N: "Ok."

S: "How does that feel now?"

N: "No it's alright, it's fine."

S: "Would you be able to go to this person there and show him your nose, close up?"

N: "Yes, sure."

<audience laughs out loud as man pretends to be horrified>

S: "How are you feeling? Is it ok? Did it hit you anywhere?"

N: "No its fine. It just went through and out. Straight out."

S: "Well thank you for putting up with that, that was a nice demonstration."

<audience claps and laughs>

So, this shouting insults at each other was actually how we discovered this in the first place. We had a lot of fun with it. Shouting insults at each other, noticing where that hits you in the body, working on the energy behind the sensations, not the emotions, not the memories of what your father said to you 75 years ago, simply giving the energy the instruction to soften and move through its requisite paths and it just slithers off without a backward glance - without an argument, without a care in the world, and when you do it again and it flows swiftly, you get an energised end state which is very nice as well.

Incoming energies from the universe - and they could be from people, they could be from sunsets, they could be from colours - are blocked in people. That's the first problem. They are blocked from ever entering the energy system at all and we call this shields.

When I was doing the demonstration with Nicola and said that her nose was horrible, it didn't even hit her. It was shielded and deflected off and an energy barrier that wouldn't even let it come in. For those of you who are that way inclined, try that on your Doors of Perception. Something interesting happens when you open those.

Now shields are always a problem because they lead to scurvy and starvation as there is no energy coming in at all.

You are sitting behind that shield and no-one and nothing can get to you.

The shields were established by direct conscious command as a response to avoid suffering - obviously.

A man looks at a woman and says, "You are really beautiful." She thinks, "He just wants to have sex with me." That is a shield. Then she goes home and cries in front of a mirror because no-body likes her, no-body loves her and she's ugly, because in order to feel differently, that man's statement would have **needed to come in** to be utilised, processed, made a part of her energy system.

Sometimes, instead of being deflected outright, the energy comes in a way but then gets stuck and what we have then is a pressure cooker effect. The energy builds up and up and when it reaches a certain threshold, it turns into a physical sensation, then into a pain. The example where someone is told, "You are fired!" and they curl up in pain and say it was as though they had been punched in the stomach is an example of what happens when emotion bridges into physicality.

That means already that the emotion is so dense, so stuck, so blocked that it has nothing else left to give, it has nowhere else left to go, the whole feedback system as to what's going on in the energy body is long past breakdown point, and now it's physical because it goes, energy body -> emotion -> physical in that order.

If energies get blocked in the energy body, this creates our emotional problems and if it gets dense enough and goes on for long enough, then it bridges into physicality. If it still doesn't stop and it gets denser still, you have to do something to relieve that pressure - have a nervous breakdown, an anger tantrum, you name it.

All energy workers know this, what does energy needs to do?

Right, it needs to flow. Always. Always needs to flow in and out. And these energies that we are blocking up carry nutrients that are systemic requirements for the energy body's immune system to bounce back from injuries.

You know, shit happens. Logs fall on your head, bad leylines appear, you can stand in a bad place - shit happens. But a fully functioning energy body, with it's immune system intact and in place, working as it should, might even be able to handle ... Jehovah's Witnesses.

I know it's a stretch, but the hope is there.

It is important to notice that these blocks are actually not the problem in themselves, or not by themselves.

Yes, that's where it hurts, that's where the pain is, yes that's where you get your ulcers, tumours, or whatever you get, but what's happening below that blockage?

Those systems below the blockage, they are arid lowlands, deserts which have not seen rain or energy for years, where there should be flowers growing and there is nothing - because it all got blocked up here.

But there is something else. So you have your desert areas behind the blocks, but blocks also happen by holding on to any kind of emotion. Giving a direct instruction that an energy be held there in perpetuity - and these are direct instructions by the conscious mind, this is not the unconscious at work that does this, these are fully conscious decisions and instructions - "I will NEVER forgive you. NEVER!"

And on the other hand, we have the Guiding Stars. "I wish this one second would last forever." - "I never want to be anywhere else but here with you, NOW."

A powerful example of this was a lady whose husband had died five years ago and she was just in a terrible, terrible state. In her own words, and that was so fantastic, she just said it like that, "You know, just before he died, he was just lying there and they told me he'd have perhaps 10, 15 minutes left. And I stopped time. And there is this place where he is still alive and everything that is good about me is still there, holding his hand."

She gave a direct, conscious command to stop time and her energy system did the best it could, without killing the physicality, took out everything that wasn't needed to run the body on like an automaton, and made it happen for her.

It was fantastic. And you know, this is a metaphor. But what's a metaphor? Metaphor is the label on a jar with energy inside it so we can tell what's underneath. A can of peaches has a picture of a peach on the front so you know there's some peaches inside. A picture of a peach is not a peach and a metaphor is not the energetic reality.

How was that resolved? Any ideas? Logical, re-establish the Even Flow?

Well what was needed was for her to let him die.

Rescind that instruction. Let time move on. And yes, although he's been dead for five years, as far as this lady's energy system was concerned, he died last week, in my office.

Blocks and energy kernels are those things that people hold onto so tightly, that one moment of glory in their lives. You can see people in old people's homes, going over the same stories, time and time and time again, that one time when they were in Paris in 1964 and took part in this dance competition, they won and a famous French singer came and gave them a trophy and it was the best moment of their lives.

This causes havoc in the energy system, just as much havoc as the "I will NEVER!! forgive you." or the "Stop time! He must not die!" Other variations of this are "He still lives in my heart." and I have even once heard someone say about a moment of transcendence, "I enfolded the moment and held it close to me so it would be with me forever."

Everything in the energy system has got to flow, it must be flowing. You can't block out the rubbish, or even avoid it. People will be people. They will stomp on your foot, give you a bad response, you will be getting wet, cold and frightened - you can't avoid it. No more than you can avoid the good stuff. But you must not hold on to either of them because it really, really plays havoc with your energy system.

Let's go back to the core ideas to be sure.

Emotions are nothing but feedback devices to the existing conditions in the energy body. An early warning system. This escalates into physical sensations and then into physical illness to draw attention to itself.

Intention ONLY acts on the energy system level. When you placing your attention on the physicality and you try to change the physicality, some of this will ricochet around the system and with luck, you'll get a bit of fall out benefits as some of it reaches the energy system too. Which completely confuses tests and research - it works a bit but not reliably and is totally unpredictable because of this wrongful targeting and just get lucky with the odd ricochet here and there.

How do we work with this insight?

Well I propose to work with it in the simplest way possible. A lot of people are appalled by this and they say, it's too simple.

In 2001 I wrote a course called Energy Healing for Animals, and it's about pure energy healing and probably the most amazing piece of work I've ever written.

Animals are interesting because they don't get better just to please you or so you don't feel you're a bad healer. Thus, energy healing with animals is a fantastic feedback device in order to find out if you are completely deluded if you think you're a great healer or whether there is really something going on.

I recommend this highly. Try some lame horses for a change. Put your hands over them and then observe. Are they really now stretching out their legs, moving more freely? If they are not, back to the drawing board.

In Energy Healing for Animals, the core statement I repeat over and over again is that we need to develop a feedback system to teach us the difference between really touching energy realities and when we're only hallucinating. That is to me - and this might not be so for you - the absolute essence and core of the task ahead.

We must make clear distinctions because people can and do hallucinate so amazingly. They can build complex delusions and live in them their entire lives and never see the true light of day. This is a terrible state of affairs because the real world is so much better than the most candyflossed delusion could ever begin to be. That's the difference between true magic and nonsense - the difference between a real sunrise and a painted cardboard fairground with a few candles and if you get close you'll see it's all peeling.

Over here is reality and there is delusion. For the love of god, let's make sure we're going in the right direction.

Especially with energy healing with people, they want to have a nice happy thing going on, "Oh yes this is great, I can really feel it and ooh I'm having such a good time..."

That's nice but you know, it isn't energy healing.

Energy Healing is whoosh! power! A powerful thing that makes the lame walk and the blind see. That causes instant remission for cancer and AIDs and restores people's spines - THAT's healing. Accept no substitutes. To call anything else that isn't THAT healing is a total insult to the power of the field.

Now how the hell you teach people who are training to be healers to distinguish between illusion and intuition?

Well, EmoTrance does that by its very design and its very structure.

EmoTrance As A Healing Teacher

I am going to give you a very brief demonstration to make really clear what I mean and what we are talking about here.

I was at a healing thing, and the idea was they would be teaching people how to use their intuition.

So we had a person sitting there, and the instruction was that the person should be really focussing on their problem in order for me to read their aura and figure out what their problem is.

<Invites Chrissie Hardisty to come forward. She sits in a chair.>

Ok, so you focus on your problem and I stand behind you and put my hands on your shoulders and I imagine what your energy might be like and then I give you a guess.

Right, you were thinking about your left foot?

Is that right?

<C shakes her head and laughs>

Ok, so it's not.

Fair enough.

But that's ok, because I have this system called EmoTrance. It's a damned sight quicker.

Would you like to see how it works? Yes? Ok, here we go.

S: "Hi my name is Silvia. What's yours?"

C: "Chrissie."

S: "Do you have a problem?"

C: "Yes."

S: "Where in your body is that? Show me with your hands."

C: "It's here." <places hand on chest>

There you go. I mean seriously, how much easier does it get?

Where's your problem, show me with your hands. Now we know exactly where the blockage is in her energy system, without reading auras, hallucinating, without anything at all. My six year old can learn to this - never mind, my dog can learn to do this!

Which means that we have our hands free for more interesting and useful things, like helping the client, learning something about healing and all the rest of it.

But why I'm calling it a Healing Teacher is this. See, if you want to learn how to do this, as you are asking here, "Where is it in your body, show me with your hands.", guess quietly in your head and you can go, "I bet three quid it's in her left foot." So she shows you that it is in her stomach.

You will be getting right and wrong answers. And they **feel differently**. If you do this enough, you will very soon be able to tell the difference between when you're having a real intuition - and what is intuition? It's a message from the unconscious mind which computes a great deal more about the nature of the Universe than we consciously ever could - a reading of the patterns of reality that it has just undertaken on your behalf and delivered it's conclusion - and when you're either hallucinating or doing transference and projections.

This is another set of factors that interfere in taking proper realistic readings from other people and the Universe at large.

She might come in and say she has problems with bereavement. Where do you feel that in your body? and voom, your stomach flips over but look, that's my bereavement. HER bereavement is actually in her throat.

This totally direct approach to finding out where a problem is located does a whole array of things all at the same time.

First of all, it makes EmoTrance incredibly quick.

Secondly, if you want to use it that way, it teaches you to actually KNOW in your own self reliably whether what you are doing is intuition, hallucination, transference, your problem, her problem, where exactly the problem is located, without ever having to be afraid to feel like a fool whilst being completely confident that you will get it right, every singe time.

Much more importantly, the clients are truly happy because they get to tell you and show you where it really hurts them. This is so much safer and better than having to be in this weird position where you are all nervous and guessing best you can, thinking, "I hope I'll get it right." like when I was guessing about Chrissie's left foot. And when people don't get it right, a lot of people and especially healers who have a rather high opinion of their own opinions, they will try to convince themselves and the client that there really is a problem in her left foot when she doesn't have one and desperately wants help with that problem in her stomach.

The next step in the EmoTrance process would be for me to tell her that it's just a stuck energy, an emotional energy and what you have is a number of channels in the body through which that should be moved through and out.

I'm not even going to think "meridian system". I'm going to say to her, if this energy expands and softens, where would it like to go? Can you show me with your hands?

C: "It would like to go downward."

S: "Can we assist it in going downward?"

C: "Yes."

S: "Can you keep telling me what's happening whilst you are doing that."

C: "It's starting to move downward and just slowly going down my legs."

Now if you were a healer and you were assisting this client as a healer, you would say, "You assist this from the inside with your intention, and I assist this from the outside with mine." This makes the whole process much more smooth and elegant.

S: "So where is it going now?"

C: "It's going right down and out through the toes?"

S: "That's great. How about the original erea? Is it softening?"

C: "Yes it's softening but it's still there."

The fact is that energy lives in the quantum realms and there, there is no time. This could just be gone in a flash, as easily as that.

Now, this is a long standing problem and people have their time to do this. It is important to make it comfortable for the client.

S: "How are you doing?"

C: "It's moving."

S: "Do you think that process could continue by itself and on it's own, now that the channels have been found and established?"

C: "Maybe, not sure."

S: "Ok, now what if you were to put your hand on that place, and assist this softening yourself? How does that feel?"

C: "Yes that feels good."

S: "So you go and sit down and finish this process because that's more important than a silly demonstration."

See, this is how it works. You ask the client at every step of the way - what is it, where is it, what's happening. And it's important to remember that in EmoTrance, we are not moving metaphors, we are not moving emotions, or feelings. You are not moving 40 years of misery but only moving an energy. Softening and moving an energy.

This principle is applicable to everything. From allowing sunsets to come in, from watching a movie on the TV and all of a sudden, you burst out into tears and wonder, where did that come from? Move it, soften it, let it go, re-establish the Even Flow.

And you can do this with the most complicated, long standing problems.

One of my favourite ever moments with EmoTrance was this. There was a person and they were totally upset, "Oh dear I have this terrible problem and I've had it for ages and it's in my stomach and it hurts and I can't move it."

I said, "Ok, fair enough. It's only an energy. Start softening it."

The person said, "But it only wants to protect me!" and I don't know why, on that day I said, "It's only an energy - it doesn't want anything."

"Oh, alright then."

Voom! it simply disappeared, just like that – slid down her body and it was gone.

I went "Oops, ecology?"

But we tested and it was fine. When she said, "But it only wants to protect me!" I saw this HUGE therapeutic landscape stretching out before me, with parts integrations, calling in the angels, probably even an Indian dance, I have no idea.

Another lady at some point said, and that creased me up. She had some sort of thing stuck in her back and wasn't sure if she wanted to let it go.

I said, "Oh go on, it's not doing you any good at all, it's just stuck there, messing up your energy system. Just let it go."

She said, "Oh, alright." Then she sat up bolt upright and said, "Ouw!"

"What happened? Feedback, feedback?"

And she said, and I quote, "It just slithered off - without a backward glance!"

I couldn't help myself and had to say, "Bloody hell. After 45 years of continuous efforts to get rid of it, and that's the thanks you get!"

That is a scary aspect of EmoTrance and make no mistake, it really can be quite scary.

There's this problem you thought you would have had until the stars fall from the sky and it's this really big deal that's ruled your life for decades - and it just goes. Just like that. No ecology problems, nothing. Just an energy and it just basically goes away but for a single thought command. And that can make you feel like a right fool. Even more so than EFT ever did. It really makes you feel a fool for having had that problem for so long.

Which is why the practitioners hardly ever do what I would call pure EmoTrance with their clients - they just can't handle it. With themselves and friends they do it but for most people it's just too fast and so we talk first and take it easy, make sure people are comfortable with it.

EmoTrance Self Help

I'd like to say a few words about the EmoTrance self help protocol. Of course, ET needs a self help protocol else it would not be any good at all - if therapists don't need help then I don't know who doesn't.

It's essential the same as the basic protocol and it works like this:

Firstly, you notice where the upset is in your body.

Secondly, you show yourself where it is - put your hand on it you can reach it.

There is some merit in speaking about it out loud, and then you soften the energy to let it move along the pathways, wherever they may be. And it's surprising where the energy goes.

Once, I did a session and the energy swished out my spine, and I had a lovely energy tail! Very nice indeed.

But remember that we don't know where the pathways are - the only way to find out is to do it, and then afterwards you know where it is. And it's not always only pathways either. The energy can turn into a fine mist and rise out of the body entirely, but that's another story.

The key point in making EmoTrance work for you is to not fall into the trap of trying to treat the pain, the emotion or the meanings of the problem. You cannot move a metaphor through your energy system. That's like trying to flush a toilet roll down the system that's designed for water and soluble things. The energy system cannot handle metaphors, so in EmoTrance you can't go on about "this big black ball in my stomach". That's just an energy - it isn't big, it isn't black and it certainly isn't a ball, but only an energy. An energy can travel happily through meridians and other channels in the energy body but a ball cannot - this would cause entirely unnecessary suffering and thus mustn't be done.

So remember, "It's just an energy!" is the slogan. BSFF has, "Treat that!". In EFT we say, "Tap yourself on that, I should.", and we EmoTrancers have, "It's just an energy."

So, we have the self help protocol and the healing work. We have talked about the theoretical underpinnings and the development of the abilities of the healer.

So this, ladies and gentlemen, is EmoTrance.

Addendum 2 – Questions & Answers

Feelings, Blocks & Shields

Q: I don't feel anything in my body at all when I hear/think of the statement.

A: There are two possibilities with this. Either, it is simply not a relevant statement for you and so try something else you find "difficult to handle" - "YOU are the most beautiful person I've ever seen!" or perhaps, "You are so stupid!" - whatever, really. Also see the next question, that might be the problem in this case.

Q: It doesn't actually get to my body, there's a shield or block before it even arrives close to me.

A: That is an often occurring response - people learn to make shields to deflect the incoming energies suspect of being damaging. Unfortunately, they often end up with the energetic equivalent of scurvy or starvation behind their shields. Choose a statement of your own, perhaps something minor to start with, and do what you have to do to soften or remove the shield so it can properly touch you. Often, setting such a block or shield aside temporarily and just for this one exercise can provide the experience and incentive to know that it is perfectly safe to do it and to do it more often in future, and as your ability to unconsciously convert and channel a wider spectrum of energies grows with experience and use.

A shield can be softened, moved temporarily or made more see-through by gently touching it, massaging, or stroking it away.

Q: I can get it to come in a little way but then it gets stuck (in my stomach, in my head, in my chest etc.)"

A: What we have here are the equivalents of dried up river beds - the channels for the energy flow are absolutely there but haven't been used for so long or even ever that it might not be immediately obvious what the route for this energy should have been and it circulates around and around, trying to find a way out.

It helps to keep with it, to focus on it and to have the intention of softening and a gentle trickle in the right direction, the right channels to get underway. You usually notice then that there actually is an exit point or more but it's small and not efficient enough yet to handle this energy. By the very moving of energy through these channels for the first time, they come to life and begin to allow a flow to occur - it might be slow the first time, just a trickle that needs you to help it along, soften it's passing all the way to the final exit points where the rest of it leaves your body - through your head, your fingers and toes, through your skin, straight down your spine as though you had a tail, in all different kinds of ways.

You - or another - can help this softening process along by gently touching or physically massaging the area where the energy seems stuck. You can do this physically which is really nice and very beneficial and you can also do this with "hands of ghost" - with your intention and your imagination.

The first time is the slowest; when you do the same incoming energy (using the same statement as before) again, you'll notice it's much more apparent and will need less help from you to complete that circuit. On the third or fourth try, it moves already quite swiftly and freely and it is then you get this lovely "re-energising" effect from the process.

Q: What do you do when there is a strong fear or resistance to dropping a shield?

A: You ask, where do you feel the strong fear in your body? Show me with your hands. It is just an energy that needs to flow. When that is repaired, you can then go on to start with the pinprick protocol and take it from there.

Channelling Energies

Q: Is this practical for "real life"? Isn't it too complicated, takes too long?

A: Well, the truly neat thing about this pattern is that the unconscious mind seems to really like it and picks it up very quickly and with very little practise in a workshop or by yourself, or with a friend. Once you' have done it a few times on different topics, you can already begin to notice that you are starting to do this automatically and spontaneously in various "real life" situations - usually with much surprise and delight when it happens for the first time.

I think there are two reasons for this. Firstly, it is actually the correct way to handle incoming energies of any kind, namely to channel them in the correct channels that absolutely exist for these purposes already, through and out, removing the food in the process and releasing what's not wanted or needed without any further ado.

Secondly, it's clearly beneficial and very energising - it feels good to do this. There are no negative side effects, no ecology problems with this pattern, quite in the contrary - it revitalises and nourishes the entire ecology of a person and softens in the process many other problems, alleviates fears and so forth, so it's no wonder the unconscious mind likes it and learns very quickly how to do this!

Q: Can you really channel ALL energies in that way? Even pure evil, pure nastiness, pure aggression?

A: Try it, is all I can say. Energy is energy, very much as colours are colours. Purple doesn't hurt you any more than orange does. Allergic responses to certain types of energies clearly show that there is a problem in how these energies are handled within someone's system much, much more than that there's anything wrong per se with these "incoming energies" that exist quite rightfully both as a part of the universe at large, as well as being a part of human interaction in general.

It is a fact that there are a great many energies we clearly currently cannot channel or digest or process at all, especially high and powerful energies and regardless of whether they were labelled as positive or negative.

I have yet to meet a person who can handle pure love without really going into grand contortions of pain, regardless of what they might profess to the outside world, and as to "the light" - well. Without the filtering down delusions, the real thing is like a blasting sandstorm of such intensity, it would burn us up like the vampires under the noonday sun with the current state of affairs in our energy systems that spin out of control when a total stranger gives you a dirty look!

I would keep on avoiding these powerful energies for now and until the energy system has recovered at least some basic flow and can handle at least basic energies once again without causing any unfortunate repercussions.

Q: If I allow negative statements/energies into myself such as, "I am an idiot", does this not function like an affirmation? Will I end up believing that this is true about me?

A: In short, no and no.

It is very strange how this energy ingestion does not do at all what we think it might do. When these statements are handled not like words, at the conscious level, but as energy forms, they become harmless and energising – good statements or bad. I have seen people get into hysterics of laughter over using "You're an idiot" as an EmoTrance exercise. They are laughing because they are having a whole new position on the whole topic; most likely they'll be thinking now, yeah I have done some amazingly idiotic things in my time, but that is no longer a problem, really more like something that just happens when you are human and you are living in our bizarre environments.

It won't make them any more idiotic, quite in the contrary. I believe that we make our worst mistakes and decisions when we are afraid, energetically blocked up and contorted, worried, anxious, not thinking clearly. When your energy system runs clearly, then you think clearly too and that is all there is to it.

I can talk for hours and not convince you of this; I must invite you to try it for yourself and then you will understand how channelling energies actually sets you free from the content – and how truly wonderful that feels.

Q: I have been told that anger is a sign of stagnant chi or non-flowing chi and that it is really bad to get angry or to use anger energy. How does that tie in with the idea of channelling all energies?

A: Anger is the label given for the experience of a certain class of emotions and these emotions are derived from a change in the individual's totality which includes energy body state changes.

One could and indeed, should, make a major distinction between the actual energy being involved and the manifestations of folk who cannot handle this energy correctly within their systems.

Anger, as is vengeance, fury, and various other forms of this type of energy, are a) existing, b) extremely powerful, and c) have their rightful place in the universe.

There is an enormous difference between the experience and usage of these energies to fuel endeavour of one kind or the other, and the kinds of childish symptoms of shallow breathing, feet stomping and jumping up and down with a red face which indeed denote a disturbance and breakdown in someone's systems and which would thereby and very logically, slow them down in a fight or other suchlike situations.

Unfortunately, the big big misconception about the emotional energies is that it is their existence or their raising which causes the problem, when in fact it is the handling thereof which does.

In other words, what tends to happen is that people (especially men) waste their lives attempting not to have these emotions at all because somehow, they ended up thinking that the way to be in control is by not having them and ergo, never losing control at all.

This causes even more disturbances in the energy system and all kinds of psychosis, not to mention psychosomatics as is well known. Sitting in sweat lodges and screaming your head off for a week is definitely NOT the answer, although it does serve as a pressure valve to head off the worst side effects of the blocked up, messed up systems before they explode under the stress.

I would say that it would be useful to:

1. Recognise the energies involved as always being useful by the simple virtue of their existence;

2. Learn to raise these energies (as opposed to trying to never experience them at all);

3. Learn to ride, channel and make use of these energies successfully.

Pont 3 ends up looking as though the guy in question was never angry at all as they don't turn red or scream and shout - and that is where that weird misconception and misunderstanding about that state being about not experiencing emotions comes from in the first place.

So it's quite right then, grown men shouldn't cry. And neither should grown women. It's simply a sign of failure to control and run correctly the energies in one's system which should have been, but wasn't, learned step by step in the run up to adolescence.

So, and to go back to the beginning:

Anger, YES. It's a very powerful force.

Tantrums, NO. That's a sign of systems mismanagement.

Q: I have muscle tested people who have a lot of anger but are using it for "righteous goals", and they test strong; they also seem to achieve a lot in their lives. How does that tie in with EmoTrance theory?

A: I believe what happens when someone has a "righteous goal" to focus their anger-energies on is that they somehow allow themselves to say YES to the energy that rushes through them.

That's my ET "energy nutrition" theory - in the rushing through of the energy the system becomes energised and extremely powerful - physiologically that would come out as being faster, stronger, lighter on your feet, more aware of the environment and mentally it would be a state of highly focused yet wide ranging clarity.

When you on the other hand say "nononono!!!" to any kind of emotional energy or rather just energy because the emotion is the effect, NOT the cause (which is the energy itself) you slow it down, disturb it, distort it and that HURTS - emotionally and if you do it hard enough (aka exert enough will power!) it will hurt physically, too. Not just anger either but all the heavies - love, desperation, fear, terror, hatred, desire, the lot of them - all works exactly the same because. there is an energy principle at work below the surface of our awareness.

Which makes me think that ET might just be the most important energy drill a person could ever learn. I've had a couple of personal experiences with heavies and riding the lightning with ET and I can tell you it is an extraordinary feeling. Not at all the floaty "Oh I don't give a damn" kind of detachment but a completely different experience of the same energy - it doesn't hurt any more and the clarity is just extraordinary.

A Natural Ability?

Q: If EmoTrance is a natural ability we have, how did we lose it?

A: That is a very good question and something I've mused on for a long time.

It is my assumption at this point that the problem lies in people - most peoples these days - behaving as though there was no energy realms AT ALL.

We hear tell that "way back when" civilisations had a healthy respect for energy in all its shapes and forms, native tribes of one kind or the other talking about "everything being alive", aligning with the spirit of an animal or a landscape, "eating" their enemies in a ceremonial way to partake of their essences, using energy healing as an obvious choice for health care and so forth.

In our worlds, that's not so anymore. We don't even have words for "energy", using this undefined term in all kinds of ways that is probably inappropriate and adds to the confusion.

We don't have children's books "Susie & Her Anger Blockage" or, "Peter Meets A Powerfield".

From what I can see, in order to raise children who naturally work with their energy systems step by step just as they learn to become housetrained and their walking gets steadier over time, it would take an environment where a) this learning was essential and important, and b) these happenings were being modelled for them by their elders.

I believe that small children learn primarily by modelling and imprinting and that they model their parent's (or environments, or caretakers) ways of dealing with energy.

Then there is another point.

Because the adults are totally unaware of all things energy related, they are drowning little kids in energy forms of such strengths and severity that a freshly developing system has no hope at all to take these energies and survive without damage.

A parent who can't, for example, sort their own "anger energies" and lightning-conducts that sort of pure discharge power into a little baby must be blowing their sensitive systems to smithereens. So the first order of the day for such a kid must surely be to build barriers, and quickly, else they're going to go mad.

This is where the shields come from which then lead to energetic scurvy, all of this unconscious so no-one can rescind these decisions later on, and no culture to give guidance as to how to conduct oneself energetically at all.

How did all of this happen?

I am thinking it could be an evolutionary process and as simple as that. This is a long and convoluted story but animals have a fine awareness of energy fields and their general processing of energy is just dandy in the context of their various environments to which they have adapted.

People did this brain-growing thing and somewhere, conscious and self reflexive thought came into it and all hell was let loose. Patriarchies, for example, and I noted with interest the other day how the social organisation of a gorilla tribe was just like that of an Amazonian jungle tribe as I switched from one TV channel to the other, is one of these evolutionary things we're about to transcend which is a very nice thing indeed but demands an entire re-organisation of the human race on a pretty profound level.

But I digress I guess.

I would say that we're as energy-disabled as we are because of conscious contortions and false learning and indoctrination, which makes the conscious thought processes poisonous to ourselves and totally screws up a system that has conscious control built in as a natural and very profound evolutionary advantage.

Energy Pathways

Q: Does EmoTrance use meridians?

A: To answer this, I go to a teaching story about the human neurology.

People think of the brain as this big walnut in the skull, but that's not correct. It's much more like a super-octopus, extending tentacles basically to each and every cell in the body.

Indeed, if one was to immerse a human in a bath of acid that would dissolve all flesh, bone, tissue, muscle, everything at all and just leave the neurological pathways intact, the system would be so dense that you would be perfectly recognisable to your friends, only a funny colour.

Now that's pretty dense. That's a lot of pathways. If you add to this the systems for transporting blood around the body, from the great big veins to the tiniest little capillaries, we're getting a sense of the level of complexity inherent in just two of the physical body's systems.

I see no reason why the energy body is any less complicated. Being what it is and having the possibility of more than one thing being in the same space as another it probably is a whole lot more complicated.

Luckily for us, we do not need to concern ourselves with where these pathways are, what they are called or where they should be. Nor even what kinds or if they are this kind of energy system or another because in EmoTrance, we don't need this. We just treat what presents itself, all the time.

We use attention - where is it? how is it manifesting? and where does it need to go? - first and then intention to repair if necessary, give permission for flow, if necessary, to establish a smooth flowing in that area.

This is essentially very different from approaches such as acupuncture and acupressure which uses a "cause-and-effect" pathway system built up over a lot of trial and error, much like TFT's original algorithms, really.

It is different because firstly, we don't have any built up of experience to say, if this client says bereavement, the block's bound to be just above their nose, a bit to the right, because that's where all the other people's bereavements were too. I like this because it makes every client fresh and new and allows for absolute individuality both in experience as in treatment.

The other difference is the use of intention to resolve the problem. If you will, EFT et al are halfway between traditional acupressure or acupuncture on one hand, and EmoTrance on the other, because you stimulate the main points AND pay attention (tune in, say opening statement etc) to the problem. We, on the other hand, are stimulating what is asking for stimulation and healing, straight out feedback from the body, and the repair is by intention firstly and foremostly.

There is also one other main difference between acupressure and acupuncture and EmoTrance, and that is the fact we are NOT treating PHYSIOLOGICAL occurrences. I've always made a really big deal about this difference because it really is important - EmoTrance is for channelling energies, NOT for physiological problems. There may be a beneficial knock-on effect somewhere down the line, but I'm just not a physician and would NEVER try and teach my grandma to suck eggs - or tell an acupuncturist, for example, that I know what they are doing or could do it better.

You could say that ET is offering to cover the issues that are NOT covered by traditional energy medicine and thus, represents a co-operative effort rather than trying to take over or replace those kinds of treatments in any way.

Hope this helps if it comes up and you are asked about it.

Q: Is the perfect end state for the energy to leave the body? Or is it going where it is supposed to go?

A: Both. In the process of flow - coming in, going through the energy system and then leaving it to rejoin the Oceans of Energy - in that process something healing and important happens for the system overall. And I thank you for this question. The point of EmoTrance is not to cure someone of depression or release old memories or anything like that at all - it is only to re-establish the Even Flow which exist when energies flow in or out, are not being held on to, are not being reversed, are not being shielded out but are flowing through the energy system.

The only true purpose of EmoTrance is to establish the Even Flow.

Q: What if the client gets it wrong where it is in their body?

A: Ok let's for a moment consider that you have somehow deceived yourself that you have a pain in your stomach, and I as your therapist tell you that you are deceived and wrong about your own pain - how would you feel?

You wouldn't be very happy. Of course.

I find when people are told that what they are feeling is not the truth, and that they are completely deluded and that it takes for someone else to tell them what they're feeling because they don't know what they are feeling is a very appalling thing. I don't ever do that to people, yet people do that to me all the time. They say, "I know what's wrong with you. I know what your problems are." And I think, "Get lost! You have no bloody idea!."

I think that staying with the client and asking what the client is experiencing is absolutely perfect.

Even if that's what is being presented is a defence mechanism, it is still of the client and is still being presented and there is an energy there somewhere.

I just so don't like other people to tell me what I am feeling. How DARE they? Yes, you are right, I am indeed angry about this, and I can tell you honestly that the way EmoTrance works based on client feedback **only** and literally ties up the ETP into not being allowed to say much more than ask two questions has a lot to do with that.

Either way, it is about time that we got to really pay attention to ourselves, in therapy or out, and reclaim the right to feel as we really do, so that is a good thing in my opinion.

Q: Can we tranceform the energy for a positive application to pull something in?

A: Yes, we call that to raise or evoke energy. You can do that as simply as to say, "I am a healer" and notice where that hurts and causes contortions, move it out and through until it flows really fast and powerfully. There is an end state to EmoTrance proceedings, we call it the Energised End State when the energy really zips - whoosh! - through the system and that's a really good feeling. You can set the direction by just saying what you want to do - "I AM a public speaker."

Q: When an energy just moves through you, does that mean you are alright with that energy, on that issue?

A: Yes, when it zips through, you're fine. You might have trouble convincing people to let go of Guiding Stars and positive blockages, it happens at ET trainings all the time. Someone gets told, "You're perfect." and the person says, "Aaah, that feels all lovely and fuzzy round my heart area, wonderful."

Then you say, ok, now move it through and out and they go, "No! Get away from me! I haven't felt like that in years, I want to keep this feeling!" I then say to them, "Look you can always hire an unemployed layabout to shout this stuff at you as you leave your house to go to work in the mornings. Just let it go."

Q: Would the same pathway be used every time when you let an energy go?

A: We don't know where the pathways are. They are completely unpredictable and idiosyncratic. People have it go out their backs, sometimes it goes up, around the head, then down the spine and out. Sometimes it comes out of their eyes or mouth; sometimes it comes out of every pore of their skin. Each one is potentially different and that's why have you keep asking the client or yourself, where is it going? What is happening?

Some people have the same problem with the same ereas and channels over and over again. It is likely that you are looking at a variation of the

226

"Fault Line" manifestation in that case and you need to do healing first and then trancing later.

Q: What happens when someone experiences unwillingness to 'let go' of energies? Anxiety energy, for instance, may cue someone with the belief that the universe is unsafe to be vigilant. Without the anxiety they (their subconscious) may feel that the 'guard' is down and they may not be able to protect themselves as effectively.

A: The focus on the physiological aspects or manifestations of whatever the problem may be circumvents just about all the defence systems someone has put into place which is the neatest thing in the World.

We simply don't talk about "their old friend anxiety" at all, only where they feel something in their body. We are not letting anxiety go but are only repairing an energy disturbance, and that can't want or do anything; whilst someone is still arguing secondary gain, they are clearly not yet in that place where you are simply feeling the feelings of the body that tell you there is something very wrong which really needs to be resolved before it gets any worse and causes a nervous breakdown or physiological disease.

That is why it is so important to repeat our mantra, "It's only an energy!" to ourselves and to our clients over and over again at the beginning and until we stop slipping off into all the conscious stuff.

Another approach I have also taken to get around the protective rationalisations is to go for straight energy healing and cut all further talk. They have a long standing "issue". They tell you it's in their lower back. You go and ask permission, put your hands on their lower back, (I am a healer, full healing intentions, energies of mine, do what you need to do, flow where you will, I give myself permission to HEAL) and then just do the job like that.

Ask the client how it feels, how that other feeling they had when you started is changing, keeping the client focussed totally on the physiology all the time - there's an energy problem there, let us undo it, repair what needs to be repaired, make right what once was broken, put it to rights, put it back as God designed it should have always been.

This is the most powerful and powerfully effective version of ET.

If you can't touch the client, you can still have a go or do it proxy with them touching themselves. Touch breaks through the shieldings. It wakes up the energy system and the energy system wants it - so badly that many other things can be overridden in that way.

Depending on the context of sessions with clients, and how dysfunctional/damaged their energy bodies actually are, there may even be merit in starting slow with general alignments rather than straight into the depths of their worst problems. That would be the First Aid medicine approach of stabilising the patient before they get wheeled off to have the bullet removed.

Whenever there is trouble, going back to physiology and starting there seems to be a key point in the treatment of the more severe emotional "psychological" disturbances.

EmoTrance & Hypnosis

Q: Is EmoTrance hypnosis? It has the word trance in it!

A: Ah yes, so it has ...

Hypnosis is the art of altered states; firstly, move into altered states and secondly, to make use of the greatly enhanced and very different experiences and abilities you can find when you shift state into a different gear. Such as being able to remember with crystal clarity every little thing that has ever happened to you in your entire life or to turn off the experience of pain altogether – and then all the rest of the truly astonishing "hypnotic phenomena".

As soon as you turn your attention inwards and begin to move energy with your mind, you enter an altered state by definition.

We do not use this state to give any suggestions other than to support the client in finding out where the energy wants to go and encourage them to move it; as this is the key component of hypnosis – the suggestions the practitioner makes once the client has arrived in a trance state, EmoTrance is not definable as a form of hypnosis.

Q: How do I use EmoTrance in hypnosis?

A: Here is an example of you might want to say. I suggest for non-hypnotherapists to also read this because it contains all the main instructions and wordings to make it easy for another to run the process.

"And as you are thinking about your problem, all that confusion, hurt and pain, all those blockages which have stopped you over the years from manifesting your true will in all ways, from being who you were always meant to be, you are becoming more and more aware that these are nothing more than disturbances in your energy body, and you begin to feel an excitement rising and a hope too as you realise today is the day to let go of all of that, to clear and cleanse the channels of energy that you can feel now in your body, from the tip of your toes through your legs and into your hips, into your spine and into your neck, flowing freely across your face like cooling, gentling water, energies finding their rightful pathways at last, into your shoulders and down your arms, right out to your very fingertips, tingling lightly.

"Now, we are going to place our attention on that part of your energy body where the real blockages reside, where the real pain originates and you know where that is. You know where that is, you have felt it for so long. Understand now that it is nothing but an energy which needs to flow and you can begin to feel it softening now, slowly at first, gently the outside layers are beginning to dissipate and rise like the finest mist, finding their pathways and their channels back to the all-there-is, re-establishing the first linkages to the Even Flow as the softening and release now begins to spread far and wide, further inward, energies releasing at long last, hardness turning to softness and then begin to flow, as they were always meant to from the start, as was always right for you."

<Go on until client shows or indicates that blockage/damage has been resolved in much the same vein.>

"And now, with your energy bodies channels and pathways functioning once again, young and new they are, we allow the restoration to continue, energy bringing in the much needed building blocks to strengthen those channels and the systems who have waited for this healing for so long, and a profound healing it is, soft and respectful, layer by layer, moment by moment, coming back to health and channelling the natural energies around us with such ease and lightness, faster and stronger as the channels grow stronger in return, a rushing flow to energise you, nourish you, build you from the inside out and you can feel it, can't you, feel it flowing and how good that feels, how alive, how right and true."

Apart from that, and whatever you do, when you notice an emotional reaction, there is always a good time to just ask the basic question of where they feel it and to let it dissolve.

EmoTrance & The Auric Field

Q: Can ET be used to repair the wider Auric field?

A: I have been working with High Energy Fields for years and it's fun and truly magical in all ways. Also very useful and educational.

What it doesn't do, however, is produce reliable, recognisable, immediate and instant change in the Hard.

Of course it doesn't because it's stepped off and takes a while to filter through in the right ways, and also, cause-and-effect are not the kind of thing we're used to so whatever happens as a result of High Energy Field work has a habit of manifesting in strange ways that are often not even recognisable as related to the original piece of work. The other reason is that High Energy Field work is complex, fragile, encompassing and very subtle, and our existing conditions are a BIG unsubtle and inelegant mess that needs something very direct and as close to source as possible to start sorting it out.

The reason I made EmoTrance is as a starting point to the whole idea of working with energy systems.

Here we are, in our own body, learning to track sensations and emotions, finding energy channels and in doing so, learning something about the nature of energy itself and how it is not at all like we always think, with gravity, heaviness, time passing linearly and all the stuff we have come to expect, presuppose and all of that.

What it is, is a whole new territory, a basically alien world where what we learned about "how things work" doesn't actually help but in truth, it hinders - aka, if I've had a problem for fifty years, then it takes fifty years to deconstruct the problem, a heavy brick at a time. If my problem has arisen because of a trauma that has the charge of a nuclear explosion then it needs a counter charge of the same intensity to remove it. And so forth.

When we talk about shields, that's the first time we're stepping beyond the skin boundary and into real invisible territory. To be safe and sure about what we're doing there (even this close to the body) requires some experience first IN THE BODY for any single human to actually know what's what, to recognise the feedback they're getting inside themselves, what types of feedback there are, how they know things.

That's essential to know and have experienced properly FIRST before we move on and out into the other forms of EREAS (existing energetic realities) and begin to manipulate them with volition and in consciousness.

It is also essential to repair the most important, the biggest, and closest to the physicality in existence, structures before we go on to do more "magical" stuff.

If there was a word that expresses the word ESSENTIAL better and you know it, please insert it here.

As it stands, we're no better than hunchbacks and elephant men and women lurching around on the various planes, with the elegance of a something that totters and stumbles blindly.

The state we're in, energetically speaking, it's a blessing we're not getting to handle the high energies and the real powerful stuff that exists because it would blow us up and send us spinning into insanity and physical illness.

People who try in spite of this non-readiness get burned big time when they attempt High Magic, even at the lowest levels thereof.

So.

Having recognised this, I have taken the requisite step to sort some of this out before we go any further.

EmoTrance is designed to re-align the most important parts of our energy systems, the ones the most closely aligned to physicality and manifestation and have them working better.

Its also a form of "feeding up" the astronauts before they disembark in their spacecraft – what is the point of having weak, sick, freaked out, malnourished folk trying to go out and explore the stars?

How is someone who is running on 12% or thereabouts, burdened down with all those unhealed (energetic) injuries, no channels functioning, turned inward with their own long term pain and suffering, unable to receive and process even the most basic of energies that exist all around us, exhausted after 40, 50 years of trying to live that way, going to be in any position to be brave enough to face the universe, strong enough to withstand the storms and pro-active enough to handle it all?

I got a Chinese fortune cookie on Saturday at my birthday party.

It said, "When the burdens of life get too heavy, don't pray to lighten them. Pray for a stronger back."

That illustrates the point about what EmoTrance is in the greater scheme of things quite nicely.

Q: I have come aware of a disturbance which is outside of my physical body and I am wondering whether this energy is mine or from an external source since it was not within me physically?

A: Well in keeping with the observation that "this bird was once a mountain and will become a wave, or a tree ..." energy moves or should move in, through and out, being held in shape by matrix like structures which define what is what during an individual's development.

But apart from that, of course the energy body extends way beyond the physical skin parameters. There is all sorts going on in your wider energy body and it has all sorts of repercussions on your current state of being.

However, EmoTrance at the beginners level focuses on verifiable physiological sensations - these are the strongest of all field disturbances and a training ground for understanding how to work in these realms, and very importantly, how to distinguish between real occurrences and illusions by practicing with the stronger occurrences first.

You described the sensation of the energetic occurrence or erea as "like a motorcycle helmet but an airy one" which is very indicative of how sensations fade when they get further away from the physical body and also, how they become very different from the sensations we are used to experiencing with the physical body (and which we are used to describing in "ordinary hard terms" which neither have the reach or flexibility to be particularly effective in describing these energetic occurrences).

There are a whole lot of thoughtfields if you will, dense ereas of energy systems that do something, generate something, are an ecology in their own right which did not originate from us at all. Now I'm not even going to go down the path of "spirit attachments" which I believe is a metaphor for the most dense and cohesive thoughtfield systems but those are an example of programmes running inside our energy bodies which did not originate from us.

We also get send all sorts of energetic packages all the time by all kinds of people (and entities for all I know) which if they get "ingested" and integrated into our energy body systems (rather than passing through and out), can cause a hell of a lot of trouble and confusion.

In your particular case it might well be that the helmet was a protective device, a shield to something. I can't really say, its always difficult working from descriptions and without having been there.

But to sum up:

Yes, of course the energy body extends way, way beyond the physical skin.

Yes, there is all sorts going on in the wider energy body which we will get to in due course and when our apprenticeship with "EmoTrance Level 1" (the inner energy body) has been completed.

Yes, there are outside energy systems which did not originate from within us nor serve us at all and which will have to be dealt with in due course.

But if any of you should encounter problems in the wider energy field, know that all the basic tenets of energy work with ET hold there just as well:

- Stuck energy isn't good

- Find out the "natural channels" (only there are not really channels there anymore, so its more like, find out the natural currents of the energy in question).

- allow it to take its path as it was designed to, facilitate this in any way possible.

- heal disturbances along the path if this is required to facilitate the natural movement of the energy.

There is a whole world of this stuff out there beyond the basic ET Inner Energy Body work. I would prefer that at this time, we'd take it easy and keep working with the inner energy body.

Any work done here will help in being better balanced and more finely tuned as well as more experienced and far, far more capable when we get into the wider ereas.

Metaphors & Energy

Q: What happens when someone uses a persistent metaphor, such as a flame in the chest, and doesn't want to think of it as only energy? Can we not simply then talk about "the flame in the chest" rather than about energy?

A: It is really important to understand that ET isn't metaphor based.

It is body based instead.

It actually isn't psychotherapy in any shape, form, type, metaphor or anything like that, it's simply bit of much needed repair work for your energy body, and that's all!

So, in ET a "persistent metaphor" becomes JUST ENERGY and gets to "slither off without a backward glance" once permission is given.

If there's a feeling of "emptiness" after the blockage in the energy system has been uncorked then one needs to trace the channels further up to find further blockages that precluded a smooth energy flow in that area.

And that's it. That's all there is.

Please remember that you cannot move a flame, a sword, a glowing orb or any suchlike thing through the meridian/energy system - these are different systems which are essentially incompatible.

If there is a flame, then there must be a fire and with that fire comes an environment that includes oxygen. If there is a sword, then there must have been a hand wielding it at some point. Metaphor work is fine energy work on a very subtle level with its own rules and regulations; EmoTrance is here-and-now, instantly observable and very close to the "Hard" indeed.

IF there is a great and profound need to be working at that particular level, one might deliberately and with volition switch into a metaphor session which is a totally different modality altogether, much more different in fact than say, Gestalt is to EFT.

It is really essential to understand about ET that it's not THAT therapy where you turn a sensation or feeling into a red ball or a sword or a anything at all one can have even further emotions, thoughts and feelings about in turn, running then a relationship consultation between all the parts and transferences in question as well as working in a very different level altogether.

There are such healing and even energy field adjusting therapies, many of them very good indeed including my very own Project Sanctuary. They are very good in their own level and time but EmoTrance isn't one of them and when you're doing metaphors, you're basically NOT doing ET but one of those instead.

Q: How is talking about "energy" not also a metaphor?

A: Yes, of course, that's an important question.

First of all, we need to be clear about the fact that all communication, all language and all conscious thought is conducted as a metaphor.

All language is metaphor. All language forms are metaphor.

Maths is a metaphor, music is another type and when I say, "This is a cat" that's a metaphor too because I can't be having a real cat inside my brain nor get it out through my mouth - and nor can anyone get it in through their ears!

Talking about "it's only an energy" is what you could call a "re-frame" - meaning that by changing the word or metaphor, a whole lot more changes besides in an instant. That is the old, "She was a stubborn old witch" vs. "She was a strong mature woman who stood up for her beliefs." - we have the same "energetic occurrence" but when it is being described differently, the thoughts and actions that derive are different in turn.

The description of "energy" and especially "quantum state energy" opens up possibilities of time/space freedom that cannot exist conceptually when you talk about "a plank of wood".

Further, it really rather precludes being able to have feelings about it and to make judgments about it, even to have a relationship with it which is often based on the former, causing the latter.

This is a long story really, but the key is that all communication and thought by needs happen with metaphorical interfaces in our current formats of thinking and experiencing (and not necessarily by design).

There are different kinds of metaphorical interfaces for different purposes and it's often a question to pick the right one to get something done.

There is a class of metaphorical interfaces that is known to psychotherapists and such as "metaphor" because the way things (occurrences, collections of space time events, experiences etc) are being described is different from other forms of descriptions which are just as metaphorical if only you knew it - such as someone saying to you, "Good Morning." In this class of metaphorical interfaces (the one generally referred to as "metaphor"), objects are used and anthropomorphized, imbued with active thought and volitions, but retaining the identity of the object and it's limitations AND it's context in a restrained, gravity, distance and time bound experiential world I call the Hard.

This has uses but also, can lead one down the wrong garden path in a big hurry, which is one of the reasons why that class of metaphors hasn't really ever been properly described and explored, in spite of having been in use since history became recorded and probably long before that, too.

There are many, many other classes of MIs (metaphorical interfaces) and if one was to look at them (!!) as tools for a specific job, one can come to notice that some work better for some jobs than others. For some jobs, it's true, the right ones simply haven't been written yet, and others are as horrendous as the Windows Operating system which is full of bugs, misleading information, cumbersome as hell and slows down the power of any underlying hardware to a snail's crawl. Others are more functional like Linux but lack a good GUI (graphical user interface) and thus can't be used by most of the population.

End of the day, we try to describe experiences which is all we can have or know, in some way. Conceptualising "Quantum Energy" as a metaphor of flow and related to water is not bad as it opens up whole new realms of possibility which just weren't there before, including instant change and non-judgemental, systemic repair.

And so, what I'd suggest you say when someone asks, "But isn't energy a metaphor too?" is,

"Sure. Just happens to be a much more useful metaphor."

EmoTrance & EFT

Q: Does EmoTrance have 'aspects' similar to EFT?

A: Yes, EmoTrance has "aspects" the same as EFT. It happens that when you test the same (statement, memory, thought, topic, etc) a different sensation turns up or it's noted in two or more distinct locations from the start.

The nice thing about EmoTrance is that the aspects (or connected issues) reveal themselves nicely in the correct order and sequence quite naturally so you just clear them up as well.

When you start with two (or more) body locations just ask which one is the most noticeable or the most painful and that is always the one to start with. Sometimes they all go like domino stones even though they are seemingly unconnected after the first or most important one has been resolved. Sometimes they are just separate and you can do them (and any aspects THEY might have) then in the order they turn up.

What I've also noticed a lot again is the fact that sometimes a single channel has numerous knots in it. For example, the energy starts in the stomach, gets blocked in the solar plexus, moves happily up, then gets blocked in the throat, up into the head, gets blocked on the top of the head and only then it's all smooth flowing.

Also, and I thought this was way weird because I've never witnessed it, was an experience where someone cried floods out of their left eye whilst the right remained entirely dry and normal following some work that was very much stuck on the left side of their head. Fascinating to watch, it must be said, even though somewhat disturbing!

Q: Can you combine EFT and EmoTrance?

A: Oh yes – they work perfectly together and you can use both systems seamlessly within a single session. For example if someone is working with EmoTrance and the energy gets stuck, a few taps can help loosen the system enough for the energy to just slide away. Alternatively, if you are working with EFT and the SUDs are not coming down sufficiently, you can switch to EmoTrance at any time to rescue the session. This is particularly useful when there is a lot of conscious resistance to solving the problem (conscious contortions). You can also use the EmoTrance system of locating a body sensation, the using EFT on that body sensation – "Even though I have this barrier in my forehead, I deeply ... etc".

The reversal corrections of EFT are also useful sometimes in EmoTrance; and EFT is further a good option for clients who find EmoTrance way too spooky.

I consider a full knowledge of both systems essential for a modern energy healer; and for anyone seriously involved in personal healing/development to be able to use both is a must in my opinion.

Q: Does EmoTrance work at the same level as EFT?

A: That is an interesting question. EFT is essentially meridian based and works with the meridian system. There is of course a great deal more to the energy system than just meridians and it is indeed my assumption that some disturbances in the meridian system are actually symptoms of disturbances on other levels of the energy body rather than being the cause.

It has been noted by ETPs that if you raise a certain topic with EmoTrance that it does not always responds to EFT for resolution; and I believe that is so because the topic and the disturbances are not meridian based.

On the other hand, people who know about meridians often find to their delight that sometimes, EmoTrance sessions show the flow in a meridian on a particular topic more or less exactly as the Yellow Emperor said it would – the energy takes a path as described by an entirely meridian-unaware person "off the street" that is just like in the diagrams.

The nice thing about all of this is that although it is fascinating to muse upon such things, it is entirely immaterial in the context of healing the energy body and restoring the Even Flow – we simply don't need to know what energy level is producing these "pain calls" via the physiological system of emotions and sensations in order to **get the job done**.

In the meantime, the more we do it, the more we learn and the more information and experience we have; in the end, I am sure we will end up with a pretty good, workable AND testable new model of the many layers of the human energy system – even though we actually don't need this at all.

Q: What is the essential differences between EFT & EmoTrance?

A: EFT and TFT derived techniques have in common that they work best when target very specifically (low chunked) at a single memory/disturbance.

The MET community of developers have tried their best to get around this which becomes a severe limitation when people start trying to work on transformational life pattern stuff and complex systems such as addictions instead of wanting to remove a single phobia, one-event PTSD etc.

One way of doing this is making more and more complex protocols (with huge lists of PR reversals, grids, matrices and so forth).

Another way is going right around this limitation of the TFT based tapping techniques and do something like BSFF and ET and work differently with the energy system altogether.

The Slow EFT protocol (and Willem Lammers Consecutive Points Protocol which is the TFT version of that same thing) tries to address this and it works reasonably well for things that have so many aspects you might as well tap until the sun has died (esp. high end nominalisations such as mother, money, "I", etc) (the SLOW EFT protocol can be found in the Advanced Patterns Of EFT)

There is also another and much bigger problem, namely that in order to tap on anything you have to be consciously aware that it's there. The real big stuff is either physiologically stored or well repressed and doesn't present itself in consciousness at all, and therefore cannot be tapped on, of course.

Seems to me that there are three types of personal development.

One is symptom removal and that's well catered for with the end result being that one is able to lead one's EXISTING life EXACTLY but with some efficiency improvements in the every day running of what there is already.

Second type is life change stuff such as putting some sort of right angle into the current timeline - getting divorced, leaving the country, different job, giving up cocaine and the lifestyle derived therefrom. Long term use of METs does seem to bring that one on, but rather slowly, chaotically and weirdly, with much pain and trauma in the interim (and I'm not sure if that isn't feedback on it not quite working as it should).

Last type of change is what I would call re-birth. That's a whole new incarnation in this life, different person altogether. It's the hardest one to do but the one with the most promises, as in re-birth ALL the old "till death do us part" decisions are rescinded in an instant and one would really be able to start afresh (religions try to go for that but don't usually get it right). That is of course the ball park in which EmoTrance plays, by design because that is what I want for myself and those I love.

The most customers and the customers who will pay the most are in Group One, naturally, and thus EFT and other lower chunked techniques suit them to the ground. There is some merit in working out what one's aims actually are in personal development, that helps with the choice of possible techniques applied.

Physical Pain & Disease

Q: Can EmoTrance be used for physical pain and/or disease?

A: I expressly forbid my practitioners and trainers to offer any form of physical healing via EmoTrance. Indeed, it goes as far as making them all sign a document that states should I ever get to hear they did offer EmoTrance for pain relief or to cure any form of physical problem at all they will be immediately disbarred.

The reason for this is as follows and best illustrated by the following story.

Last night I was talking to a "cynic" who really attacked EmoTrance in every which way without knowing anything about it, making many accusations based on their unfortunate personal experiences with the older, less effective types of healing.

The whole deal of treating physical illness and being a charlatan for promising cures to the desperate came up yet again and I gave my usual speech at that point:

"EmoTrance is called EMO-trance because we ONLY deal with EMOTIONAL ENERGIES.

We don't deal with anything else.

That's what it's for. To TRANCEFORM EMOTIONAL ENERGIES and restore our energy body by doing that.

So when some comes along and they are dying of AIDs, say, we ask about their emotions - are they afraid to die? angry at the person who gave it to them? distraught because they will never grow old, never have children, never have a full life? terrified of the processes of pain and decomposition that are said to occur?

We can treat THAT. We can help them with THAT.

Do you think that would be valuable to them?"

And the cynic just crumbled and said, "Yes, it would. It would help them immeasurably - why, it might even slow the process of disease itself because they feel better, stronger inside."

At which point I said with a very evil smile, "Well but that's not the point now, is it. Because we don't deal with the disease. Or the person's physical health. Only - ONLY! - with their emotions and with their energy bodies."

They went away deep in thought and I thought, how useful it is this to have it set up like that. It makes EmoTrance bombproof to any form of accusation of snake oiling, bottom feeding and charlatanism and indeed, allows the ETPs to go where many other holistic healers fear to tread. EmoTrance deals with restoring the energy body via the feedback devices of feelings and sensations.

What you do in the privacy of your own home with thoughts such as, "Hm, that pain in my ankle might just be only an energy - where does that want to go?" or, "Where do I feel this diabetes in my body?" is, of course, none of my business.

Distance Healing, Proxy Healing

Q: Can EmoTrance be used for distance healing?

A: Yes, certainly. The form to use is the basic and very simple EmoTrance Proxy protocol, which is a simple shamanic move of becoming the other and asking, "Where do I feel **their** problem in **my** body?" and then to move the energy as usual.

Another variant is to imagine the person in a "dreamtime space" and to conduct a normal EmoTrance session with them there by asking as normal, "Where do you feel this problem in your body? Show me with your hands." This being a dreamtime space, you might be able to actually **see** the energy disturbances directly there and do some extremely effective work.

You can also treat animals with the proxy protocol. For example, someone who might have a nervous cat might think/say to themselves, "Where do **I** feel **my cat's** problem in **my** body?" and trance it as normal.

Other energetic entities, such as businesses, rivers, landscapes, houses etc. may be dealt with similarly as do past selves, people who may already be dead and even ghosts.

If you find these notions disturbing, simply ignore this more esoteric aspect and know that if you are doing an EmoTrance session and **you** are feeling **something** and then you restore Even Flow, you are always doing **your own** energy body a big favour and leave it at that.

Q: Can EmoTrance session be conducted successfully over the telephone?

A: Oh yes indeed – it was invented on the telephone in the first place and was refined in over a hundred telephone sessions before it was ever done for the first time interactively with client and ETP being in the same room together.

As the ETP is constantly asking for feedback, and with the additional feedback of the client's (or practice partners, friends) tonality, breathing patterns, rate of speech etc. it work very well indeed at the distance.

EmoTrance being quantum based, it make technically no difference whether the ETP is right next to the client or 5,000 miles away – if it does make much of a difference then it is likely that this would be based on limiting beliefs by one or the other (which may be tranced away before the actual session for the presenting problems even begins).

The ETP can help the client with intention and the ghosthands come in handy for telephone work too.

Explaining EmoTrance

Q: How do you explain the basic EmoTrance technique to someone who has never done something like that (energy moving) before?

A: Here is a short sample version of what I might say to such a person:

Everyone has feelings all the time.

Feelings are not a problem, they just come and go in an instant – in one ear and out the other – or at least, that's how it should be in a perfect world.

Feelings become a problem when they get stuck somewhere and can't move along and out as they should. Then you have the original feeling, and the next and the next all piling on top of one another and increasing the pressure until you get physical pain in that area. If the pressure gets too bad, people have panic attacks or throw a fit or start screaming and crying, they have to do something to release the energy build up but that's a desperate measure.

What we are going to do is to open up the pressure valves and let the feelings flow through and out as they should, and when we do that, you will notice that the physical sensations tell you clearly how much better you feel and how right it is to be doing this.

In your body are channels for this energy to run through and out. Some of these channels haven't been used in a very long time, but they are there and when we find them, the energy can flow through and just leave your body – sometimes through the skin, sometimes through your hands and feet, sometimes it comes out of your mouth, it's different for everyone.

We will find the pathways for the energy and release the block that causes the pain.

You work from the inside and I help from the outside and between us, we will be able to free up that part of your body so you can feel these things and they won't hurt anymore as they flow through and out as they should.

Q: When do I need to consult an ETP?

A: When you are stuck by yourself and have tried everything you know and would like someone experienced to help you get back into the flow; when you have "issues" that frighten you to approach by yourself; when you have the strange feeling that there is "something you are not thinking of" but that, if discovered and treated, would help an awful lot; when you would like an unbiased second opinion, and when you want to learn more about what you can do with EmoTrance and would like someone you can ask personal questions of.

Q: How do I get to be an EmoTrance practitioner? Are there any qualifications I need?

A: You get to be a licensed EmoTrance practitioner by successfully completing a training with a licensed EmoTrance trainer. You can find these listed on http://EmoTrance.com

This is a two day training and you do not need any qualifications to attend other than a true desire to learn how to give and receive healing of the energy system with this unique modality.

However, a certification in EmoTrance does not give you permission to **practice therapy** – you will need to check with your local legislation as to what you need in the way of insurances, licenses and education in order to be practicing legally and safely.

In general, EmoTrance practitioner trainings are taken by those who are already practicing as counsellors, coaches, therapists, psychologists etc. and who wish to add EmoTrance to their toolbox of techniques.

Q: I really enjoyed this book and find the ideas exciting and fascinating – what should I do next?

A: I can't recommend it highly enough – get together with some friends and play! Try it out on every form of emotion and sensation that comes your way; on thoughts and memories that hurt you, and on the other hand, start "taking in" some energy forms you might not have tried before.

Learn with friends and with practice partners about yourselves, how your energy systems work, what you let in and what you need much more of, where your shields are – in other words, **please USE the system.**

I have made it as easy as possible and I don't think a day could go by where you would not find some new uses for the basic technique of saying "Yes!" to the Oceans of Energy, and in doing so, saying "Yes!" to life.

ADDENDUM 3 – EMOTRANCE ARTICLES

In this section, you will find a number of popular published articles on the concepts and ideas of EmoTrance which were originally written with the general public in mind.

I have included these because firstly they explain the concepts very simply and you might find the wordings, metaphors and teaching stories helpful when you come to explain EmoTrance to others; and secondly because these articles highlight certain aspects of the main EmoTrance concepts from different angles which is helpful in the context of learning the structure of the system, its techniques and applications.

Introduction To EmoTrance

After having worked for four years intensively with EFT and having observed, experienced and facilitated the very real miracles Meridian Energy Therapies can produce especially in the treatment of all things which have a basis in emotional "disturbances", I had developed a healthy respect for METs. I had also come to learn many things about the human energy system and the energy body along the way - and all of these things I learned entirely by watching and observing, making changes and testing the responses but NOT by studying acupuncture charts or ancient texts.

The original METs relied on a limited number of points to produce change in the energy system which by extension, leads to change in how a person feels, acts, behaves and experiences their lives after the treatments. EFT uses a "total redundancy" approach to clear all the major channels during a session which is extremely successful, especially if repeat treatments are used to catch aspects that were missed or address further energy blockages. I'm not sure why it took me so long but in 2002, I had an instant insight into the relationship between the energy body, emotions and the physical body - namely, that **all** emotions are nothing more (and of course, nothing less!) than simply feedback devices to alert us to the existing conditions in the energy body, just the same as physical pain is nothing more (and certainly nothing less!) than a feedback device to alert us to existing conditions in the physical body.

It is well known that repeatedly experiencing the same strong emotions has a very direct correlation to the onset of physiological symptoms and this was the bridge I used in the system I called EmoTrance in order to show and demonstrate clearly to everyone concerned just exactly **where** in a person's body the disturbances occur at the energetic level.

Back To Physicality

When conditions change in the energy body, subtle feedback exists immediately which we generally are not aware of at all as we are too busy with our attentions elsewhere all through the day. It is only when these subtle sensations turn into strong feelings that we are **made to take notice**. We really only become aware of the strongest emotions as they turn into absolute physiological sensations.

A simple example would be like this. Someone gets told unexpectedly, "You are FIRED!" and they will report that "it felt as though they had been punched in the stomach".

That is not some kind of metaphor or a psychosomatic aberration, but a complete and correct recognition and diagnosis of a real and severe disturbance in this person's energy body. The **physical** sensation tells us exactly where this disturbance lies - in EmoTrance, the one who is working on their problem or disturbance will be asked to "show me with your hands where that is" - "that" being the problem, the bereavement, the anger, the pain, or whatever label of emotion is causing the problem.

It is crucial to EmoTrance to know that we work from the assumption that people's energy bodies are NATURALLY DESIGNED to handle just about any kind of existing energy in this World. That there are channels and pathways which, if they are clear and functioning properly, can and will channel even the most powerful of energies we can imagine into us, through us and out in an Even Flow movement.

Re-Establishing The Even Flow

EmoTrance works to re-establishing a full and functioning flow of a **very wide range of energy types** in, through and out a person's body in three ways:

248

1. Firstly, by teaching and learning the basic EmoTrance technique to find the pathways for energies that need to flow rather than be stuck, held on to or deflected out;

2. Secondly, by softening and releasing old energy blockages (which show up directly and uncontrovertibly through the medium of **physiological sensations** in a person's body);

3. Thirdly, by repairing channels, networks and areas of the energy body to enable these areas to once again allow a smooth flowing of incoming energies into, through and out of the system.

Repercussions & Energy Nutrition

When EmoTrance was originally being developed, the intention was to **reduce** firstly the physiological sensations related to high stress emotions, secondly and as a direct effect of this, to entirely release the **emotional experience** and finally, to basically re-teach the energy body to begin flowing energy again in, through and out as it was always designed to be doing and to do so automatically and in reflexive response to the environmental conditions which we may expect to be challenging often and constantly as we live our lives.

But very early on it became apparent that there were unexpected "side effects" to working with the underlying energies in the energy body in this way.

Rather than simply "not feeling the negative emotion and pain anymore" from incoming or self generated energies, it turned out that when these energies were being taken into the system and "tranced through" their correct and requisite channels, it produced a **huge** increase in a person's actual energy levels - expressed through laughter, delight, pro-active ideas and thoughts; in other words, through the movement of energy from intake, through the systems and release something very important was being **gained** in the process.

As people were learning to once again, opening themselves to energies from people for example, such as can be found in expression of admiration, gratitude, praise and so forth ("You are beautiful." - "You are intelligent." etc), they finally were able to derive what can only be described as long needed "nutrition" for their energy bodies which expressed itself in very different mental states, body postures and thoughts after an EmoTrance treatment.

But this extended much, much further than just "positive" energies. Allowing negative forms of incoming energies into the energy body too, to be moved through the requisite channels and systems, in, through and out produced even more profound state changes and shifts in return. Being able to handle an incoming (or self generated) thought form energy such as, "You are ugly." and to simply trance it through and out directly causes people to feel stronger, much more balanced, much less afraid of criticism and of failure, more determined and more resourceful.

Playing In "The Oceans of Energy"

Doing EmoTrance, perhaps to begin with to release easily and without much ado (because we are working directly with the energy/physical body and NOT in the head with thoughts, metaphors or other logical contortions) old burdens, blockages, shards, hurts and pain, does a number of very beneficial things for a person.

Firstly, users and practitioners of EmoTrance report that they become far more attuned to what is happening in their bodies and how their emotional states are actually expressed in their body. This is a very grounding and healing change of attention and for many, a first re-connection to how much their bodies have been crying out to them for help and release at last. Further, in the act of learning or re-learning to move these energies and to let them flow every person who practises EmoTrance begins to learn about the actual realities of their own energy body - where the main channels are in their body, main centres and entry and exit points for energies and much, much beside.

Secondly, and once we start moving beyond immediate trauma and emotional drama reduction, it becomes very clear just how much energy there is around us for us to use to heal, grow, have, be and do.

Opening oneself and "drinking in a sunrise" fully and completely, for example, is an extraordinary experience and not to mention, *physiological sensation*. Opening oneself fully to energies from plant life, from animals, from the sun and the sky, from the Earth and indeed, from every little thing around us makes every day quite extraordinary and provides literally ENDLESS and totally abundant sources of energy for life, work and play.

Learning to "take the energy from a thing" rather than trying to possess or ingest or own the thing itself is a wonderful gift in and of itself - it can satisfy needs and wants that were previously totally out of reach and even out of possibility and has inordinate applications for addictions of all kinds, and even radically reduce food and shopping bills into the bargain!

There is also the magical aspect of deliberately *raising energies* such as, "I am a healer" and being able to trace and track any blockages, smooth them out and have this - and basically, ANY - form of energy flow powerfully and very intentionally through our systems.

Endless Possibilities, Endless Applications

EmoTrance is at its most basic level, an incredibly simple and intuitive method because it relies upon naturally existing systems of the human totality - the intention of the conscious mind, the feedback devices of emotion and sensation from the physical and energy bodies and the co-operation of the unconscious systems and the body mind. Simply put, bodies love EmoTrance. Because it is entirely natural and following the direct evidence of physiological feedback, EmoTrance is amazingly easy to learn and easy to do.

As EmoTrance is entirely and strictly focussed on the movement of energy in, through and out the energy body, it is "content free" in the best sense of the word and can be applied to just about anything that humans can think, worry or feel pain about - this includes past resolution, forgiveness, bereavement, relationship issues, old wounds, burdens and pains, current instabilities, feelings "in the moment", and all things future related, including goal setting, planning, self identity and so much more besides.

For psychologists and psychotherapists, EmoTrance can be the bridge into energy psychology and healing as it does not require touching, tapping, or muscle testing and although it is in effect, a *pure energy healing* modality it is also close enough to a "talking therapy" to be easily accepted and accessible.

For healers of any kind, EmoTrance offers a new doorway to exploring energy healing with direct feedback rather than to have to guess or rely on intuition. It does not demand any special talents or abilities from either the healer or their partner in healing, and represents a beautiful, experientially based system for a healer to develop their natural healing skills which everyone is blessed with simply by having been born to be human.

The EmoTrance systems and techniques are not at all an end product but rather, a starting point and learning tool to how much more we can all do, be, have, achieve and experience right here, right now - simply by re-learning to use the systems we already have and once again, stepping back into a true appreciation of The Even Flow.

First Published By The Association For Meridian & Energy Therapies,
October 2002

Starving For Love Amidst The Oceans of Energy

People spend an absolute fortune on diet gizmos, pills and fancy foods.

They study nutrition in great detail, weigh their calories and exercise themselves into early arthritis. They have plastic surgery to keep looking young and spend £90 on a tiny tube of wrinkle cream. They take drugs to speed them up, mellow themselves out, have a bit of artificial ecstasy in their lives once in a while - and after all of that, end up starving to death in completely different way - quite literally.

For at least 6000 years it has been well known that the human energy system has the most profound impact on all levels of health, happiness, and fitness to live more than just a half-life of unfulfilled hopes and dreams.

Isn't it about time we turned our attention to the requirements of this total mind/body system, what it's resident energy immune system requires for maximum functioning, why it is that our energy systems are so disturbed, blocked, disconnected - rivers that churn but do not flow?

Isn't it time we would ask the questions of Energy Nutrition - what is it, how does it work, and what you can do to avoid the equivalent of "energy scurvy" across your mind/body systems which absolutely lead to cancer, all forms of degenerative diseases and the most serious of mental health problems?

No Even Flow ...

Any practitioner who deals with the human energy system - acupuncturists, Kinesiologists, acupressurists, energy healers, touch healers, Reiki practitioners, holistic healers working with chakras, with auras, and all the other disciplines such as the New Meridian Energy Therapies (EFT, TFT et al) - can tell you clearly that when they see someone, all is definitely NOT well.

- Chakras are displaced and spinning backwards; they are distorted, disconnected, dried up, atrophied.

- Meridians have major blockages all over their complex river networks with vast areas that have become nothing but a desert where any life is struggling desperately to even be able to make it from day to the next.

- Auras and Energy Fields are disturbed, full of attachments, dirt and dust; with swirling vortices that drain energy the whole time, twisting and churning here and radiation-too-bright over there.

Even if you're not working with the energy systems, just take a look around. Look, really LOOK at people's faces in the street, on the underground in rush hour traffic, in the supermarkets, at Mind-Body-Spirit Festivals. Look at how they move and how walk - this is NOT dancing through life with eyes wide open and ready to find out what else there might be from one exciting day to the next!

So, this is how it is. We try to combat these dreadful states of existence with everything we can lay our hands on - with vegetables, with potions, with pills and with gurus, with illusions, with mantras. We overeat, we abuse substances, we try and trance out with movies and computers and work - in fact, anything - ANYTHING! - at all to **remove the constant pain** we're in, a droning, grating background noise that is ever present, always there, always always nagging, nagging, dragging us down, sucking our energy away no matter what we do and slowly over time, eroding first our will to live with joy, then our health, then our will to live, and finally take away our lives.

This is the half-life I mentioned earlier. This is the catastrophe of the Western World.

It is simply so that we have NO IDEA of how to feed ourselves correctly in the energetic sense.

We were absolutely NEVER TOLD how to take care of ourselves and our energy systems in any way, and what we WERE told is useless at best but far more often, intensely damaging instead.

How to USE YOUR ENERGY SYSTEM as it was designed was NEVER modelled for us or even acknowledged as something that's so incredibly vital to living successfully at all!

We have NO IDEA at the conscious level of how BADLY we are mishandling the currents and components of the "Oceans of Energy" of which we are a part and how much we are HURTING ourselves in the process.

254

I believe we have a deep remembrance of HOW IT WAS SUPPOSED TO BE deep, deep down inside our minds and bodies, and we have a tremendous anger and behind that, fields of sadness the size of Galaxies that pervade us all as we continue to live and act AGAINST the Even Flow, day in, day out, from moment to moment - whether we're consciously aware of it, or not.

I have researched this particular phenomenon all my life, in one shape or form or the other.

There is something so **profoundly wrong** about the way we conduct our lives that it hurts. All the time. All of us. And through us, all and everything we touch and thus, pass on the **wrongness** that seems so interwoven with our very beings that often, I simply stood in tears and didn't know anymore where to start, or if there was any point at all, any hope at all to do **anything**.

I have worked and studied and researched, endlessly and ceaselessly, for as long as I can remember because there IS A PART OF ME that KNOWS we can do better. It's not a feeling, a hope or a theory but it is an absolute, incontrovertible KNOWING - and that's what made me pick up the pieces, time and time again, and go on, after the dark hours had passed once again.

"Could Do Better ..."

We are **structurally designed** to do better. You could say, God made us with the potential to **do better** and to be able to change the experience of this World back into something altogether different, something so **other** than what we've been doing so far that truly, I don't think we can begin to have any idea, picture or conception of what this **other** might look like, be like, feel like.

In the olden days, people came up with lions sleeping with lambs and rivers full of milk as a representation of what that might be like - yes, it's pathetic, but the best they could do with what they had. But that's beside the point.

What is the point is that we now have **a starting point** in the right direction.

After 25 years of working with energy, one way or the other, I am beginning to see the patterns unfold, and as I do, I am beginning to see just where we are going wrong.

- Going wrong as in "against the Even Flow";

- Going wrong as in "mishandling our natural, God given systems through sheer ignorance, superstition and false indoctrination of the ages".

- Going wrong as in "stubbornly refusing to replace the old illusions with EXPERIENCE, no matter how much it hurts us".

To find our way back to how it's all supposed to work requires, however, that we let go of just about EVERYTHING we've ever been told is right or true about the World, about people, and about the energy system and go right back to the drawing board, challenging EVERYTHING and demanding that EVERYTHING prove itself to be real, workable and effective - not as a faceless herd of statistics in a laboratory but FOR ONE PERSON AT A TIME, in their own World, in their own life.

Now, in this brief article there isn't the space to get into the details of what, how and why - all it is designed to do is to start your thinking and investigation into your own energy households, what you do with energy, where you lose it, what's REALLY going on WITH YOU, where there are shortcomings in vital nourishments in YOUR LIFE. I'll give you a tip though - if you start with the forms of energy I referred to in the title of this article and do nothing else but pay some attention as to what YOU PERSONALLY are DOING with those types of energy, you will gain some very interesting insights, right away.

I would like to leave you with one "little" exercise to back up my assumption that in order to make a brand new understanding, one person at a time, of how to work within the Oceans of Energy and experience this World, this life in a "first person", "you and me" LOVE AFFAIR with the Universe that NEVER ends, we HAVE to challenge ruthlessly what has gone before.

Kundalini ....

I went through a stage where, just for fun, I would do the exact opposite of what it said to do in a learned, dusty book of the ages.

You know about Kundalini, right?

Goes up your spine and when it rises, you're supposed to get instant enlightenment (and/or madness, just so we have some severe reservations and can't be congruently willing this occurrence any longer!).

Just for fun, try the following. First, try the standard "Kundalini Rising".

Start with the base chakra and try and make the energies go up and out to your star chakra.

Consider how that felt.

Take a break for a moment (walk around, drink some water, "break state").

Now, try Silvia's "Kundalini Falling".

Start at the top with the star chakra, connect it up with the Universe, and then let all that boundless, incredible energy run **downwards** through your chakras.

Compare the two experiences.

Especially, answer these questions on the following points:

- Which is more "user friendly"?
- Which is "easier to do"?
- Which "feels better" whilst you're doing it?
- Which "feels righter" whilst you're doing it?
- What is your overall state of mind/body/spirit **AFTER** these two exercises, respectively?
- Which one of the two would you do again, tonight perhaps, tomorrow and every time you need a boost?
- Which one of the two do you reckon does your energy system more good, and which does more harm?
- Which one contributes more to a sense of connectedness to the Universe?
- Which one contains more aspects of information transmission and **GAINING** something from the exercise?

- Which one would you show to a loved one, or a child?

Ok. It's a personal experience, what can I say.

JUST YOUR EXPERIENCE, not some holy guru's declaration straight down from Heaven or a hugely expensive "scientific" study by important people with heads the size and weight of those found on the Easter Islands.

Just what **YOU** felt.

I would tell you though that what you feel isn't right or wrong, it is what YOU FEEL and that is what is THE ONLY TRUTH AND THE ONLY REALITY for your own energy system.

Keep paying attention to the Oceans of Energies **and your perceptions and experiences** amidst their manifold currents but most of all, **keep on playing**.

That, as they say, is always a step in the right direction.

And the **ONLY** way to learn to **KNOW**.

First Published by The Sidereus Foundation 20. 05. 2002

Energy Nutrition – Essential Health For The Energy Body

What Is Energy Nutrition?

There are all manners of energies coming in to the energy body at all times. We live in a veritable "Ocean of Energy" which is generated by literally **everything** - from the ground beneath to the radiation from the sun, the moon and the stars; every living being exudes vast quantities of energies all the time on a very wide bandwidth and this includes people, animals, plants, insects.

Human beings are probably the only species on this planet who have the ability to actively and consciously "shield" themselves from certain types of energy and actually are able to reject energies that exist, and may very well be most beneficial to them.

This is specifically achieved by the mechanism of "thought" or "intention".

Intention & Energy

A very common saying is, "Where intention goes, energy flows."

Although we cannot move a rock by staring at it, we can indeed influence energetic realities with intention. This is because intention and thought and energy are **of the same realm** and structurally designed to work with one another.

This process is natural and in action all the time; humans sometimes turn deliberately to trying to shape energetic realities with their intention, for example in the act of prayer, spell casting, making a wish, or the more modern versions of affirmations, goal setting, visualisation and so forth.

What has been forgotten and this is proving to be perhaps one of the most major causes for ill health and unhappiness amidst a well fed, well sheltered and well supported population in the First World today, is that **our intention is interfering with energy exchanges ALL THE TIME.**

This is entirely unconscious; "energy awareness" is restricted to the few in our societies who make an effort to find out more about energy healing, come into contact with the powers of the energy system because of ill health or because they are studying martial arts perhaps.

Energy Reversals or "Saying NO To Healing"

In Energy Therapies there exists the concept of a "reversal". Simply put, it means that a part of the energy system has gone into reverse and works **against** the rest of the system, much like an engine that has been switched over to run backwards instead of forwards.

Most often, this becomes apparent when there was a major trauma which caused such an occurrence. On the simplest level, it could be said that any time we say, "No!" to something, this is a command - a direct command! - to a part of the energy system to stop and go into reverse.

These reversals in the energy system express themselves always in something seemingly being stuck and unmovable - an injury that simply will not heal, no matter how much ointment and bandages are applied; a psychological reaction that simply won't recede, no matter how much therapy and healing is given.

The Energy Therapists talk about "specific" and "massive" reversals, for indeed there are people who show in their bodies that they have said, "No." to healing.

Many more people show in their behaviours, their bodies, their real lives absolute evidence that they must have said, "No." to prosperity, to happiness, to success, to loosing weight, to living without an addictive substance - these are the people who endlessly and desperately try **everything** to overcome their problems but their problems remain, no matter what the treatment, no matter if it is successful with everyone else who has undergone it, no matter how precarious or even life threatening their situation is becoming.

The power of intention and decision over the behaviour and activities in the Energy Body is simply extraordinary.

A simple decision, once it has occurred as a by-product of trauma or experience, will remain untouchable and out of view for an entire lifetime, causing endless suffering and misery - in the Quantum spaces of energy, time is no healer at all and something that happened perhaps 75 years ago is as red raw and as "now" as it ever was.

However, in the Quantum spaces of energy, there also resides the possibility of even the most extensive trauma being healed right now, in an instant, but for the asking. Please note that this does not mean instant healing on the **physical** because we are talking about the Energy Body here; yet it is clear that when the Energy Body functions as it should, the physical body will be supported in its own self healing endeavours from the ground up and true healing has a chance to take place.

Particularly the "reversals" are of prime importance in Energy Nutrition, because it is in the simple act of saying, "No." to an incoming energy, a barrier is created to that energy which keeps it out of the system - a malnutrition situation cannot help but ensue.

All You Need Is Love ...

It has been said by every great prophet, every great religious leader, across time and space of humanity, that love is the greatest healer and that the energy of love creates healing miracles.

There are, indeed, hundreds if not thousands of scientific studies conducted all around the First World to the effect of human attention - which is a precursor for human love - on healing, well being, symptom alleviation. One of the most famous of these had nursing staff withholding attention from newborn babies in an orphanage in the 1950s, yet giving these babies all the physical caretaking and food they could only require.

The babies began to fade and when they began to die, the experiment was abandoned as the staff refused to go on any further.

Attention energy relieves measurably the symptoms of every disease, every illness. It "makes people more intelligent", calmer, more sociable, more resourceful. It helps them live longer, even if this attention energy is provided by non-human species such as dogs, cats and monkeys, even birds as studies conducted with the effects of having pet animals in old people's homes and geriatric wards attest to.

Attention energy is an **essential nutrient** for the energy body and when people don't get this energy, they fade away, go mad and they may even die.

With the population density of the First World, how can it be that this vital life energy seems in such short supply?

The answer is simple and profoundly sad. This energy is NOT in short supply; rather the problem lies in the fact that individual humans do not receive and process it correctly. Indeed, the ability to receive and process attention energy from other humans is probably the most likely and directly related factor that decides on any given person's health and happiness throughout their lifetimes.

Shields To Joy & Ecstasy

When a man goes up to a woman in a bar, looks her in the eye and says, "You are very beautiful.", what kind of response on the energetic level would you expect to see if energy exchanges could be made visible by a special video camera?

Would this energy travel across to the woman, be openly received, taken into her many systems, moving through these systems as the energetic equivalent of a digestion takes place, powering and re-charging all manner of sub-systems in it's travel, and then smoothly flow out to leave the lady in question vibrant, happy and glowing?

Clearly, the answer to this is a resounding NO.

Indeed, the lady in the bar may have put her shields up before the man even got close enough to send his message to her. Her reaction to the energetic wave travelling towards her would most likely be more shields still, as she thinks, "He only wants X from me, he doesn't know me, he's lying, I don't like him, he looks ugly, etc." ... and many more thoughts of the same kind, all of which create an impenetrable barrier to what could otherwise have been a highly nourishing energy exchange.

This strong example was chosen to illustrate a basic point about energy exchanges in humans. It also brings up the most common objections to "taking energies into the system" - would this not be a disaster? Would the lady in the bar not end with AIDs **if** she didn't have all her shields to keep these energies at bay?

The answer to this is that such considerations are clearly coming from a very different place and NOT from considering the Energy Body and it's requirements.

Allowing the energy from the compliment to pass into her system, through and out and as a result, feeling better, more nourished, more powerful, more **energised** does NOT lead to our lady in the bar becoming stupid all of a sudden - quite in the contrary. Someone with a balanced, energised system tends to experience great mental clarity, not to mention **emotional stability** which clearly, is a good place to make decisions about what courses of action might be for the best.

Human & Other Energies

One of the reasons that people in the First World often turn to pets for energy suppliers is that the barriers against love, affection and attention from other people are not in place and the energies can flow freely. There is, of course, the other side of the coin. Animals do not have barriers as a rule to **incoming** energies and they will actually accept attention **from** humans who are bursting to give these - but cannot find any fellow human recipients for their energies, only barriers upon barriers where their contributions bounce out flatly too.

But of course, there are other energies that are not received, to which we have said, "NO!" at some point and which are no longer available for the essential nutrition and widely varied energy diets our Energy Bodies require for full functioning.

Weather is a good example of this. Storms, rainy weather and cold weathers are **tremendous** energy providers - if one would open up to this. Current group consensus in the First World, however, is that anything other than a sunny, warm day with a cloudless sky is "bad weather" and must be avoided, bemoaned, and shielded against in every way possible.

The very act of saying "NO!" to "bad weather" in and of itself reverses and disables parts of the energy system and this leads to people who hold these views to becoming more acutely affected by cold or rainy weather in return - with mental depression or psychosomatic flare-ups, for example.

There are many other naturally existing energies that are blocked by individuals. Many people have strong colour preferences - someone might say, "Orange is not my colour." or, "I don't like the colour orange." which is the equivalent of saying, "NO! to orange."

Thus instructed, the energy body deflects that particular vibration and we are very literally, in scurvy conditions.

It is important to note that the processes which have been described in this article are not an addition or a new invention, but simply represent an observation about naturally occurring exchanges in reality.

It is impossible to repair a person's self esteem, for example, who hold it to be the truth that they are worthless, with counter-examples or by sending them (telling them, showing them, demonstrating to them) that this is a false decision IF this person is INCAPABLE of receiving the energies associated with this sentiment.

Thus it is possible that the most beautiful model on Earth is in tears because she is convinced that she is ugly; the most beloved person who has innumerable family members and friends who all care deeply about them is entirely convinced that "No-body loves me."; and the most talented and gifted people can state with absolute conviction that, "I am worthless."

It needs to be clearly understood that it is not the **meanings** of such words or phrases which will heal and put a great many things to rights, but the **energies** these words and phrases contain and carry.

These energies go to the Energy Body and there, fulfill tasks of repair, of healing, of renewal. In doing so, they correct at the underlying energetic level what is wrong which then becomes reflected in psychological and physiological changes too.

In the case of psychological changes, as a person "takes readings" of their internal energetic landscapes, this translates directly into self concept understandings and realities.

The Essential Flow Of Energies

If we go back to the example of the lady in the bar, who was told, "You are beautiful." we will remember also the resistance to let such energies into ones system for fear that they might be believed and thus, become a reality.

Many of the human energy exchanges suffer from this false understanding, namely that if one was to open oneself and accept such incoming energy or information, one would necessarily **become** that in turn.

This is the fear and misunderstanding about energy exchanges of the "You are beautiful" kind just as well as about energy exchanges of the "You are ugly" kind - either way, it must not be "believed" because that would be a very bad thing.

It is of the essence to really understand that energy exchanges have absolutely nothing to do with believing something, thinking one is something or another as a result.

Indeed, a catastrophe for many people is that at one point, someone might have said something positive which on that occasion actually **did** enter the energy system. It felt so good that they attempted to **hold on** to the energy involved to keep feeling like that for longer.

This causes the most severe forms of disturbances in the Energy Body as it instantly blocks the channels designed to transport this kind of information - no further energy can come in from other sources in the future.

Also, as the energy is not passing through the system as it should, behind the blockage lie veritable wastelands of empty channels and the energy organs they were meant to supply, causing severe disturbances which will firstly manifest in emotions and if they go on for long enough, physiological sensations, pain and then actual illness.

This process is also in action with forms of energy that were stopped halfway through the system as they were being perceived as damaging, and energies that never get to enter the system at all because they are being blocked off before they get into the central Energy Body at all.

But apart from the damage to the energy system, there is another aspect to this and this is best explained by example. This is the report in my own words, written down only a few hours after it had happened.

Here is an extraordinary case story about a moment of intense love, experienced 30 years ago, a moment which should have been an instant transformation of the person who experienced it but was not because they took the energy and "enfolded it within their heart", keeping it there as a keepsake of the best moment in their lives. And there, it remained and it stopped any further flow or experience of something similar or even better - ruining this person's life entirely in the process and keeping them stuck in the past. What happened when they understood that they must complete the process that was started all those years ago?

Re-Learning To Process Energy Correctly

We are indeed, energy beings in an Ocean of Energies.

All we find in the Universe, all life on Earth and that includes human beings is **structurally designed** to process the flow of energies and to take part in the vast, vast cycles of life.

Energy needs to flow to be naturally correct and doing as it is designed to do. What we need to do in order to move closer to what is called The Even Flow of natural balance, is not learn something new, but to re-learn to correctly use the systems we were given.

We all have the ability to block energy and we have used this to our own disadvantage as a species for many thousands of years at least.

By definition, we all also have the ability to remove these blockages that were simply a side effect of living in a culture that seems blind to the Oceans of Energy.

We all have Energy Bodies, and within these Energy Bodies the channels and systems exist to truly feast in the Oceans of Energy.

What it takes to make this happen successfully, and easily, is firstly and foremostly to pay attention to how energy exchanges work and manifest "in the real World".

Energy manifestations are simply everywhere and once one starts to open ones awareness of such straightforward examples as energy exchanges which exist between humans, and between a single human and their environment, a great many things become very clear and obvious that never made any sense at all.

Energy nutrition, i.e. the understanding and realisation that our energy bodies have absolutely nutritional needs, is one of the aspects of this.

Further, even a base insight into this extraordinary realm will very quickly reveal which kinds of energies are missing, sorely needed, in desperately short supply in a person's body.

It is simply amazing how many previously insoluble problems become not only understood as to how they structurally function, but also how easy it is to find "energetic solutions" to what were in essence, always "energetic problems" in the first place - and thus could not be solved from other places and with physical/mental approaches at all.

Addictions, weight problems, identity problems and replacement activities of all kinds begin to make sense at last when viewed from the Energy perspective - here are people trying to use physical means to compensate for an injury, deficiency, disturbance in their energy systems which is absolutely and structurally doomed to failure.

In Conclusion

A wider understanding and experientially based exploration of the human energy body is of the essence if we wish to solve human mind/body problems that have been out of reach entirely for as many as 2000 years or more.

It is not suggested that caring for the energy body take precedence over care for the physical body.

What is suggested, however, is that there are many aspects of human health and well being that simply cannot be solved AT ALL from any other place or using any other means.

The human energy body exists. It is real and many hold it to be the very foundation of **all** physiological functioning in the long term.

The topic of "Energy Nutrition" is one of the most exciting avenues of exploration to make true, lasting changes in any individual's health, happiness and levels of satisfaction and achievement in their lifetime, that has been discovered in many years.

We might just find that, after all, we really do live in a Universe of total abundance that really does supply everything we need and more beside, and that's it there for everyone - simply for the taking.

First Published by Om Place December 2002

Heal Your Energy Body

In human healing in the First World, we have a clear distinction between the fields of healing the body and healing the mind. Indeed, practitioners who seek to heal the mind in many officially acknowledged modalities are not allowed to touch the body, literally and metaphorically both, at all unless a problem is held to be "psychosomatic" – not really physical at all but just "all in the patient's mind".

Holistic practitioners have been seeking for a long time now to overcome this mind-body division because it is so obvious that the two are not separate, that one causes another and that they are inter-related, intertwined and to treat one in the absence of another is basically non-sensical and less efficient than it should be.

One thing the First World allopathic and holistic approaches have very much in common still, however, is the drive to symptom reduction.

First World inhabitants do not consider health unless there is a problem.

There are aspects of First World behaviour which seem as though health is being considered – health food, fitness and dietary supplements are indeed a thriving business – but it isn't health people are after, but to look healthy and to function with efficiency and as though there actually was underlying health.

This, of course, is putting the cart before the horse as people who had an understanding of what health and healthy living is all about as far back as the Yellow Emperor.

When someone is actually healthy, it is then that they:

- look healthy (appropriate body proportions, muscle tissue where there should be, shiny hair and eyes, glowing skin, warm and supple body)

- think clearly (logic and intuition working together, creativity, problem solving skills);

- are emotionally balanced (able to experience the widest range of human emotions and being energised by the process; being able to approach life without fear and in the knowledge that they can experience);

- live pro-actively (being focussed and joyful, effective in one's actions, relating successfully to others, having the energy to build your dreams).

All these things arise from an underlying state of health quite naturally, without any struggle or hassle, without having to spend hours in the gym, grimly counting the calories at each meal, doing "mind gym" exercises or seeking personal development in therapy, courses and classes.

When the underlying state of health is absent or the underlying state of being is one of non-balance, chaos, disturbance and non-cooperation between the many systems that comprise the totality of a human being, no amount of fire fighting the symptoms can do more than mask the problems for any length of time.

Energetic Bodies, Energetic Health

Take any First World person, at random, from anywhere out of their busy lives and sit them down in a white room, on a white chair, right in front of you and look at them carefully.

Chances are, they are not getting enough exercise of the right kind. The right kind of exercise for a human body being NOT strapped to some machine which makes a part of the body move backs and forth repeatedly to build muscle or to lose weight; and it is also not running around on concrete surfaces for hours on end.

The right kind of exercise for a human being is to run some then jump and dance, to stretch and flex, to move fluently in many different ways, many different positions throughout every moment of every single day.

Clearly, they are not doing that.

No matter how dedicated to health this person would declare themselves to be, they are not moving around like an unfettered three year old would and it shows in their body – the older they are, the more it shows.

Now, we could tell them about that, show them the evidence, explain it all and surely, they would nod most earnestly, may make a resolve or two to re-organise their lives to "do more exercise" but there we are.

The cart is once again, before the confused looking horse and we already know that nothing will change.

This person is going to right back to their lives as they had previously; doing their eight hours in front of a computer screen, lying on a couch or whatever it is they do and returning to their lives exactly as it was.

Thus it is with the legions of dieters, health seekers, exercisers and all those other First World folk who want to make changes for the better in their lives because their lives hurt to live the longer it goes on, but in the end, simply can't.

But WHY? That is the question I have been fascinated with for as long as I can remember.

WHY are we like this? Why don't we stop hurting ourselves with our daily lives and do something else instead?

In my quest to find the answer to that particular question, I turned to the mind as the driving force for behaviour – I looked into psychology.

A Healthy Mind in a Healthy Body ....

When I began to investigate what happens with health of mind, or the absence thereof, how it was treated and how it came about, I noted right away that exactly the same processes were in action as were happening with the body.

People would have real problems with their mental functionings, and as with physical fitness, it is as easy as pie to spot where things are going wrong and what they should be doing instead. Instead of being nasty to themselves, they should be more supportive of themselves, for example. That would work with just about every form of problem, just as eating a healthy diet would work with about every physical problem to bring about a real and noticeable change for the better.

So simple and so obvious the solutions – but once again, here is the vexed question of WHY yet again. The mind holds the answer no more than the body, being engaged in exactly the same kind of inverted happenings as the physical body was also.

And then, there was the matter of "emotions".

Emotional "Freedom"?

Roger Callahan, a Californian psychologist, began a true human revolution in the early 1980s by discovering that emotions could be made to disappear by treating the human energy system.

He had patients tap on major meridian points which were disputed by First World science as to whether they existed at all but had been in use by other human cultures for at least 10,000 years at that time and this resulted in emotions, such as fear, anxiety, stress, anger, sadness and so on simply "disappearing".

From this groundbreaking discovery, the whole field of Energy Psychology began to grow at a rapid rate almost immediately, as the First World inhabitants jumped with desperation on the idea that you could "simply tap your emotions away".

If you were not afraid anymore, then you could do all sorts of things that were out of reach before – just as someone who might have lost 100 pounds in weight might all of a sudden have access to public swimming pools, glamorous clothes and the approval of their friends and neighbours.

Now, it's true what I just said, namely that the First World inhabitants "jumped onto the idea in desperation". Of course, they were and are desperate to find a cure for emotions. Emotions are inordinately powerful pains and pleasures that can rip you apart, turn your life upside down or simply condemn you to a hell of nothingness and suffering until you die.

I, of course, was one of these "First World inhabitants" and I tapped to destroy my emotions just as desperately as the others who got hold of a pain relief at long last and after decades of suffering.

And I do believe it was because I was able to remove the most intense of these pains which caused my mind and body to live in a constant state of confusion to one day, wake up and look around with amazement and to say, "Wait a minute. What are these emotions we are removing? What is it that we are tapping away so happily here? Why do we have emotions at all? If we are natural systems where everything has a place and an important function, then what is the function of emotions?"

It took me a while but I do believe that I can answer that question now – what emotions are and what their function is and from that starting point, a whole new idea of health and health care was beginning to emerge. New, you should say, to me – what I found was echoed across the ages by those who had worked with the human energy system before, and it was this which finally convinced me that I was right about my assumptions.

What Are Emotions?

Simply put, emotions are the feedback devices through which the energy body communicates with the conscious mind, just as physical pain is the feedback device through which the physical body communicates with the conscious mind about its states of being.

These "feelings" which I prefer to call "sensations" because they always have a physiological component too, whether we recognise this at the time or not, are cries from the invisible dimensions of our own self, that actual reality which I call the energy body.

This energy body does actually exist; it has systems not unlike the organs of the physical body; pathways not unlike the veins and arteries of the physical body; nutritional requirements, an immune system, and all of that is true and real in spite of the fact that all knowledge or occurrence of this has been edited out of awareness by the First World medical science for the past 500 years or so.

When we "tap an emotion away" we are not actually tapping a pain away – to be able to make a pain go away, you have to heal the underlying injury which caused it in the first place.

The Energy Psychologists and especially the ones who use the tapping techniques to stimulate the main energy body meridians, often talk of "removing blockages" in the system. You could think of the emotions resulting from these blockages as the equivalents to the inordinate physical pain one would feel with thrombosis – a blocked flow causes the entire surrounding erea to go on red alert and the pain is spread far and wide, much further than the original seat of injury that may only be the size of a pinprick.

The Progression Of Disease

The ancient systems of Indian and Chinese medicine clearly say that any disease starts with the energy body being out of balance. Now I never really understood this properly and like most if not all First World inhabitants, gave it little thought beyond that it sounds nice in theory but hey, I've got a raging toothache, pass me the painkillers!

This is the cart before the horse again, or rather should I say, that is the Caesar and Jupiter confusion.

The Romans, a very practical people indeed, used to say, "Give to Caesar what is Caesar's, and to Jupiter what is Jupiter's.", thereby acknowledging that there are times and places for the energetic and the hard and you shouldn't get them confused, or else nothing good can come of it.

What we have been doing is giving only to Caesar and paying attention to Caesar only, leaving Jupiter quite out of the equation and that is a very costly mistake indeed.

There is a completely clear and logical transition between the happenings at the energetic level and the manifestation of physical disease in the Hard (my term for physical reality).

It really does all start with the energy body.

When this energy body is getting stressed or injured, the warning calls and warning signs are put out and they are our emotions – small fleeting ones at first, then building up in direct correlation with the severity of the imbalance which tends to get worse when no action is taken to put right what went wrong.

Think of it like this – you step on a small thorn. It hurts and you know it is there, you have sustained an injury. The natural response would be to stop, to sit down, extract the thorn, lick the wound (or engage in some other activity to stop infection), then favour the foot for as long as it takes for the wound to heal when walking is of the essence, and when it isn't, to sit down and keep the foot off the ground.

But that is NOT what we First World folk do.

When we step on the metaphorical thorn, we ignore the pain. If we happen to be on the warpath, we will manfully walk on and on, even run into battle. When the pain gets worse, we will exert our will power to think of something else. If it gets worse still, we go and take some painkillers, then stronger painkillers, and it is only when the whole foot has become so infected that walking has become entirely impossible and our entire life is filled with nothing but the pain of this is that we finally STOP and seek some treatment.

This is so for metaphorical thorns in our psychology as well as it is in our physicality.

We may accuse our allopathic healers of throwing all this heavy duty, nasty war based stuff at our injuries and that they are not really proper healers and so forth but look what we are presenting them with! How can they possibly be healers in the true sense of the word if all they see is rows upon rows of people who should have sought help with the tiny thorn a year ago when it was still easy to heal – we have literally left them with no other choice now than to cut off the entire leg to save our lives.

This is how the unsubtle and seemingly brutal First World health care systems have come into being, namely as a response to a population which doesn't understand that you need to understand health first and that living follows suit from there, and not the other way around.

Our injuries start in the energy system.

From there, they show up by the means of emotions which get successively worse and more profound. Now, these emotions turn into sensations – physical sensations like the proverbial "being punched in the stomach" as someone might describe the emotional feeling of having being told, "You're fired" only there was no physical fist involved at all, at least not one that anyone else could see.

These physical responses, if repeated often enough, just simply become physical disease, just the same as if the person who was fired indeed was physically punched in the stomach repeatedly – the stomach will become damaged and physical sickness manifests.

That is the simple, direct, cause and effect progression between the energy body, via emotions into physical disease – there is nothing metaphysical about it, there is nothing spooky about it, there is nothing weird about it; it is a simple, plain fact and the evidence is there for all to see who wish to open their eyes to it.

Healing The Energy Body

And now, we come to a simple result of the above processes which is entirely logical and for many, will bring a huge sigh of relief, may they be healers or suffers, or most probably, both.

We cannot force ourselves to lose weight with willpower alone over a lifetime – what a struggle! What an energy expenditure! What a never ending battle! What an outlook – a nightmare that never stops, can never stop and will wear us down, more and more as time goes by.

But what we can do is to heal the systems of the energy body that are causing the malfunctioning thoughts and behaviours that arise directly from the injuries of the energy body.

When we do that, there will be no more malfunctioning thoughts and behaviours.

They will simply cease to exist, just like those emotions that were simply tapped away because the basis for their existence has been removed – the original energetic injury has finally been healed and now, the pain simply STOPS.

If you recall, I said that the progression was:

Energy Body Injury -> Emotion -> Pain -> Physical Disease

Along the same lines, we have this progression:

Energy Body -> Emotion -> Pain -> Psychological Disease

... because the energy body underlies of course all health for the totality (the mind/body/spirit unit a human being represents).

Now, it is my desire to not so much heal what is already fully fledged and broken out disease. There are many who do this professionally and they are good at it – be it the last resort allopathic healers who amputate that leg because their owner failed to seek help when it was still just a thorn in the sole of their foot, or the holistic healers who point out that the likelihood of infection would have been a lot less if they had eaten a proper diet, taken care of the wound properly in the first place and have remedies to re-stimulate the systems of the body that might be able to cure this still; or be it the psychologists who would try and make a change to the person believing that it was a good thing to walk around for a year with a thorn in their foot or that winning the war was more important than losing a leg.

What I want to do is something else entirely.

I want to talk about true health – about healing and restoring the energy body from the ground up, to repair the energetic injuries that cause all the psychological and physiological suffering which is already there and to prevent any further suffering in the future.

I want to do this because repairing the energy body is so easy – all it takes for it to happen is to have the will to health, because the energy realms are absolutely responsive to thought and intention.

Healing In The Quantum Realms

You might have heard me say this before, but I will repeat it because it is so centrally important.

When you stare at a wound, you cannot will it to close. Well you can, and it might make the wound close in statistically, 15% - 18.5% less time than if you hadn't stared it at solidly for a week but that is just basically a huge waste of time of energy and effort, because the effort expended is in no relationship to the results achieved.

Energy healers across the ages have driven themselves mad because of this – it does a little so there must be something there that works but there seems to be no proper cause and effect between effectiveness and mental energy expended (as in praying for a sick person, hands on healing and so forth).

The fact is that actually, energy healing isn't supposed to heal the physical body at all. That is the wrong tool for the wrong job – like trying to hammer in a nail with a fine screw driver.

Intention (as in spells, prayers, wishes, attention, sending love and so forth) MOVES ENERGY.

That is what it is for, that is what it is designed to do, and it is incredibly efficient at doing just that.

The energy body exists in a kind of quantum space – no time, no distance, that kind of thing. Here and if attention is focussed HERE, the energy body responds immediately and instantly to intentions of restoration, of healing, of re-establishing the Even Flow.

Here, and ONLY HERE, we can heal the most complex injuries for the price of a simple thought.

Here, and ONLY HERE, we can heal what lay broken and fallow for decades in a single instance.

That is the most marvellous thing imaginable.

If we focus our attention where it belongs, namely on the energy realms and the energy body, cause and effect is restored and effort and reward work smoothly, quickly and with immediate results.

This does NOT mean that when we focus on the energetic injury underlying a physical disease, that the physicality is instantly repaired, please let us be clear about that in all ways.

What we repair is only the energy body – that is my only desire and outcome for the system which has been called EmoTrance.

It is a healing system that does NOT seek to alleviate psychological or physical suffering; it is not a symptom remover, not a response to a pressing practical need of the "Please take this sensation away so I can go on with my busy life."

EmoTrance is a healing system without direction or cause other than that it is logical and sensible to restore that which was broken, to heal that which was injured, to bring back to flow that which was perverted and blocked, and to have the energy body be what it should have always been – a glowing functioning entity of such perfection and beauty, it shines in all ways in the realms where it resides.

It is not that I am not aware of how much suffering there is, nor that I lack compassion for the suffers.

It is not that I don't want to help people who are in pain.

But the fact is that there are millions who do this far more effectively than I can.

What I want to know is what happens when you repair the energy body and bring its systems back online, back to a true state of health.

I can't begin to know or imagine.

We are talking about a state of being that might never have existed before in human history, that might have never been sought because it has never been modelled.

A fully functioning, fully nourished energy body, with all systems on line and exchanging energy freely with the Universe at every level is something that I have never seen or even thought to seek – before now.

But it is something that we can have – and I for one, would want to experience what that would be like, for the possibilities inherent beyond our current states of being and not just so the pain will stop.

In magic, there is a principle which states that when you need something, and you ask for this from a state of neediness, you cannot ever get it – the very state of neediness precludes the flow of that exact thing you need towards you and blocks you from being offered it at all.

This "law of magical nature" has been the greatest headache, despair and conundrum for all and any across the ages who were desperate for help and begged for it on their knees; it has brought so many to magic and to healing who otherwise would have never given these states of existence the time of day in the first place and left them bitterly disappointed in the process.

I believe that when we work in the energy realms, with the intention of restoring our own energy bodies, not from a state of neediness but from a true desire to bring back to being an Even Flow we have never experienced before, we will open the doors to a form of magic we never had within our reach before.

This is a kind of magic that cannot be found by searching with intelligence; by disciplined study or self deprecation; not by following a guru or a teacher but only by experiencing it first hand, one human being at a time.

This is the magic I seek and for which I have developed the EmoTrance system that reminds us of the basic principles of true healing from the ground up.

I know that it is used primarily at this time to alleviate suffering and to repair symptom based problems of one kind or the other and that is fine too, because any repair work you do, any steps you take towards restoring the Even Flow in your energy body is a step towards that state of being we don't know yet what it might be, what it might feel like, what it might be like to experience.

Heal your energy body.

With volition and just because you want to bring it back on line in all its potential perfection and beauty, as an end in and of itself and not just so you can make a few extra bucks, work a few hours a day more, get rid of that headache, find a new boyfriend or impress the neighbours.

That is nothing compared to what just might be within our reach to do – at the energetic levels, for the asking and for the focussed desire and intention that it should be so.

First Published by Positive Health, January 2003

ADDENDUM 4 - EMOTRANCE SESSION STORIES

These session stories are contributed by ETPs who are daily using EmoTrance in a healing setting with their clients as examples for you of what it is like to be in a session – both as a client as well as a healer.

EmoTrance is used by practitioners and healers from many different modalities because it is so easy and flexible. Even in the most rigorously supervised "psychotherapy" style settings, it sounds not very different from some form of talking therapy or metaphor treatment; there are no strange holistic tools, no wording which might give away that we are doing nothing but pure energy healing here instead of standard psychology!

EmoTrance combines beautifully with all other forms of Meridian & Energy Therapies (EFT, TFT, TAT, BSFF etc) and can slide in and out of physical treatments such as massage and acupuncture with absolute ease and even without the clients being any the wiser as to what the ETP might have been doing.

When combined with Reiki, Therapeutic Touch, Quantum Touch, faith healing, laying on of hands, EmoTrance becomes truly magical and especially if the practitioner has truly accepted that "I am a healer", you can expect to see truly outstanding results.

EmoTrance also lends itself perfectly to the more "cerebral" or "logical" approaches to changework such as coaching and NLP, fitting seamlessly into the paradigm, the treatment forms and the techniques whilst supercharging their effectiveness simply by removing blocks and shields to have those techniques really work as their originator intended.

The same of course applies to the more esoteric schools of healing, of magic, of shamanic work; being structural and so very basic, EmoTrance has never an issue with the techniques being used, with the mindsets being used, and even Catholic priests can use it to help their clients, just as well as a Reiki practitioner or a Reflexologist might.

EmoTrance really does fit in with everything but there is one modality that sparkles more than most when the "fairy dust" of EmoTrance has been added, namely all forms of hypnotherapy. With a practitioner who has an experiential understanding of trance states and no fear of working in those different layers and levels, truly profound changes can be had that literally change lives.

But enough of the introductions; here is a short selection of "real life" session stories from EmoTrance practitioners and their clients for us to consider, to learn from and to enjoy.

Fibromyalgia And Old Emotions

Contributed by Kath Baker, ETP

This client is in her 40s and was suffering with Fibromyalgia.

During the consultation she told me her grandfather to whom she was very close to died when she was 10.

At the age of 11 she was experiencing lightening pain in her wrists, had many inexplicable pains later and various operations. She always had a bad back, was allergic to tea (used to drink 40 cups a day, but had cut down to 20). For the last 6 years was unable to work due to the fatigue, headaches, and pain. Although she knew tea upset her she was unable to cut down any more.

When we talked about granddad she told me she missed him a lot but she did not cry when he died. I knew she used to sit on granddads lap to be very close to him and they used to drink tea together. I felt that this loss was contributing to her illness in some way. I used the ET process during the reflexology treatment whilst she was getting in touch with the feeling of how much she missed him.

As the energy moved through her body it was at times intense, and exactly the same as that experienced during a fibromyalgia attack. She was able to describe clearly the routes it was travelling and these mirrored specific meridian pathways exactly. After two such sessions she was experiencing hardly any pain, when a stress occurred she was able to go and lie down and soften the energy and allow it to leave, massively reducing the duration of an attack.

After her second treatment she experienced such a rush of energy she was awake most of the night! She felt this was her cue to try to cut down on tea. I gave her dietary advice to eat as unprocessed a diet as possible , no wheat and dairy and plenty of water. She also began taking a whole food product consisting of dried fruit and vegetable juices in capsule form to supplement her diet and aid detoxification. She dealt with her cravings for the tea and the accompanying headache when she tried to remove the last cup easily. After just three sessions her doctor and her physiotherapist were amazed, she has gone into remission after 6 very painful years.

The bonus of working this way I think she would say was how it really showed her how emotions were affecting her physicality. We continue to use ET during reflexology sessions for all stressful situations In total this lady has received 7 sessions and is now doing a part time job, hardly any pain. The pain in her back is now gone also.

Kath Baker, ETP - Hayling Island, PO11 9SN, United Kingdom

Low Self Esteem

Contributed by Jeanette Pettiford, MA, PhD, EFT, ETP

A young lady presented with low self-esteem as her main problem that was affecting all areas of her life and her current love relationship. She stated the low self-esteem came from childhood abuse.

We started with the usual listening and validating and some pre-explanation of what EmoTrance does. Once the client understood and was willing to proceed I asked her to tell me more about her low self esteem until she was tuned into it at which point I asked her where she felt that issue in her body as she thought about it.

From there we followed the basic EmoTrance protocol, which worked very well and seemed to make time fly for us both (an hour felt like 15 minutes.) The energy in her body softened and moved to various places and then the client had a strong urge to exhale. I told her that was a good exit point and she continued exhaling very long, even out breathes that seemed to make her feel lighter with each one. She said she could feel it leaving her body. I supported her to continue until she felt it was all out. She breathed for a long time, over and over, out it came. The majority of the session was basically her exhaling.

When she felt she was done, I challenged her with her presenting issue and told her she would always have low self esteem because of her abuse.

She responded with a completely calm, serene voice and stated that that simply wasn't true about her any longer. She needed no further explanation and neither did I because it was so true and matter of fact. She stated it clearly as fact and then kept saying how amazing this was. She repeated a few times "that was amazing!" that got me feeling very good about ET all over again and it struck me how amazing it was for energy that was stuck for years to come out and the issue be altered for the better as a result. We both agreed if everyone knew EmoTrance there would probably be no wars.

This session was different than many others I've had in that there wasn't a lot of visuals or needing to check in and keep reminding them to soften and move, etc. once it moved it did and kept moving out through the breath the whole time and she just surrendered to it and kept breathing until she felt done.

I followed up a week later and she said she still felt the low self-esteem was gone, she was practicing EmoTrance on herself and sounded very calm and that she really didn't have anything to report other than she had a great week and was feeling fine. She expressed her desire for a session in the future on an entirely different matter.

Birth Issues

In contrast I had a recent session with someone who had an issue since birth since she was born a preemie and then "given away" and that the resulting feelings about it permeated her entire life and threatened to end her love relationship which she did not want to happen.

With this case, I jotted down all the words she used in describing her issue and then went ahead with the ET protocol. Her energy softened and moved but each time it did a new aspect or visual or metaphor came up that she felt the need to speak on. Each time she did I listened and then asked her where she felt that in her body and went into the ET protocol. This continued on for several rounds of ET protocol and then her responses about more aspects coming up.

She was very honest about how she was doing and what she was unwilling to do - (which is very important feedback for the practitioner and shows the importance of safety to be honest session. Giving an accepting, supportive presence, and being interactive with the client, is supporting their empowerment to take care of themselves.) The client mainly did not want to cry in someone else's presence. I said tears could be a good exit point but since that made her uncomfortable I said to soften the energy around her eyes, brush away the energy of the tears and support it to move, which it did and she did not have to cry it out.

Her energy continued to move, we utilized ghost hands and it seemed it would never end. I'd challenge her on one thing and another aspect of it would come up, I'd ask her where she felt that in her body and so on. This session ran over time, but I felt she was moving exactly what she needed to move.

An interesting thing about this one was that as her energy was moving out she didn't want it to be "wasted" and just fall out onto the floor or into space. She felt it was her love energy leaving and not having any place to go or be received. I went with that by asking her where did she want to send her love and she replied that she wanted to send love energy to orphanages and I said how I'm sure they'd love to receive her special love, so for a long time she sent this energy out. That really made her feel a lot better.

When this part was done she sort of got into her head and her practical concern of not knowing where to look for a job, that she wanted to work in an orphanage but still felt her love wouldn't be received anywhere and this caused her a distressful feeling. Where do you feel that in your body I asked? And so we moved that. After some time I challenged her on that one by saying that no matter how hard she looked she would not be able to find anyplace that would receive her love and her response what a resounding "F*** you" and anger, I didn't skip a beat as I asked her where she felt that in her body and that was a hard, deep energy that needed to soften which took some time and then proceeded to move out. There was relief with that round. The anger was gone and she felt it was possible that there were lots of orphaned kids out there would love to receive her love.

I felt this was good progress and a good stopping point.

Again, at the end of the session I hear the client say, "that was amazing." It gets me excited about doing EmoTrance with people.

Upon follow-up a week later, the client reported feeling good and still practicing ET on herself here and there and a desire for another session on her relationship in the future.

PTSD From A Car Accident

Another session that went well had an unexpected outcome. I used EmoTrance on a person's PTSD symptoms, which had returned upon being involved in a car accident. Her original PTSD was from years back being in a major earthquake. The session went well, we went with her feelings and symptoms and where she felt them in her body, softened them and supported them to move and at the end of the session she felt not only were they all gone but the pain in her neck and shoulder from whip-lash were also gone (which we didn't even address or focus on or intend to move at all.)

Upon a follow-up e-mail she said she felt much better but had some "residual", I responded by reminding her to ask herself where she felt that in her body…soften…move…support it to find it's exit point. That was like a 'light bulb' going on for her as she realized that whatever she felt anything she could tune in and could use this simple technique. She requested future sessions for her and for the other person who was in the car accident with her, which we are in the process of setting up.

As with everyone I tell them I have homework for them: 1. I tell them to drink lots of water as water helps conduct energy 2. I tell them to get some rest and give themselves some time for their energy to "settle", 3. I tell them to keep practicing EmoTrance on themselves when anything came up by getting in the habit of asking themselves where they feel it in their body and 4. To call me a week later at a set time for a free follow-up.

These session stories were brought to you by (Jnet) Jeanette Pettiford, MA, PhD, EFT, ET, who can be contacted by phone in the United States at (619) 507-5152 or via e-mail at DrNet@earthlink.net

Johnny

Contributed by Tina Cooper, ETP

By the time 'Johnny' asked for help, he had been unhappy most of his life, but his unhappiness had now turned to despair following the breakdown of his third marriage. Friends had beseeched him to get help, as his slide down the slippery slope of depression was gathering pace. He was already receiving counselling through his GP, but this was about to come to an end as the practice would only fund a short course of treatment, which given the continuing problems, was not proving to be too successful anyway.

Johnny believed his problems originated from the abandonment he had experienced when his mother and father had left Johnny and his sister Carol with their grandparents whilst they moved several hundreds of miles away and started a business.

As soon as the EmoTrance process began, it was clear Johnny had constructed a very effective shield. The counselling had given him the idea that he should feel bad about his parents leaving, but he actually felt very little. When questioned, the only sensation he felt regarding this major incident in his life was a slight pressure in his chest. We ET'ed this away, (like fog lifting and being blown away) which proved to be a great introduction to the EmoTrance process, but it was clear that Johnny would need to do some work on his shield if he wanted to progress any further.

Using word triggers, ("Your mother left because she didn't want you"; "You were a disappointment to your parents - it's no wonder they didn't want to take you with them"; "You were useless so why would they want you around?" all of which had come from Johnny himself), we worked at slowly allowing some of this energy inside the shield.

Firstly Johnny used a very fine needle to inject just a few 'drops'. The result of this was a vague bubbling feeling all over his stomach area. He gathered this together into the one place and allowed it to raise, much like the bubble in a bottle of soda, until it left via his mouth. A little belch confirmed its departure.

We repeated the process, this time using a larger syringe. The sensation was stronger this time, and concentrated around his left side. Johnny described it as akin to having trapped wind.

He wanted it to depart in the same way as the bubbles, so it took the same route, up and out. I had asked him to track its progress with his hands, and he was pleasantly surprised at how his hands seemed to move of their own free will.

I think he was probably convinced I was the one who needed help when we begun, but ET was working its magic and Johnny was becoming more reassured that he could cope. What he had believed would be an overwhelming experience was proving to be no more stressful that a spot of daydreaming.

Buoyed up by his success so far, Johnny decided to 'open a window' on this shield - just the fanlight to start, but enough to cause a stabbing sensation just below his heart. I reminded him it was only energy, and that he had the skills to shift it. This he did, quickly and effectively by softening and moving the energy out through the top of his head.

The smiles should have given me a clue, but I asked him how he was feeling just to be on the safe side. Giggles were all I got in response. It had been such a long time since he'd felt so good he simply couldn't help himself. The rest of the shield was deconstructed in a similar way - opening the small window first, then the large one, until the energy was literally blowing through Johnny like a spring breeze into a stuffy room.

Now Johnny was actually feeling, over several sessions we were able to do a lot of work on the issues surrounding his parents' departure, all of which was very effective. The biggest success however, came when I suggested he telephone his dad and tell him he loves him. A previously stony, cold person unable to connect to the hurt he had carried with him all his life, became animated with so many sensations it was akin to watching a sack of snakes wriggling for freedom. Johnny had energy moving up and out of the top of his head, down each leg, flicking from the ends of his fingers, spewing out of his mouth. He had become very adept at the ET process and moved very quickly to shift whatever presented itself.

But did he meet the challenge? With a laugh he reached for his mobile and dialled!

Tina Cooper, ETP. 49 Southwell Road, Lowestoft, Suffolk NR33 0RW,
Tel. 01502 518913 - Email - meridianpsycho@aol.com

A Poor Relationship With Father

Contributed by Regan Duggan MH.CT, ETP

I would like to tell a story of a lady who had mentioned several times about the very poor relationship with her father. She started on about the years of mistrust, emotional and physical abuse to herself and family, for a while I made the age old mistake of trying to reason with someone who had a preconceived idea, this went on quite some time until eventually I conveyed the notion that there was no point hearing the same scratched record over and over and no desire at all to change it.

"There's no way you'll ever change the way I feel about my father," she me told me.

This lady had never been able to sit still for 5 minutes, couldn't watch a film, never had a decent nights sleep, was always on edge nearly all the time.

She believed that this stemmed from her father always telling her she was useless, would never achieve anything.

We started to do EFT on various issues such as I hate my father, he makes me sick, I can't stand him near me. Things were moving gradually when I suggested how would she feel if her dad came in the room right now, sat on the arm of the chair and reached over to touched her – immediately, she pinned herself to the back of the chair and an expression of total fear and shock came over her.

Right now it was time for EmoTrance!

"Where do you feel it." I asked.

"In my stomach, I feel sick."

I followed the standard process then as you should be aware of by now, and in the space of about a minute it had found its way out down to the feet and the feelings were gone. Her words were, "How the f*** did you do that!!"

I said, "I never- you did!"

When I heard from her again some time later, she told me that about a week after the session her father unexpectedly came into a pub she was at. She said, "There was absolutely no reaction at all, no feelings of anger or rage, just a 'Oh, that's my dad there' – I was totally calm."

She also told me that she now sleep like a log a night and can sit down and watch films all the way through.

In summary she has taken back a huge amount of power, which she had willingly given to her father, this in turn has allowed her to live her life as she sees fit.

Contributed byRegan Duggan MH.CT ETP

Anxious About Being Too Far From Home

Contributed by Gunnar Moritsen

I work with Hypnosis, Regression and Healing, but I have also been in UK two times, year 2000 and 2002, to learn EFT.

When I got a mail about EmoTrance something said to me "this I for you", but I didn't knew why?

I have had a block about EFT, because it seemed too "easy" to get results.

In November 2002 I was in UK and learned EmoTrance and one of the first work we did, was to clear my limitation to speak English and my "easy" limitation about EFT, and I stood in the room, I didn't knew what to say, my blocks were gone, so now I asked a lot in English and I also tapped EFT on another person!

At home in Denmark I have worked a lot with a client, he was anxious to be alone home, so his wife had always a phone with her so they could be connected. He was also unable to walk more than about 100 meters from his front door.

Now he feels safe at home, and he is also walking a longer distance, but his walking area is still only about 3 kilometres around his home.

Sitting at home I asked him to visualise he was walking to a shop he had mentioned (before last week, he had not been so far away for 26 years) and where he now was still safe. I said to him, "please walk longer down the street and tell me if you get an emotion". The emotion was some anxiety, "where in your body is this anxiety?" - "in my legs". I said "It is only energy so please focus on it and let it out".

A little later he said "I can't feel it any longer, it has gone".

"That's fine", I said "take on your coat and lets walk". We walked to the place he had visualised, walked a longer distance until a new aspect came up.

He was very satisfied so he didn't want to make more work this day, but he is now working alone and has mailed me, his walking distant has been even longer.

Severe Depression

I have also worked with a lady who has a very bad depression and the tablets don't help any longer, so she had received electric shock treatment several times.

We have had good results with Hypnosis/Regression, but the problem has not gone.

At the end of the last session I saw, she had some emotions when we talked, and I hadn't told anything her about EmoTrance, but I said "Where do you feel this emotion?" - "In my stomach". We did EmoTrance and she said by herself, very confused "What has you done to me? I don't feel anything in my stomach".

It is only energy.

Contributed by Gunnar Moritsen, Gronlokke 5, 4622 Havdrup, Denmark 4618 6029 - change@tdcadsl.dk - www.energychange.dk

A Wonderful Person ...?

Contributed by Ananga Sivyer, Dip Kin, CTAMT, ETP

Graham took to using EmoTrance easily for processing incoming negative statements, but was reluctant to use it when someone told him they thought he was a "wonderful person".

He winced and shifted in his seat and said that the statement made him feel very uncomfortable. When asked where in his body he felt that discomfort he said it was in his chest and felt hard and heavy.

He put his hands over the area as suggested and began softening the sensation by rubbing his hands around it in circular movements.

After a while he said it felt like something was moving down into his stomach but he didn't want to move it any further. He wanted to hold onto it and keep it there and not let it go.

We talked for a while about what might happen to a river that held on to its water with no sense of flow and movement and Graham readily volunteered that it would soon stagnate. He decided to hold the feeling in his stomach for a few moments more before moving the feeling through and out of his body as an experiment. When he felt ready he moved the feeling on. I repeated the statement to him again and watched as he breathed it in, put his hands briefly on his chest, then moved them down to his stomach, and noted that as he did so a trace of a smile appeared at the corners of his mouth as he moved the energy on and out of his body.

Again I offered the statement, by now he was smiling broadly and put his head to one side as if listening as he moved the energy through more quickly this time.

Then he opened his eyes and said, with a big grin, "Say it again"!

Contributed by Ananga Sivyer, Dip Kin, CTAMT, ETP –
http://Ananga.net

Changing A Life Pattern

Contributed by Sandra Hillawi

This is a case of using EmoTrance which was quite amazing. It is detailed, but I thought it might be useful to relate because of how we started and what the outcome was.

The client came in having a "sense" of some big issue coming up that she did not know quite how to deal with, nor even what it was (gulp! I thought!) and she proceeded to talk about her relationship and how she observed a pattern of her partner becoming aggressive and how she was blocking that energy and him getting worse as a result.

She related childhood patterns of her not being important or worthwhile when she had an opinion to express and was repressed then as she is in her relationship now, although wanting to change these patterns but being unable to do so.

We started with visualising the aggressive energy coming in from her partner. She felt it in her throat but also sensed a barrier outside in front of her face. We started to clear the energy in the throat and came back to the barrier which she would not even open a bit due to fear, which she felt in her stomach.

We went to the stomach to find a great pile of old dark energy, black coals which needed burning, energy never been moved before. The energy could only move so far up the body and was blocked. She then felt aware of another area, a treasure chest, never been opened. We opened it and what started to unravel was a network of channels which became her "tree of life" but outside of her body. She had to accept this whole tree into her body for all her energy pathways to be fully present. Then this sapling (her inner strength, herself, identity) had to be supported with stakes & wires (being so new, never having been there before). I asked her to run time faster so the tree got stronger, which it did, and only then could all the old blocked energy dark coals (original fear) fully flow out of her body. We also ran time faster then too, as the coals were taking ages to burn! During this whole process the client was burping continuously!

We finished with some cleansing & refreshing water energy and tested the original response to the incoming energy of her husband.

Her response was interesting. She said, she no longer needed to heal pains, as she now had inner strength & support that she'd never ever had before and that she could now relate differently with her partner and the world around her. It was like she'd found herself.

I have gone into this much detail to illustrate the point of the potential of this work, in this case, changing a life pattern! Amazing. And also to illustrate and re-emphasise, probably more to myself, to just trust the process and work with the person where they are at in their energy system.

Guilt

Another case today, came in for EFT for her guilt she was feeling since leaving her boyfriend last year. She was now in new relationship, pregnant but the guilt was causing her depression and beginning to effect eating patterns. I thought I would try EmoTrance instead. It took all of 10 minutes to clear it all up completely using the standard approach, clearing energy in the stomach, behind the eyes and back in the stomach again. I was amazed yet again.

Weight, Insecurity, Age Issues

The client is a singer and model, age 27. She has great insecurity issues about her age, about whether she'll make it in music since she is getting older and because she is so insecure she cannot go away from home and leave her partner to do recording work.

She also wants to lose weight and sees her IBS (irritable bowel syndrome) as stopping her and her sugar & chocolate cravings. Her passion is music but she's frustrated and trapped by her issues about age and insecurity and so cannot see herself ever being fulfilled. She has been feeling this way for years and had been to all kinds of therapists for help.

We started on the belief that she's past it in music at 26, using EFT, which then opened up to her having a few more years and now feeling more relaxed about it, and we did the rest with ET.

We looked at how she feels about her age, her insecurity about other beautiful younger singers, her insecurity about working away, her insecurity about her weight. I then paid her a compliment (she's stunning) and she received it, which amazed her as at her last visit she batted it right back to me. I checked her confidence levels, they'd gone up to 9 1/2, the last bit being due to her wanting to lose 1/2 stone. We then looked at what is stopping her from losing the 1/2 stone - her IBS and her chocolate & sugar cravings.

Interestingly, she'd felt a whole block of energy in her abdomen regarding her IBS from under her chest to the pelvis - we cleared this up with ET. Also, having reduced her actual sugar craving that day with EFT to 0, she still had a sense that she had a craving in general and that it was only 0 for today and it could still be a problem. After clearing the energy attached to that thought she said now chocolate & sweets just seemed to her like any other food and did not have any hold over her now and she was confident she could eat sensibly and lose the excess.

I was just amazed at how much we got through and how quickly she cleared all this up. It was so fast and she was totally clear on all the issues as we tested and tested afterwards to check.

Experiences From A Training Weekend

One student who had learned EmoTrance previously always wondered whether she was imagining the energy flowing and was not sure if she really could feel anything. When we did the shields exercise she had some BIG shields! On allowing the energy in bit by bit (and there was big fear to clear in the abdomen before we could start with the shield), she got to a point where she felt comfortable to drop the rest of the shield and let the remaining energy in ...... well the last bit of energy came rushing in and she literally jumped backwards 2 feet with the impact of it, and laughed in amazement! I think she's now a believer!

Another student decided to tackle the shield she had against her mother, who always used to grab her face and kiss her on the lips, right up to when she died, which made the student cringe and want to pull away! Although she had a good relationship with her father, she never had a loving relationship with her mother, who she felt was always wanting to drain her own energy.

Anyway, she was the volunteer for the shields demonstration. It was a big issue for her, which incidentally she processed in no more that 10 minutes, but it was so moving and beautiful. She said afterwards that she now felt love for her Mother which she never had felt before. It was interesting to observe that her whole demeanour had changed afterwards. She became so much more gentle, so beautiful and the absolute embodiment of love. It was amazing. She said it was the most important 10 minutes she had ever spent working on herself yet!

Contributed by Sandra Hillawi MH,CT,MT,ETP, Passion for Health Centre for Natural Healing, 96 Sydney Road, Gosport, PO12 1PL. Tel: 023 92 433928 - Email: sandra@passionforhealth.com - Website: www.passionforhealth.com

Panic Attacks & Pain In The Heart

I was working with a client who suffered from panic attacks and who had booked in for an EFT session.

Even beginning to talk about the problem caused the young lady to become very upset as she was thinking of a major core issue; she was crying hard and nearly abreacting, she was suffering massively.

I asked her to tell me where the 'failure' lived in her body and she told me it hurt in her heart; she put her hand over it and was crying quite loudly. I suggested for her to start softening it and it began to move. The more it moved, the calmer she became until she told me the 'failure' wanted to come out of her little finger.

I almost started to cry myself because, as you may or may not know, the little finger is where the heart meridian point sits and at just about the top joint it got a bit stuck.

So I reached over, tapped on the point and – out it shot!

YES!

The client was absolutely amazed, feeling much better than she had for a long time and I – felt almost evangelical after that, I must admit.

Gaura Dasi, APAMT, ETP. Chandra PDS, Kent, United Kingdom.

Email info@chandra-pds.co.uk Website http://chandra-pds.co.uk

Fear Of Criticism

Contributed by Susan Courtney BA, CTAMT, ETP

This client was a 27 year old lady with serious self confidence problems and in particular, an inability to deal with criticism and a severe fear of criticism.

I explained EmoTrance to her and she was willing to try it.

When the idea of being possibly criticised came up, she immediately described a tightness in the center of her chest that was very painful to her. This energy began to soften slowly and then move downwards. She followed the movement with her hands down towards the root chakra area and I noticed that a small smile began that became bigger and bigger the lower her hands went. Then the energy found its exit and she had this great big smile on her face and was eager to do it again because it felt so good.

We talked about the experience and she said that she felt completely different about being criticised now. She laughed and wondered if it would feel this good, certainly not something to be so afraid of any longer.

During our conversation I mentioned the idea of taking energy into yourself and she was eager to try this. There was a glass of water on the table. I was observing; as she put her hands around the glass and began to draw this energy into herself, I had a strong sensation of water splashing – I felt as though I was standing right next to a waterfall! We both said, "Wow!" and sat grinning at each other, that is the energised end state, when words simply fail.

This lady has become a dedicated fan of EmoTrance and has used it by herself on lots of issues since then, including treating herself for hunger pangs as she has had weight issues in the past; she is no longer so afraid of criticism and treats herself with EmoTrance if any old thoughts of failure or rejection occur to her.

Contributed by: Susan Courtney, B.A., CTAMT, ETP.
London/Tonbrigde, Kent, United Kingdom.

Email info@truechange.org - Website http://TrueChange.org

Understanding Shame In A New Way

Contributed by James Stanbridge, PhD

This client was a young lady who had been the victim of a multiple rape approx. 3 years ago. Since then, she suffered from severe anxiety attacks, paranoia, suicidal thoughts and sleep disturbances.

She had never visited with the same psychologist/counsellor/support group for more than a maximum of four sessions as she felt they did not understand her and did not care enough to try and understand how difficult things were for her.

She told me that in these groups and with the other psychologists she constantly felt pressured to do all these things, admit to all these things and this was all wrong. So I asked her where she felt the wrongness in her body and with surprise, she indicated her forehead. I explained EmoTrance a little and she was perfectly happy to let the "thick, nasty, slimy" energy soften and flow down her face, down the front of her body and out. She told me she felt much better after that and was surprised; then she made a quite off handed comment about shame. I picked it up and said that often people who had been attacked felt ashamed; to my surprise, she did not respond at all negatively to that suggestions but simply stated that she was extremely ashamed of "the mess they had made out of that girl" back then and that it was "the mess" who was ashamed of herself and now presented such a problem to her current self.

It was natural to ask her to look at "the mess" and to enquire where she felt the sensations in her body as she looked at "the mess". There was a shield in the way but once again I was surprised how the young lady immediately and eagerly worked at resolving this. It seemed natural and easy to her. When the shield between her current self and "the mess" had gone, she experienced strong emotions in her throat and under her eyes; another location was in the collarbone area. When these were cleared, she sat upright and surprised me by calling out loudly, "Oh my God, oh my God!"

She told me that she had mistakenly thought that "the mess" needed healing but when the energy from the collarbone area had began to soften, "something had switched" and she had understood that the mess did not need the healing at all – it was she herself who needed to be healed of the shame.

She said, "That – I don't want to call her a mess anymore – that girl didn't do anything wrong. She doesn't have to be ashamed. She is hurt of course, but there is nothing wrong with that at all, it is all me! Don't you see, it is all me. It is me who needs the healing!"

It was extremely emotional for me to observe and facilitate the client's energy tranceformations as she kept looking at the injured girl and using EmoTrance to move her responses, one after the other – shame, guilt, anger, disgust, sadness, compassion – with every emotion that went away, the client became brighter and more centred, more powerful a presence in the room.

298

When she said that it was all done, she expressed the desire to sincerely thank the girl from the past who had not needed any healing at all but who, in the contrary, had shown her who needed to be healed.

"She healed ME", the client said.

Contributed by James Stanbridge, PhD

Aspergers Boy's Fear Of Others

Contributed by Silvia Hartmann

I conducted an EmoTrance session with an Aspergers diagnosed 12 year old child relating to fear of being noticed and being looked at because he had to attend a public concert at a local school with his group from the special unit and had a lot of fear about it.

The boy in question accepted EmoTrance readily and easily, much more so than EFT which had been attempted but which he didn't want to do at all and rejected completely. The mother had made some progress with proxy work, which didn't help though with his real time problems at his special school especially with other children or his own state control because he wouldn't do it himself.

I explained about feelings being stuck energy that needs to leave somewhere and he accepted this readily and without argument. It took a little while to have him locate the physical sensations relating to the fears but once he had found the first one, it all went astonishingly smoothly and easily from there.

First there was fear of being noticed by the other children, in his stomach, which moved up and came out through his mouth. He was much calmer after that.

Then, there was a fear of being looked at directly, in his head. This moved all around and came out through his skin.

Next was fear of what they would say to him - comments about his looks, about being stupid. Once he had the hang of it, he actually started to giggle when I told him sternly that he was a total idiot and useless as well.

Then he mentioned another fear, namely that of his parents being upset when the staff told them afterwards about him "having had a bad day", producing looks and demeanour of disappointment in the parents, and silence. This was in his chest and took the longest to move, half went up and out of the top of his head, the other down his back.

I then offered him to do "one on me" – I don't know why, it just happened - and he readily yelled some abuse at me which he truly enjoyed and also, was paying intense attention to me and fascinated with how it moved around and out for *me*. For whatever reason I cannot fathom, I asked him to tell me that "You have failed, I knew you would! I knew it all along!"

It was fascinating how this boy who is normally very, very reserved and expressionless really got into that and shouted it at me, flat out, with the intensity of an Oscar winning actor and with full meaning AND eye contact (he doesn't normally give eye contact).

When he did, it really did something extraordinary to my systems, a huge effect and sensation that led to me saying to him that I understood now that it's not the winning or failing, but having had the guts to TRY in the first place that takes the medal.

I'm really not sure what happened there or why I did that, if it was for him or for me or for both of us but it certainly wasn't like any therapy session I've ever conducted or experienced, ever.

The practical outcome was also very interesting, strange. He didn't "freak out" and actually said he had looked forward to the public performance and had even had noticed the unusual thought that he wanted to respond to someone who said something to him.

He also at one point during the performance at the school, got a pen out and wrote his own name on his arm, upside down so that one could read it if one was looking at him, and stated that he "had no idea why he did it and only noticed after he had done it".

I suggested the idea that there was a part of him that really wanted people to know his name and who he was, and this other part that was still traumatised and needing to hide away after having been bullied and hurt at his previous school and he agreed that this was the most likely reason for the "name writing". He was very accepting of it all, very open, perfectly happy to talk to me about it - that in and of itself is totally unheard of with this boy, such a breakthrough, it's extraordinary.

I have known this boy for quite a while and today it was like I've found myself in a totally different country with him, that wasn't therapy or anything like that, something different altogether - I just don't know quite how to describe it. But it was good, and I just can't think of him as a client or a child at all now but I'm thinking of him as a fellow person, just equal in some way - very strange and yet immensely perfect, indeed.

Low Self Esteem & Depression

This gentleman suffered from "low self esteem" and "depression". When asked where he felt this problem in his body, he indicated his jaw with his hand whilst still consciously thinking about it for quite some time, then finally he said, "In and around my mouth, like a hard tightness."

This was treated straight up with no further discussion as to his history, past or any other treatments he might have had and within seconds of the energy disturbance having been resolved, he began to shout out loud, "I know what it is! How can anyone take me seriously if I never speak out for myself, never tell them who I am, and that I'm worth something!"

This is a good example how with these "sensation based" treatments often incredibly obvious connections come to light.

However, they are only "incredibly obvious" with the wisdom of hindsight, and one must wonder how many years it might have taken to find out the connection and resolve it, if ever.

Completing The Diamond Transformation

I know we probably know this about EmoTrance by now, but it is true that I was really blown away by doing this spontaneous treatment with someone on a - well, I guess you can call it a "super issue".

The life defining deal, the real big thing, over 30 years in the past and having spawned innumerable symptoms, related occurrences, formed life patterns, belief structures and values hierarchies, had the deepest possible tie ins with people and objects - a huge big deal in all.

Now, this "super issue" had at the core of it a massive Guiding Star (epiphanic positive experience or anti-trauma) with a "lost love" and all the rest of the system grew around this, as is so often the case with such experiences and their aftermath and basically, the person in question had been holding on for dear life to this memory/energy from their end and had build their entire life more or less like a shrine around this Guiding Star moment of feeling loved and loving totally in return.

The idea turned up that they were very tired and weary of their role as the priest to that temple they'd build to the one experience but that there was no way, even though it was as clear as anything that they would be wasting the rest of their lives just as successfully in that function and set up as they had done so far with what been going on for the previous 30 - unless they would allow this system to become liquid and "let it go" at last.

Talk about resistance to the very idea! Wow. That was really something. The emotional responses and pleading, absolute refusal, just everything in full out reversal at the mere suggestion that this would be a good thing.

So I actively took this whole deal and switched it into the ET world view and here, what we had was not emotions and love and contortions and entanglements and constructs and feed back loops and and and and and, but instead, this total clarity and simplicity of an energy that they had enfolded and held in their heart.

Literally, in their heart.

An energy that was so intense and so dense that it was hard as a diamond, and if anyone would try and remove this, the person would fear that their "heart was being torn from their chest".

Rightfully so, as the diamond had grown into the very structure of their energetic heart.

And in this view of clarity and logic, it was incontrovertible

- that this diamond hard energy represented a structural problem of extreme proportions;
- that it physically and practically entirely blocked the flow of any kind of energy through the heart;
- that the systems below and around were parched and atrophied for the lack of flowing, living energy;

- and even that this energy had never done what it should have done to the entirety of the system because it did not complete its pathways and did not ever complete the entirely positive and beneficial transformation to the energy body its movement through the system would have initiated.

From this viewpoint of clarity and logic, there was simply no doubt as to what had happened.

It wasn't a tragedy.

It wasn't a blessing.

It wasn't Karma and it wasn't God's will.

It wasn't all those contorted meanings or anything at all, it was simply there, cause and effect, with the pathways to what needed to be done laid out in crystal clarity for everyone to see, to understand, to appreciate.

There was no doubt at all as what needed to be done, and no resistance at all to having it happen - it was so perfectly and so clearly the right thing to do, the only thing to do that the person spontaneously said with complete conviction, "The transformation has to be completed, the diamond energy must be allowed to move."

As the person began immediately and without any hesitation to soften the very outside layers and ingrown connections to have them rise like mist and begin their journey through the dust dry pathways and channels which had not been used for 30 years, I was watching them with a sense of amazement and awe.

This was the same person who had thought that they could not ever let go of this; that it was the only thing in this life for them and they could never hope for anything better.

This was the same person who had virtually fought to the brink of death to protect the diamond in their heart from any intervention by any healer, psychologist, therapist, well meaning friend and from themselves, too.

This was the same person who now, after just one look at the clarity and logic of the energetic realities in their energy body was feeling the 30 year old diamond energy beginning to rush through the channels in their body, beginning to breathe faster and glow, trembling as the transformation which had begun all that time ago finally was allowed to be completed right in front of my eyes.

They were absolutely at a loss for words afterwards and so was I.

We were just sitting there, looking at each other and this strange sense of epiphany? rebirth? righting a wrong? holiness? was right there with us in the room and nothing needed to be said - what could you say to that?

I came away from that with a whole new found respect for the basic principles of ET and a whole new respect for how that simple switch into the viewpoint of energy and flow had simply side-stepped all the energetic injuries, all the emotional pain entanglements, all the beliefs and decisions, all the thought constructs designed to protect the status quo and to make some sense of it.

And in this place of clarity and logic, how there was a compassion to be found that totally touched both the person and myself so intensively - this was not a cold and barren place, bereft of feelings but in the contrary, a holy space, a space of awe that takes your breath away.

Now that's what I call energy healing!

Silvia Hartmann - http://StarFields.org

ADDENDUM 5 – EMOTRANCE IN THE FIELD

EmoTrance was always designed to help one individual person "in the field", i.e. not necessarily in the magic circle of a therapist's office but when things happen in real life, at home - that is exactly when I needed help the most and that is why I made that aspect such a priority in designing EmoTrance.

So these little stories are not case histories. They are not meant to be scientific and they are not here for testimonial purposes.

These "in the field" stories are **personal experiences** from all sorts of different people, under all sorts of different circumstances, and for all sorts of different reasons, told as they were told and in their own words.

I have included them here in order to give you, dear reader, an idea of the sheer **scope and flexibility** of what you can do with EmoTrance; so that when you have your own experiences you can see for yourself that it is ok to feel like that because others have experienced this too.

These are also all learning stories and teaching stories which tell us a lot about how people's problems and the energies below are correlated, interlinked and how we actually work as people, in real life.

All contributors names apart from my own have been changed to ensure privacy. These stories came by mail, by email and by telephone; some I was privileged to have experienced personally or witnessed.

This is by far my favourite section of this book and I am delighted to have this section as the closing chapter - written by the people who are using EmoTrance where it should be used - in the field.

No More Tears On The Pillow

Contributed by "Julie"

There's a personal issue I've been working on for more than two years using at various times most of the techniques I know. The pain has been temporarily relieved, but any of a vast number of triggers, both external and internal, can drop me back into it at any time. Last night, as I went to bed, one of those triggering thoughts crossed my mind. I gave my usual sigh of pain and longing and grief and self-pity and all the other things that are wrapped up in this (a recent loss with deep roots in early life and who knows how many earlier lives, as well).

And then something incredible happened. Another thought crossed my mind. One I hadn't been able to imagine thinking before. "Well, that's one way to respond to this, but you could have a different response." Simple? Yes. Obvious?

Yes. The intended and desired (well, with parts of me, at least) result of all the other work I'd done on this issue. But I'd never got to that point before. I've been stuck so deeply in this one for so long. I'd been locked into my previous response.

Now here's the important part. I hadn't even got to the point of doing an EmoTrance procedure on it, but the shift in what was possible happened apparently without effort or intention on my part. With that shift suddenly available, I could easily do a bit of EmoTrance more with it, and go to sleep contentedly and full of awed gratitude for what Silvia has offered us, instead of with my customary tight chest and jaw and tears on my pillow.

My hypothesis is that something about doing EmoTrance – which we all did LOTS of during the Training last weekend – has shaken loose or opened up all sorts of possibilities that simply weren't available to me before. And I saw this over and over again in many others during the weekend – most noticeably, of course, in those I already know well.

I am a changed woman.

Old Car Crash Pain In The Heart Area

Contributed by "Marian"

About 18 months ago I was in a nasty car crash, taking the full impact of steering wheel in chest when car hit a tree.

Since then, from time to time I have terrible pain around heart area, which builds from a sensation front and back in heart chakra. In the past it has taken about half an hour of not knowing what to do with myself, for the pain to work itself out (!)

A while ago when I was somewhere that I really didn't want to go through that, I tranced it as soon as I recognised the warning signs, and that sorted it immediately.

Just sitting here now I recognised the signs again, thought "it's just energy", put my hand to the area, closed my eyes, had the intention that it would soften, and find its pathway.

Almost immediately I started to yawn like a hippo, then had urgent message to run to toilet, and ... guess what? I'm still yawning, but the discomfort all gone.

Thank goodness.

There In The Present

Contributed by "Alison"

I was feeling generally out of touch with myself and my surroundings. I sat in a concert I had been looking forward to for months and felt as though I wasn't there at all. When the person on the stage began playing a song that I had been longing to hear performed live I decided to use EmoTrance and see what would happen. I took a deep breath as if inhaling the music and, at once, felt a heaviness in my throat and around my ears. I put my hands to her jaw and let their warmth sooth the feeling and ease it. Soon I felt the heaviness pouring into my shoulders and, as I returned my hands to her lap, it began flowing free and fast out through my thumb and index finger.

The energy continued flowing freely through my hands for the duration of the song, and as it ended and I began clapping wholeheartedly I became aware that I now felt very much "there" in the present moment, in the crowd and enjoying the concert.

Aging

Contributed by "Jaya"

In order to try EmoTrance for myself, the challenge was to deal with something painful, something I had truly consigned to the bin as not being ever wanting to see again – and quite literally as I had just thrown away a pile of highly unflattering photographs of me, taken specifically to illustrate an article and needed by the designer over the weekend.

I decided to retrieve them and do an EmoTrance™ procedure while looking at each one.

Now here's the really exciting part. I actually WANTED to do it. I felt, not just interested, not just curious while wondering how I'd fit this into my heavy workload, but impatient, with a shiver of excitement. I wanted to do it right now. So I did. I retrieved the photographs from the trash.

What a range of feelings I encountered as I worked through them, one after the other.

Pain to see how ageing is showing in my face, the jowls beginning to sag, anger at the photographer for not noticing that my hair was astray, for not having chosen a better angle, for not correcting the sharp shadows from the flash, anger at the camera for taking so long to click that the expression on my face was sometimes glazed, sometimes moronic, sometimes creased with puzzlement and impatience, anger at myself for not having powdered my nose, even disgust that I've done nothing about my eating and exercise patterns to counteract the heaviness I was seeing so graphically.

'I know how I can look, could look, should look. I've been letting myself go. What a stupid pose. Why didn't I button my jacket? Why didn't I do something different with my hair?…' and on and on.

'This isn't me, can't be me. Oh, but the camera doesn't lie. Is this really what people see when they look at me? Yikes, how much my self-confidence has been based on the security of my attractive appearance.'

And that was just the first photo!

I'm sure you can imagine it, and more. By the time I was finished, though, in just a few moments, not only was all that gone, but I was able to say, "Well, if we have to use some of these, then I think that's probably the better one.'

What a contrast to the panic I'd felt the day before when the designer told me he absolutely, positively had to have them over the weekend, so there was no chance to re-shoot. Not only that, I could even appreciate the warmth and sincerity and openness I saw in my own face. I could find the person in the photos appealing, likeable. "Hey! That's me I'm talking about!".

I've never experienced such a shift from fear and doubt to... 'Oh, WOW!'

I'd caught the scent of this, the scent of something truly different, truly new, of enthusiasm and eagerness. But I had to eat this pudding for myself to really taste the difference, the keen, avid, glowing, buzzing, FUN of doing EmoTrance.

I can think of it as a means to break out of the trances we're locked into – the trance of 'I'm not pretty enough, and I have to be pretty or...' And many, many others.

And as I write this, I've got those photos sitting on my desk right here, in front of me. I look at them and I feel affection, a real warmth for the person on these photographs and that is ME.

I can still see the faults, mistakes, and it's just fine, I don't want to throw them out, they are fine, nice even, I am fascinated by that look in my own eyes. I like the photographs and I like what they are showing me about self, so much more and so other than just the skin type beauty.

I'll do whatever I need to do to be there for a full EmoTrance training. This is so good, I want more.

Calmly Facing A Turning Point

Contributed by "Debrah"

I just had my first session of EmoTrance over the phone and I have to tell ya... it saved my marriage and gave me a new freedom, and another choice before submitting to medication (for anxiety).

I can't tell you how calm I was in facing a huge turning point and confrontation.

All went well. But it was more than my marriage, it was facing a long standing fear that has to do with all types of stuff "labels" and explanations but can be summed up in a regular shot of adrenalin and fear in my chest that is now gone. I tried it again on my own and it worked fine. I couldn't believe that it actually lasted and my anxiety is much, much less but getting smaller each time I do it.

My thoughts have evolved quickly as to how to handle the intent from will it work, I hope it works, get out, can it get out, to a demand to get out and labelling it good/bad and then a sort of "your free to go, keep what I can use and let go of what I no longer need". I feel more of a communication with the energy in myself, with myself and with All-That-Is.

This is amazing stuff!

Lost Lover Found

Contributed by "Angelina"

I've had a really wonderful experience with a very old emotional thing that really knocks me to the floor each time I go near it - or should I say, used to!

I was doing some furniture shifting and found a picture that is rather meaningful in above context and whoosh! there it was, huge charge of energy, immediate tears, the lot. But then I thought very clearly through it all, "I can handle this energy!" and said it out aloud.

Immediately, a really strange sliding sensation started up on the left hand side of my face and the pressure and tears receded noticeably. So I said it again, loudly, "I can run that energy!" and that sliding sensation started up on the right as well, slower and more thickly but going down, nonetheless.

A few moments later and there was clarity.

I just couldn't believe it. I have held on to this agony for - 20 years? 25? Before that moment with the picture it was always as though the emotion itself was connected to something so holy and important that I just never wanted to mess with it in any a way, no matter how painful - I didn't want to touch it with counselling, hypnosis, healing, EFT, NLP, TAT, you name it.

But that moment there, I did it - I ran the energy through my body.

The effect afterwards was just astonishing. It was not at all flat but the emotions were of a totally different order and nature. There was what I can only call a deep respect and love for the person in question that was quite amazing, mountainous if you will but it didn't make me want to sob and cry at all, rather it felt empowering to have known him and have had him be in my life. Also, it felt as though he was still there and I think that's correct, I probably invoke him or his energies every time I think about him or am reminded of him and whatever happened there, allowed me to actually experience that real presence which may well be why there were no bereavement related abreactions afterwards as there always were before - instead of tremendous loss and sorrow. just love.

Weight Issues

Contributed by "Alice"

I thought I'd tackle weight issues, and got out a photo of me early 20's posing in a gownless evening strap (from my Latin American dancing days!!), anyway, a couple of sizes slimmer than now!!

What an interesting experience, very very emotional. In fact, all I could feel was emotion and nothing in my body. Looking closer the emotion became intense as I thought of bringing this image into my body. It was trying to come in at the solar plexus and couldn't get in (intense emotion) so I had to let it in strand at a time. This big shield was a belief barrier about the fact that I couldn't possibly look like that again, it was like I just couldn't get it into my body, this energy, this belief that I could be like that again!!

Anyway, after taking it in strand at a time eventually increasing the flow I could step into this energy and felt congruent with it.

On reflection, I thought this idea of ETing photos was excellent. It handles so many aspects all at once.

Getting More Luck Into My Life

Contributed by "Ross"

I had an epiphany in a taxi this morning! I was on my way to give a presentation and talked to the driver about it as we got stuck in a traffic jam. When we got to the place and I had paid him, the driver said to me with a smile, "Good luck on your presentation!" I immediately said right back, "No luck needed, I'm very well prepared." when it struck me what I had just done in EmoTrance terms.

The man had send me a real present of "luck energy" - and what did I do? Bat it back just as quick as you can as though it was a red hot potato! So I took a deep breath and said to the driver, "I'm sorry about that, could you wish me luck again, please?"

He was surprised but laughed and shook his head, and said again, "Hey man, good luck with that presentation."

I took a deep breath and let it in and - wow! It was amazing! As though I'd taken a drug - it just swished and sparkled through me, woke me right up and felt just great. It really was a wonderful gift from this stranger.

I thanked him and that feeling stayed with me and still comes back when I think of him laughing and saying, "Hey man, good luck."

The only thing is that I am now asking myself, how much luck could I have had but did not because I kept it away from me?

Falling In Love With Your Demons

Contributed by "Patricia"

Right now anger is my favourite thing in the world. As soon as I notice that I am feeling pissed off, I know that I get to ET another issue. I'm in near automatic mode at the moment and all I have to do is fully intend and whatever I feel is clearing. Barely have to locate it.

Almost not at all with anger --fear still requires a little concentration.

Things are clearing so fast it's disconcerting. I may transform into a totally unrecognisable being any minute!

ET Romance you say? I think that's as good a quick description of EmoTrance as any. I am in love with the entire universe, cause everything brings new change and all of it feels good.

Either Silvia has invented access to ecstasy, or I'm succumbing to mania for the first time at the ripe age of 40.

Btw, If you really want auto-ET to kick in big time, do something that has scared you to death for years while getting only 1/4 your normal sleep for 2 nights or more. ET every fear and wobble, till you don't have to do it anymore cause the universe is doing it for you. Wheee!

312

Yesterday morning I woke up with a very strange feeling, and realized that it was annoyance that I have not arranged my life to make it possible to write all the time.

I said, "What???" and the voice in my head said, "Well, I am a writer, and my life must accommodate that."

ET on, something in my gut went clunk, and I couldn't scare myself with the idea of doing what I've always known I was supposed to do, no matter how hard I tried. As opposed to the last 40 years when I ran and hid in fear, over and over and over.

Nothing on earth has prepared me for the feeling of dancing wildly with my demons. And falling in love with them again and again.

Love, Patricia (Writer).

Frightening The Relatives With Emotional Control

Contributed by "Anna"

I totally freaked the living daylights out of some relatives today (sister-in-law, her three kids, mother-in-law and my kids).

We are all sitting round the kitchen table having coffee, talk comes up of some very traumatic, sad past thing. My voice quavers in mid-sentence, tears start up. I stop in mid sentence, sob, "Just a minute, must do ET." It was instant and easy, just blocked both sides under the eyes. About five seconds later, I continue on the same sentence in a perfectly happy and conversational fashion, look up and see all of them just staring at me in a mixture of fear and horror.

But none of them asked what had happened or what I did just then - I guess they were afraid of what I would have said! However, it was not all in vain. Nephew (16) upon leaving whispered to me, "That thing you did, when you were crying - can you show me how to do that sometime?" and I gave him a conspiratorial wink, a nod and a knowing smile.

EmoTrance rocks!

Calming a Severely Distressed System

Contributed by "Rosalie"

Four weeks ago we went on holiday abroad with some very old friends and, sadly, our friend died whilst we were in Italy. I thought I coped very well and was reasonably strong for my friend - it was all very sad. I seemed to be holding up until the day of the funeral when I just went to pieces. I felt worse than I had done at the funerals of some very close relations, including my father. I don't know about any of you but when I am immersed in a problem big time I sometimes "forget" to help myself.

The day seemed to get worse and when the night time arrived I was a wreck. I went to bed and then it struck me that I really should do something to help myself, but what? Tapping, TAB'ing, BSFF, TAT?? I know!!! EmoTrance!!! Believe me or believe me not, within 5 minutes my whole system had calmed down and I went straight to sleep. It is such a simple but amazingly effective procedure. The therapist does not necessarily need to know details of their client's problem so, used in this way, it is an extremely respectful way of working and I would think can be incorporated into almost anyone's practice.

Of course I learned a lot more during the workshop and, whilst there, worked on the fact that I find it difficult, almost impossible, to accept compliments. If someone says I have done a good job or I look nice in a particular outfit I cringe and want to curl up. It always makes me feel soooo uncomfortable. Wow, the problem went within minutes and I am totally fine with it now. This is truly amazing, great stuff - thanks Silvia for inventing it and making it so easy to learn!

Physical Awakening Of An Abused Energy Body

Contributed by "Sue Ellen"

In a nutshell - I was raped by all and sundry from age 3-21 yrs, hanged twice (someone intervened each time, so I'm still here), and experienced and witnessed violence and atrocities of many flavours. ET has come along about 10yrs into my healing journey, and I knew it was going to have a mega impact.

My guides said it is the next evolutionary step for mankind, and having heard how it is developing some people, I can't wait for my turn!

For me, ET really has been all about the physical body!

It was my physical body that was terrified of coming on the course (ill for a week before and during) and being asked to take down the 'safety' barriers. I really identified with what was said about a 'closed' system. During our practicals, I was hopeless at receiving energy (even the offer of money or a little compliment) and it really illustrated to me why I'm impoverished, burnt-out etc. (God, don't I sound a sorry case!!)

Day 2 of our course was the turning point for me - working with a practitioner / healer. It really got things moving, and I experienced enough shift states to convince me all was not lost. What I noticed, however, was that I needed (demanded!) lots of very physical interventions, like thumping and pummelling down the shoulders, back and pelvis.

By myself, it's not been so easy either. Every time I tried ET, the energy kept getting stuck in the same old places, and wouldn't budge with intent/healing alone. I've been giving my lower back lots of deep massage which is gently dissolving one of my biggest blocks. In fact I'm gradually starting to massage/love all of my body - at long last. It has really brought home to me the value of the physical therapies in combination with deep energy therapy.

Something that did work for me from the start, and is getting easier every day, is dancing the energy through my system. That seems to keep things moving, and I find my body seems to mirror what the energy is doing, drawing it in from the Universe or the Earth, undulating it through in waves and spirals, concentrating it in my heart or power centre, and radiating it back out again etc. Looking forward to dancing with my demons too ... and falling in love with them again and again ...

Speaking "His" Name

Contributed by "Jeannie"

Some years ago I had a relationship that came as near to my dream of how 'it' should feel that I've ever been. Not that it was perfect, as it wasn't.

But it made me realise I was capable of very intense feelings without being the mushy idiot I had previously assumed was part and parcel of the job.

You see I had been brought up in a family almost totally devoid of any feeling that wasn't anger. Love was expressed as anger, caring was expressed as anger. There were no soft feelings, and should any ever creep their way in, they were very quickly squashed with; yes you've guessed it, anger.

I believed myself unable to demonstrate affection, a belief that was reinforced by every man who accused me of being hard, cold, controlling. But this time was different. Different in so many ways I would sound like something from Alice in Wonderland if I tried to explain. Needless to say I found myself so plugged in and turned on by this guy, I was totally smitten and unable to hide it. When he left I was devastated. I fell to pieces, much like a carrier bag with too heavy a load.

Time didn't heal as promised, but I did find myself a changed person, changed for the better. Life moved on, weeds grew in the garden, the children became young men and I lost other things that were dear to me. All the time though I held onto that time in my life when I had felt alive. I prayed I would feel that way again some day.

I didn't of course, and it wasn't until I was giving myself a good going over with ET one day on a winter sun lit beach that I realised why. Part of me was stuck and I couldn't find that part no matter how hard I looked.

So I took to my bed with a Tachyon cell and worked the EmoTrance™ magical spell. I spoke 'his' name, I recalled the smell and texture of that soft skin in the place my head would nestle in his neck. And there it was. Not shielded out but shielded in. A love so intense, a love so true, preserved in a sphere and held apart from everything else to prevent spoiling.

Common sense told me I had to let it out, but I so wanted to keep it. How did I know this and where did that knowing reside in my body? I softened and moved all my objections (a bit like the apex effect in EFT - I can't remember what they were or how they felt), until all that was left to do was to melt the shell of the sphere, which was by now as easy as sucking chocolate from a Malteser.

The release was much like that moment when you slide your cold, exhausted body into a hot bubble bath, or curl up in a freshly made bed in the middle of a rainy afternoon.

It sounds corny to say I now view the world through different eyes, but it's true. I laugh so much more, I live and love so much more. Many years ago I remember a friend had a poem on her wall. I was always fascinated with one the phrase, "Love wasn't put in your heart there to stay; Love isn't love 'til you give it away." Now I'd finally got what it meant!

The Sandwich, The Enemy ...

Contributed by "Petra"

I'm very overweight and every so often I think about doing something about that. But as I suffer from aerobophobia (a fear of luminescent rubber sportswear) I leave it where it is.

I did notice a couple of days back that although I eat food, structurally and mentally I say NO to it in a big way. It's like every bit of everything at all and every sip of everything no matter what is going to make the fatness worse and there is a groundswell awareness of this "being so".

So, experimentally I said to a ham sandwich, "Ok, come join me and do something for my body."

My young daughter glanced at me, then got up quietly and left the room ...

But anyway.

The ham sandwich didn't actually say anything back but I did become aware of a virtual screaming all over my systems, No! Oh dear god no! Don't you know that every single bite will just make you fatter and fatter???? What are you doing??? It will make your life even worse than it already is!!! No-one will ever love you again!!! Stop!!! NOOOO! Don't eat it! NOOOOO!!!!

Wow. Now where did I feel that in my body?

In my stomach. In my ovaries. In my cheeks and jaw. Between my shoulder blades. In the back of my neck. In my throat.

Everywhere, really!

I can only wonder what that actually does when you are indeed eating and drinking things and at the same time, energetically everything is fighting like crazy to not have anything to do with the food at all - is there some slim energy body ghost of mine leaving the building every time I have a cup of tea???

I am sure this could this slow down digestion in the hard body - fat people move food through their digestive systems significantly slower than thin people.

But back to the sandwich.

I looked at it and immediately, the storm and sensations started up again. This time, it occurred to me to think, then say out loud, "This sandwich is ONLY AN ENERGY."

That was a good idea because it calmed me down significantly and what I did then was to take a bite and treat the sandwich going down just like a normal EmoTrance experience, only this time it was sandwich energy!

It was a really interesting experience. I undid all sorts of blockages in my jaw, in my throat, there were stuck things under my eyes, in my stomach, in my heart - all over the place. When I was done, I wasn't actually hungry anymore, either and put the rest of the sandwich away for later.

Love For My Father

Contributed by "Heather"

My aim was to have a loving, connected, affectionate relationship with my Dad. The problem was that in thinking of that, his energy coming towards me, I felt a hard lump in the solar plexus AND a BIG barrier in front of me to my right.

I felt the barrier to be about the awkwardness of physical expression with a male family member, due to rejecting some kind of sexual aspect and something else about my Dad's personality that made me cringe. I worked on softening and clearing the solar plexus. It was a very hard energy, which took a lot of softening.

318

Then we went to the barrier. It was all I could do to allow a tiny pin prick of a hole in the barrier to allow a tiny thread of this energy through and into me and through me. But it felt good.

I opened the hole a bit more and allowed a flow into my right shoulder and down my arm and right side of the body.

Oh, did it feel good. I finally dropped the barrier and very gently allowed more and more of this beautiful energy to flow into me until every part of me was full to the brim. I felt, warm, I felt complete, I felt full, oh it was so good. I was moved to tears at the experience that I never felt ever in my life before. The energy of my father's love filling me.

I basked in the fullness of this beautiful gentle energy for sometime, as it flowed in to me and through me, before a soft gentle misty rainfall to start to cool and refresh me. When I came round, all I could feel was this fullness and completeness and had a big satisfied smile on my face.

I think about my Father now with a new warmth and loving feelings. There's no barrier now. No coldness. I still feel the fullness now as I write. I look forward to our new relationship building. I actually feel love for my Father

4am Chakra Expansion

Contributed by "Gloria"

My personal experience with EmoTrance has been wonderfully rewarding. The day following my initial phone session with my ETP I was the victim of a robbery: my car was broken into, and my purse, containing money, credit cards, check book, driver's license, automobile registration (and who knows what else) was stolen.

That night I awoke at about 4 in the morning feeling rotten.

I did EmoTrance on the spot and felt all of my chakras go from feeling knotted and collapsed to feeling light, twinkly and expanded.

I fell back to sleep feeling peaceful and the next day I calmly went about setting things straight, without feeling victimized or resentful.

A few days later, in conference with my ETP, I had the opportunity to experience guided EmoTrance.

The ETP and I were discussing a chronic relationship problem of mine, and I said I felt "slimed around my heart." Following their gentle prompting, the slime around my heart changed to warm compassionate tears.

A few days later, I had the opportunity to speak with the person I'd felt slimed by, and amazingly, I still felt warmly compassionate and able to feel their love instead of their intrusiveness!

I am very excited and eagerly anticipating learning more about EmoTrance and becoming a practitioner myself.

The Energy Of Best Sellers

Contributed by "Hazel"

I was in town yesterday, waiting to be picked up and having concluded my business about ten minutes early. So I wandered into a book store and was faced with the "Top Ten Best-selling Softbacks" shelf which held innumerable copies of each one of the Bestsellers.

"Hm," thought I (who has dreadful contortions about the whole topic of writing, publishing, editors, etc etc etc), "I wonder what would happen if I sucked a bit of that Bestseller energy into my systems? Well, let's have a go."

So I went and pretended to be rather indecisive as not to be removed by the security guards for strange behaviour in a public bookstore and just floated my hands over the No.1 books (a cooking book by The Naked Chef (!)) and did a bit of EmoTrance there. Fascinatingly, there was extreme shielding of many layers, many types and all sorts in between me and the whole display through which I had to fight my way first before a "door of perception" was established.

Face to face with the bestsellers, so to speak, was very strange. Cold, sharp energy. Very focussed. Very interesting. Very painful as it hit internal blockages with force (which would account for the past necessity of all those shields to keep it out). No gentle softening here, I just put up with the unpleasant sensations as it basically smashed through the various blockages in an entire non-holistic fashion. Ouch. But then when it was all done, it ran clearly and I ended up feeling very focussed, very sharply aware of things around me.

Strangely, no thoughts about writing. Or books or anything like that. Nor any memory flashbacks, insights or anything else. Over 24 hours later, still nothing about books came along, so I'm beginning to think this whole deal never had anything to do with writing or books at all.

But that I must say is one of my very favourite things about ET all around. Things, it seems, are not at all what I always thought they were. Which gives me some hope of solving some seemingly insolvable puzzles.

Since then, I have noticed the following changes in my behaviour. Firstly, I find it difficult to recall even how I used to feel about publishers and "writing for markets" and "artistic integrity" and such. I remember I used to have problems with that, profoundly, but I don't feel like that anymore. I just write now!

Secondly, I noticed that anger, jealousy and bitterness at "more successful" (aka best-selling!) authors has completely disappeared. They are doing their thing, and I'm doing mine, and good luck to them is my attitude these days. As a piece of behavioural evidence, before that day I was spitting acid at the mere mention of "Harry Potter". After, I went to see the movie, enjoyed it tremendously to my surprise and then went on to read all the books with keen interest and admiration. I would make the comment that this particular energetic adjustment has done a lot to make my life nicer, more pleasant, more open and I am very, very glad I did it. I can only recommend to anyone who has real jealousy/anger problems on any achievement topic to have a go at this, it is an excellent piece of very welcome and long overdue changework.

ET Makes Housework Easier!

Contributed by "Sally"

45 minutes was well spent time for a young lady who felt overwhelmed so much by the thought of doing housework she sat down, had a cigarette and felt bad. At the beginning of the ET process she realised there was a heaviness all over her body, this energy came out of both legs leaving her toes tingling, she was then aware that there was an area in her head which felt blocked, this was softened and it left, this happened three more times in different places in her head every time we introduced the thought of the housework until, finally, breakthrough, she

was feeling happy and visualising herself cleaning in every room of the house, playing music and feeling good about doing it. An interesting point about this story is, she did feel really tired that evening but awoke early, feeling good and telling herself, get up , get on with it. "

PERSONAL NOTE: This is my daughter, what a difference. My daughter does not have a house like a palace but she said the benefits are still in place she can motivate herself to do it happily. This did have a speeding up effect on her elimination system as well and she lost a couple of pounds in weight.

Friendship Is ...

Contributed by "Julian"

A friend called me this afternoon. I was really glad to hear his voice, get me out of repetition of work for a bit, and said, "Oh hi! How are you darling!"

Friend: Actually, I'm depressed.

Me: Oh! Do you want to give me a bit of that?

Friend <surprised>: Are you sure you want some?

Me: Well it's only energy and I could do with some right now.

Friend: Oh ok then - here goes ...

Me <gets a sensation of a deep grey wide ocean type of cold but very powerful energy washing through her entire body>

Friend & Me <sigh deeply and exactly in unison>

<a moment's silence>

Me: So, where are you? Do you want to come over for a coffee and a chat?

Friend:<very brightly> Oh that'll be great! Ten minutes ok for you?

So and whilst waiting for friend to arrive, J thought many things to himself. About the man in the movie Magnolia "who had all this love inside but just didn't know where to put it."

About the amazingness of someone saying, "I'm so sad." and another responding with, "Would you like to give me some of that sadness, lighten your burden?"

About the possibility that if people exchanged energies like that openly, might some folk then not to have wring that energy out of hearing animals scream, or other types of victims for their "sadistic" impulses.

About how cool it would be if I could say, "Oh I am so happy!" and instead of responding with an immediate dampener, someone would say back, "Oh dear, that's wonderful, can I share it please? I haven't been happy for years! I've quite forgotten even what it feels like!"

There is so much we can do and learn to do differently - it really sometimes takes my breath away.

Even Sceptics Can Heal ...

Contributed by "Gary"

Has anyone else noticed a real noticeable increase in their "healing powers" since the onset of ET?

And/or a serious attitude change to the whole thing since we did the "You are a healer" exercise at the training?

I found myself, much to my surprised horror, calmly offering someone who had had a tooth extracted two days ago which broke and had to be chiselled out of their back jaw and who'd been in agony since the Novocaine started to fade, some "healing".

Before I knew it, I was sitting next to them, feeling around near their jaw with my hand about a foot away and before I knew THAT, my hand had sharply flipped over so it was palm away from their face and I was drawing massive amounts of energy out of their jaw that raced up my arm and rushed all through my systems. At the same time, person literally shouts, my God, what are you doing, this is an incredible feeling!

A part of me is standing like five foot away with eyebrows raised and arms crossed as "the other me" just as calmly and with quiet efficiency goes on to clear a very old blockage/shard higher up on the person's cheek, sort some channels in their throat, neck and back and then says, "There we are."

Person totally astonished, moving jaw from side to side, pain gone and also, long standing always present ear ache which I was (consciously) entirely unaware of.

Total time spent, about three minutes. No EmoTrance, just straight energy healing.

And that is not like me at all!

The Realms Of The Psychics

Contributed by "Rani"

You asked if anyone else noticed a real noticeable increase in their "healing powers" since the onset of ET?

Yep! :) but I had put it down to being as a result of a certain ETP accusing me of being a healer!

I learned some Reiki healing a few years back and took the attunement (as did much of the population of the UK!) but never really used it other than for family and close friends and then only very occasionally - until the ET training weekend I had the kind of notion that healing was a lovely thing to be able to do for people but wasn't really "my thing".

That has changed for me personally big time. My first realisations here arrived during the lunch break on the first day when we were playing around, were trying something out on me and ended up doing "healing" on my knees (yes healing for sure - it felt very "healy" and fantastic!) and I, in return helped out one of the other participants with something around their shoulders...

I know a few tricks with acupressure, tui na, holding neuro vascular and lymphatic points etc which have helped friends and some clients out many times - these are things that I've always considered kind of mechanical/adjusting techniques - I am aware that when using these things now something's different - I'm getting more positive feedback and I can really feel things moving through my hands.

It was this that was on my mind when I wrote my EmoTrance review and made reference to my experience (see below):

"It took a little while for me to get going with EmoTrance. Although my very first tryout over the phone with an ETP has had far reaching repercussions in my life of the most positive and exciting kind, I wasn't consciously aware of them at first (i.e. the "you are a healer" experience). Now things are very different. By the end of day one on the training I was feeling things I thought I never could, by the end of day two I was feeling things I thought belonged to the realms of others - healers, psychics, mystics, and by the closing of day three... well, to be frank, I'm still processing here."

The Onion Induction

Contributed by Silvia

At an energy therapies conference, I was in my rooms, having coffee with some folk and including a couple of non-therapist visitors. We were just messing around, telling stories and such, when one of the non-therapists mentioned something that really took the sun from the sky, metaphorically speaking, and darkened the energy in the room instantly - clearly something very traumatic from her past that must have been causing much pain and suffering on a daily basis.

One of the happy campers chirped up, "Where do feel that in your body?" and oh dear, there we were, with a massive life issue touched and presented and NO WAY that something of that severity could be dealt with there, in those surroundings.

So I took control of it and suggested the slightest of softenings round the edges of the "giant hard block on her heart" so that a little mist would begin to rise and show us where the channels were. Found them easily enough.

So then, and seeing the entirety of the situation, I said the following to the poor person:

"Now that your body has found the channels, it can begin, in it's own time, and no sooner than you are ready in all ways, to let this energy go, a small layer at a time, like the layers of an onion, as and when it's right, taking all the time you need to gently begin to dissolve this, a gentle mist moving from the surface and as it does so, making this blockage just a little smaller in turn.

"Are you happy for this to be so?"

(Person nods wholeheartedly, tears in their eyes.)

"Then let it be so, let this process continue, a layer at a time, in your own time, whether you are paying attention to it or not, until all is restored, re-balanced, and working better even than it ever did, all things healed, all things resolved."

Person was very grateful to me for both giving these gentle suggestions as well as NOT forcing the issue in any way - it was a pretty beautiful compromise really and a useful pattern which I used again when a demo subject at the ET breakout session was going into something that would have taken longer than I had time for, and revealed much more about the process to the audience than I was willing to share with them.

I had it go on "automatic pilot" and got her intention, permission and consent to have the process continue in it's own time to full ecological resolution. This one said to me afterwards that it was a huge relief and still felt really good, and that they had felt as though I had really taken care of them properly and were very moved by that.

I would offer this for any situation where the deal's too huge to be facing all at once; where people are afraid and need more time; when you run out of time; whenever you feel it's appropriate to slow things down a bit for the rest of the person to be able to catch up with themselves and their changes, cognitively or energetically.

Now I appreciate it's not as fast and furious and there's the real possibility that you won't be getting thank you letters as the thing resolves so gently and gradually that the client never knows it's gone but what the hell.

Some folk deserve it after all they've been thru and I guess there are things I'm still carrying that probably cry out for just that kind of treatment, i.e. giving them time to dissolve a little at a time and in their own time.

EmoTrance - The Ultimate Challenge ...

... A Week in a Caravan with my Parents!

Contributed by Ananga

I begin my tale in the true tradition of family revelations "I love them dearly but…"

I have just returned from a "holiday" in France with my daughter and parents in their touring (i.e. small) caravan and spent a most interesting time playing with EmoTrance during the many and varied opportunities that such a dwelling and combination of personalities can manifest.

I've done it before, twice, they love taking my daughter out and they are most attentive to her and she really does enjoy it. I, however, find it a shifting mix of a break away from e-mails and work, the pleasure of seeing my little girl, have huge fun and horrific oppression!

It's a joke among my friends that I'm a good person to travel with – I take things like Swiss army knifes and torches, wet wipes and the like – the kinds of things that people mock you for taking and continually ask to borrow. On the last two visits I was sure to take EFT and diverting reading such as Project Sanctuary they were both essential to my survival.

This time I took EmoTrance too…

From feeling trapped amidst the waves of one of my father's "serious depressions" and instantly being transported to childhood times of walking on eggshells for days on end (done in about 2 minutes) to clearing a most uncomfortable pressure in my head when he did an emergency stop on a dual carriageway and reversed back to a turning he'd missed that my mother had pointed out to him well in advance (about 2 minutes again including aspects such as "he always talks to her like she's stupid" and "he never listens to anyone" and how this makes me feel since he's my Dad).

This one I really loved doing. How does/did it make me feel? Bloody frustrated are the words that spring to mind - he's arrogant, you can't tell him anything because he can't/won't listen and on it goes… But where do I feel it… such a huge pressure across my forehead and down my arms, my fists were actually clenched and I wasn't at all aware of this until I decided to do some EmoTrance right there and then and really take notice of how this affected me.

I'm 36 years old and have always felt tense around my father, for sure the degree of tensions varies greatly, from light hearted and affectionate exchanges where it is absolutely minimal to the strain of us being very different people with very different ideas to the overwhelming stress of being around him when he's suffering more than anyone else in the world - it's always been there and, no doubt, I've spent years with teeth and fists clenched, tension in my head and who knows where else.

Once again here I am seeing EmoTrance as the most profound tool for dealing with anything that comes our way in the here and now and, pause here to reflect on the vast healing potential, getting things moving that have been stuck for years.

So here I am back home unscathed and unscarred and not, as so many times in the past, feeling like I really deserve a good holiday after all I've been through!

I advise all travellers to update their checklists... passport... tickets... EmoTrance...

Learning From Our Children

Contributed by "Stella"

Following the out of this world experiences at my first EmoTrance training, I was high as a kite and the very next day, when my three year old "little monster" came rushing into my bedroom at the break of dawn (!!) I sort of automatically dropped shields and reversed the usual resistance - you know, oh go away and leave me in peace! especially first thing in the morning.

But I was not prepared for what happened when I did.

The energy charged from him into me and I burst out into tears immediately - how could I have ever rejected this being, this star? Oh good god, what have I been doing all these years thinking of him as a burden? I immediately started the EmoTrance process, and an emergency it was too because I really didn't want him to think he'd "made me cry" - poor darling!

328

We ended up cuddling in bed and I have never felt so close to him, so loving, and so totally energised by his presence - what a total difference to trying to hide under the blanket and trying to block him out. I can only say that was a complete transformation for me in too many ways I can see.

I am so grateful that I was allowed to experience this. It would have been a miracle gift to just feel it the once but I can feel it all the time and it has raised me, made me into a much better mother, I feel better, happier in my own skin - thank you for EmoTrance. And that really doesn't convey what I really feel.

Throwing Away Books

Contributed by "Verity"

This is a story about moving house, letting go of a part of your life but it need not be a bereavement.

This lady had to leave the house she had raised her children in and move into a small flat and one of the things she simply could not take with her was a huge room full of books.

Many of these needed to be thrown away, others sorted into boxes to go to a charity shop, but none of this could be done because the lady was incapable of putting the books into the bags and boxes and stood crying instead.

So she phoned her ETP.

The ETP suggested that she did not need the physical books because she had read them all and to take whatever energy she needed from the books and make it her own, permanently.

So the lady started with the first one, allowing the energy from the book to go into her. It got stuck near her collarbone area and needed a little encouragement, but then flowed away freely and she found that she had no problems at all placing the book in the garbage bag as it had become simply paper and print and nothing beside.

Once the process had begun, it became faster until all the books were sorted successfully and the lady felt perfectly happy, calm, steady and energised.

She had also a third pile of books, those she would take with her because she still wanted them in some way - a thought that had not even occurred to her before.

Following this, the house move went perfectly well and there was virtually no bereavement or regret to the change in the days and weeks that followed.

First Successful Complaint

Contributed by "Charles"

My 12 year old son bought himself a computer game with his own pocket money. When he got it home, it didn't have a free special something in it which had been promised in advertisements and which was the main reason for him buying the game.

He was distraught so I suggested he should go back to the shop to get it sorted out.

He didn't like that idea at all, saying that the shop owner would think he just wanted to get another of these valuable collector's items for free.

I suggested that he should try it; that he was a good customer there and he had never taken anything back maliciously before. But he was clearly too scared at the idea.

I asked him if he would allow me to show him one of my "weird tricks" and I was lucky that time because the thing meant a great deal to him and had wiped out his savings too, so he was motivated for once and grudgingly said, "Ok then but it'll never work."

The fear of going back to the shop was in his lower abdomen and it moved real quick and easy - zoom and out, just like that. I was surprised and even a bit jealous how easy he made it seem. I have to struggle to even start the process, I don't find it easy to feel where these emotions are kept.

Anyway, it took all of two minutes and he took a deep breath and said, I'm ready to go now. Worst that can happen is they just refuse to give me a new one.

I offered to take him in the car and wait outside for him (I believe in letting kids do these things for themselves, they need to learn to get along without us). He went in, upright and full of purpose. Eventually he emerged triumphantly. They had opened some more packages and found that all of them missed the special offer item from that particular box, so they opened another fresh box and those were ok. He got one of those, no problem. Not only that, because he had saved them embarrassment from other customers, they even gave him a free gift for telling them about it.

A triumph of personal development, and a triumph for EmoTrance, I'd say. And - did I notice a look of new found respect for old Dad there in the car?!

The Nurse Who Dared To Care

Contributed by "Anna"

I had the most amazing experience today. I work in a geriatric ward and learned EmoTrance because I saw a practitioner for a personal problem. The next day when I went back to work, something happened that I believe has changed me forever.

We have this old man, an ex-army colonel. He is 83 years old, doesn't have any relatives and cranky as hell, dying of cancer, waiting for a place in a hospice.

That lunchtime when I went to bring him his meal, he was obviously in severe pain and when I came in he broke down for a moment and made this tiny gesture with his hand, like he was saying, help me, when he couldn't say it if you know what I mean. He doesn't say please or thank you ever, when he's up for it he just barks orders and complains all the time, nothing is ever good enough and no-one likes him.

As I looked at him there in such pain I really felt the shields I made around me, thick as a glass wall all around me, more like a tower really where I was safe inside and I don't know what happened I just dropped it and let him come to me, let him touch me.

It was the most amazing thing. I went over and took his hand and looked into his eyes and it was like falling in love with him, with that old man but it wasn't sad, it wasn't like I had always thought it would hurt to care for them - it was completely different. It wasn't sad at all, it was - just amazing, that's the only word I have. Amazing and energising. He stared up at me and held my hand tightly and went very quiet, and then he said, "Thank you."

Conclusion To Vol. I

EmoTrance™ is a brand new system and it is under **constant evolution**.

Because of the underlying simple yet profoundly useful pre-suppositions on how the energy body works in humans, the possibility for developing patterns and applications for EmoTrance™ are virtually limitless, and there will be many, many more patterns and techniques that will arise from these underlying presuppositions.

As is usual, lower chunked special applications are also under development – ET for weightloss, ET for prosperity, ET for healing and so forth.

My personal interest lies in the more magical applications but even so, please know that what you have seen, read and hopefully experienced so far is **only the beginning**.

At the end of the day, EmoTrance is a system of exploration, of learning on a very personal basis on what goes on in the Universe and with people who try to make their life here in our world.

I trust you too will use ET in this spirit and I look forward to hearing about your contributions and experiences on the forums, lists and in magazines, bookshops and articles on the Internet.

Please make a point of visiting the new portal on http://EmoTrance.com to stay in touch with important developments and new discoveries, techniques, patterns and practical applications.

I thank you for your interest and I sincerely wish that you will take ET for a real good test drive, really take it to its limits and then some.

Silvia Hartman

GLOSSARY OF TERMS

Attachments – Ereas in the wider energy field which were not generated or derived from the individual whose field it is.

BSFF – Be Set Free Fast, one of the METs.

EFT – Emotional Freedom Techniques, originally engineered by Gary Craig from TFT (Thought Field Therapy by Roger Callahan). Revolutionary and user-friendly system to clear energy disturbances by paying attention to the problem and tapping on 14 major meridian points.

Energy Nutrition – Thinking of energy flowing as the equivalent of nutrients flowing into, through and out the physical systems and, in their passing and interaction with those systems, bringing the building blocks for existence, growth, repair and energy for all living functions.

Erea – Short for "existing energetic reality", an erea is a dense field or system with a purpose and a personal identity. Ereas can be parts of the inner energy body in the sense of "areas", in the greater energy body and even self sustaining outside any one originating individual or occurrence.

ET – EmoTrance

ETP – EmoTrance Practitioner

Evocation – The act of raising energy by intention.

Fairy Wish – An EmoTrance reality creation pattern whereby one makes a wish and removes all blockages or disturbances for the energy thus raised to flow freely, and powerfully.

Fault Line - A highly damaged ereas that are simply hyper sensitive and the first to respond to stress of any kind. Fault Lines draw attention to themselves even if the actual problem is in a different part of the energy system; in doing so, they often massively confuse cause-and-effect attributions.

Guiding Star – A single moment of epiphanic joy or an enlightenment moment which people try to hold on to and re-create mistakenly by actually trying to recreate the circumstances and people and objects present to make it happen again.

Hands Of Ghost – Two or more hands made of intention to touch where you cannot touch in physicality in order to assist the flowing of energy through their own channels or to soften energy blockages. Hands of Ghost can be warm and healing, cool and soothing, powerfully massaging or just gently touching subtly in response to what is needed at any point in time. You can, of course, also have Arms of Ghost or an entire representation of your intention enfolding yourself or another in a full embrace if so desired.

Intrusions – Ereas which were not generated or derived from the individual whose energy body it is and which have become part of the energy body (grown into the energy body). When this happens, they are mistakenly classified as "being of me" and all the protection devices that would normally protect the energy body are called into action to protect the intrusions just as well, making them very resistant to any attempts of removal or healing.

MET – Meridian & Energy Therapies, meaning the new forms of energy based mind-body healing techniques such as TFT, EFT, BSFF, TAT, etc. and EmoTrance.

The Hard – All that usually known as "the real world" – credit cards, people dying from cancer, global warming, pain and suffering and all of that.

Shields – Existing Energetic Realities (ereas) which block an energy form from coming into the central energy body or even into the wider energy body. In order to find the correct channels for the energy that has for some important reason **at the time** been kept at bay, we make a tiny pinprick hole like a laser hole into the shield to find out where the energy comes in, what it feels like, tastes like, what it does in the body and to move it through its own channels. With a very small quantity of incoming energy, which is less stressful for the client or for yourself, this can be discovered as can be discovered if there are areas, channels, parts of the system through which this energy passes needs to be unblocked or repaired first before the shield can be dropped completely.

Storm Drains – Specific major channels designed to be capable of handling the strongest and fastest energy situations – **if** there is no damage to these channels or blockages in those channels and **if** they have developed properly as they should and have not become atrophied.

TAT – Tapas Acupressure Technique, one of the METs.

Totality – An entire human being, the mind-body-spirit-energy-etc. totality which is one single person.

Trancing – The act of moving energy deliberately through channels or layers of the energy body. Term used by ETPs to describe the act of doing EmoTrance.

About The Author

Silvia Hartmann PhD is a highly qualified and experienced trainer of Hypnosis, Hypnotherapy, Energy Therapies and Neuro-Linguistic Programming, author, international lecturer and motivational speaker. She is the Co-Founder and Director of The Association For Meridian & Energy Therapies and founder of the oldest established MET internet newsgroup, Meridiantherapy, as well as being a Contributing Editor to Gary Craig's EmoFree List.

With an extensive record in trainings design, she is well known for her outstanding ability to create trainings that allow the participants to understand and integrate even highly complex materials and making it easy to learn, easy to do and easy to replicate.

She is the author of numerous highly acclaimed original works in the field, including "Project Sanctuary" and "Guiding Stars 2002".

Silvia Hartmann's best-selling EFT Training Manual "Adventures In EFT" has to date been translated into four languages and is acknowledged to be "The Best Book on EFT".

After studying and re-searching Energy Psychology & Meridian Energy Therapies approaches in-depth for four years, Silvia Hartmann created EmoTrance™, a truly groundbreaking and entirely innovative approach to working with the human energy system for mental and physical health.

For Further Information about Silvia's Work please visit:

http://sidereus.org - News & Library Portal Of The Sidereus Foundation

http://starfields.org - Complete Online Catalogue of Manuals & Trainings

http://dragonrising.com - Hard Copy Books, Courses, CDs etc.

http://emotrance.com - The EmoTrance™ News & Library Portal

Adventures In EFT

Adventures In EFT is the World's best selling guide for beginners to Gary Craig's Emotional Freedom Techniques EFT.

Now in its fifth revised edition, Adventures does not require any previous knowledge of healing, counselling, psychology or human health or changework at all – anyone who can read can pick up this book and start to make their lives feel a whole lot better, right away.

Yet, in spite of Adventures' easy to read, friendly and informative style, all the base patterns of EFT are here – modelled on Gary Craig himself and with additional modelling from the leading EFT therapists in the World, Adventures is also a fine handbook for any healer or counsellor wishing to begin to make use of the extraordinary powers of EFT to make profound changes in people's lives.

Sparkling with ideas, enthusiasm and lively suggestions for how to take the Classic EFT protocols and make them come to life for you.

Adventures In EFT

The Essential Field Guide To

Emotional Freedom Techniques

by Silvia Hartmann, PhD

ISBN 1 873483 63 5

Available from

http://DragonRising.com - 44 1323 729 666

and all good bookshops.

The Advanced Patterns Of EFT

Primarily for professional therapists, psychologists and students and researchers in the field of Meridian & Energy Therapies, The Advanced Patterns of EFT by Silvia Hartmann, PhD, re-writes the limits of what used to be.

The first part of this advanced manual concentrates on the EFT treatment flow and describes essential patterns, techniques and variations on the Classic EFT process which move an EFT treatment into the realms of true quantum healing.

The second part consists of the advanced patterns themselves – treatment guides, techniques and approaches for guilt, bereavement, high end addictions, parts healing, shamanic applications and the original Guiding Stars patterns, released for the first time.

The Advanced Patterns Of EFT is an outstanding, original contribution to the emergent field of Meridian & Energy Therapies and an invaluable resource to any serious student, practitioner and researcher in the field.

The Advanced Patterns Of EFT

by Silvia Hartmann, PhD

ISBN 1 873483 68 6

Available from

http://DragonRising.com - 44 1323 729 666

and all good bookshops.

Project Sanctuary III

So now, we are working with the energy body, with thoughtfields, with meridians and energy shields and in the Quantum spaces where what we have learned about time, gravity, distance and more is no longer applicable. If we go into those spaces with our limited four-dimensional thinking, formed by the cause-and-effects of the physicality and after a lifetime of conditioning in the Hard, we will never be able to be at home here, never be able to actually **understand** and never mind affect these spaces and their processes as we should and as we can.

What is required is to learn a whole new way of thinking.

A logic based on entirely different principles, on entirely different laws of nature – quantum logic. Project Sanctuary is probably the first training manual ever written in the history of humanity to be a self help guide and device to teach quantum logic and to make it easy for anyone who wishes to learn.

Fascinating from the start, utilising immediately what we have remaining by the way of connection to our intuition, creativity, magic and the wider realms of the universe, Project Sanctuary is easy.

Indeed, it is surprisingly easy and what so many find so much more surprising still is the fact that this is not head-hurting school learning at all but exciting, fun, stimulating, sexy, funny, breath-takingly amazing and on occasion frighteningly exciting, too.

And that IS our first lesson in quantum logic – FORGET about learning being difficult or painful. FORGET THAT. That was learning the hard way and you can't learn hard amidst the flowing, glowing vibrant Oceans of Energy from which we came, and to which we will return in glory and delight, a homecoming of such wonder and awe, it will take your breath away.

For anyone seriously interested in getting really serious about learning, it's time to seriously lighten up and start learning for yourself, by yourself, in yourself – a one-on-one tuition between you and the universe itself. Project Sanctuary is your manual, handbook and tour guide - if you want it.

Project Sanctuary III

by Silvia Hartmann, PhD

ISBN 1 873483 98 8

Available from

http://DragonRising.com - 44 1323 729 666

and all good bookshops